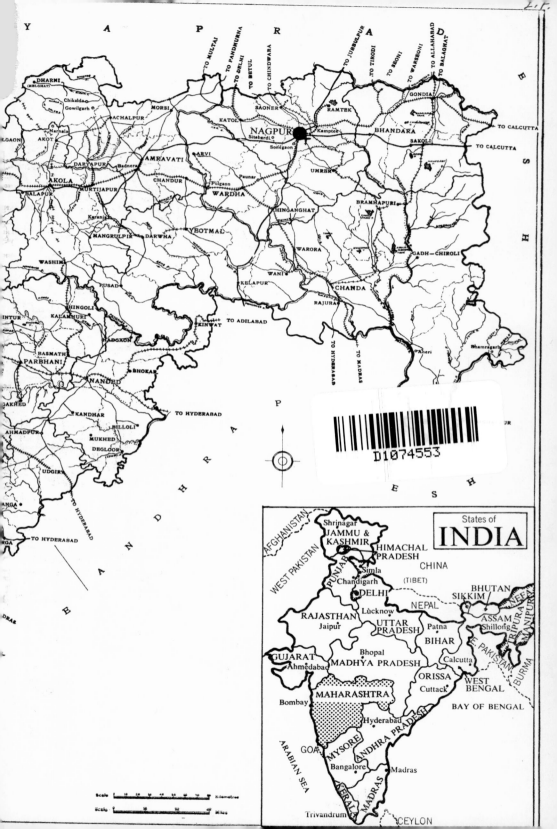

THE NEW BRAHMANS

The New Brahmans

FIVE MAHARASHTRIAN FAMILIES

Selected and Translated by
D. D. KARVE

with the editorial assistance of
Ellen E. McDonald

UNIVERSITY OF CALIFORNIA PRESS
Berkeley and Los Angeles, 1963

University of California Press
Berkeley and Los Angeles, California

Cambridge University Press
London, England

© 1963 by The Regents of the University of California
Library of Congress Catalog Card Number 63-11389

Printed in the United States of America

CONTENTS

GENERAL INTRODUCTION

A glance at the map of India will show Maharashtra sprawling across the mid-part of the Indian peninsula, halfway between the northern plains and extreme northern mountains on the one hand, and the extreme southern tip of the peninsula on the other. Its geographical position has made it a meeting ground for influences from the cultures of northern India, which from the thirteenth century until the British conquest was under the domination of foreign dynasties drawn from the Middle East and Central Asia, and influences from the very different culture of southern India, which largely escaped foreign conquest.

Thus, for example, the language of Maharashtra, Marathi, is the southernmost member of the Indo-European language group spoken on the Indian mainland; but in another aspect of Maharashtrian culture, that of marriage customs, the south Indian pattern is generally followed, and the approved custom is for a young man to marry his mother's brother's daughter or his father's sister's daughter.

But Maharashtra's importance lies not so much in its mixed culture as in the distinguished role it has played in Indian history from at least the seventeenth century until now. This is my native region, where I have resided for practically the whole of my active life; and it is my familiarity with the region and its language, as well as my conviction that what has happened in Maharashtra is significant for the understanding of the development of modern India, which have prompted this book. Let me explain further:

It was in Maharashtra that sustained and successful resistance to the rule of the Central Asian Moghul dynasty first arose under the leadership of the valiant and resourceful Shivaji (1627?–1680), a Maratha by caste (the major peasant caste of Maharashtra). Defying and defeating the Moghuls, he established an independent kingdom late in the seventeenth century which outlasted the declining Moghul empire and expanded until in 1789 a Maratha prince even became the "protector" of the Moghul emperor at Delhi. The British conquerors won final possession of India only after they defeated the Marathas in 1818 in a last battle near Poona.

Although Shivaji himself was a Maratha, Brahmans have always played an important role in the control of Maratha dominions. To staff his administration Shivaji, like earlier Indian rulers, utilized the ancient tradition that learning, teaching, and priesthood are the "caste occupation" of Brahmans; and Brahmans were prominent in both the Maratha judicial system and in the collection of the land revenue—the two traditional functions of an Indian state. In 1713 King Shahu appointed as chief minister or *peshwa* a Chitpavan Brahman from the narrow coastal strip along the west coast south of Bombay, the Konkan. Thereafter the *peshwas* gradually accumulated such prestige and power that the office became hereditary in their family, and they became the virtual rulers of Maharashtra, the line of Shivaji sinking into insignificance at Satara in southern Maharashtra while the *peshwas* ruled at Poona, near Bombay.

The word Brahman does not really denote a caste, but an occupation. Brahmans are the traditional intellectual elite, custodians of sacred learning in a land where until Western conquest all learning had something of the sacred about it. In their priestly functions, they serve as temple custodians and worshippers and also officiate at such religious ceremonies as weddings, investing boys of the upper or "twice-born" castes with the sacred thread, funerals and betrothals, which in India are primarily family ceremonies and are usually held at home. Finally, they have traditionally acted as preceptors to kings—advisors as often political as religious. A particular Brahman caste, on the other hand, is really a local kin group whose members do not marry outside the group. There are scores of Brahman castes all over the country, each with its own marriage customs, gods, and rituals.

The high prestige accorded to Brahmans because of their traditional connection with sacred learning has not prevented them from adopting different occupations when circumstances warranted, however. With high ritual status came the gradual accumulation of land and property, and in Maharashtra, where castes whose hereditary occupation is business are lacking, they often became money-lenders and absentee landlords renting their lands to tenants. Although Brahmans were among the leaders of society all over traditional India, in Maharashtra they may be said to have held a position of unrivalled prestige and power under the *peshwas*.

With the defeat of the *peshwas* in 1818, everything was changed. The highest positions in all spheres of public life were now occupied by the British; but the Brahmans, many of them now dispossessed officeholders, soon began to realize that new opportunities were being opened by the British attempt to create a modern administrative state in India. Macaulay's famous Minute of 1835 laid down that existing funds for education should henceforth be spent on English education, although little was done to establish an educational system until after the Mutiny with the opening of the three Presidency Universities of Calcutta, Madras, and Bombay in 1858. Brahmans immediately recognised the importance of the new kind of education, and, throughout the latter half of the nineteenth century, a very large proportion of those who took advantage of the opportunities for secondary and higher education were Brahmans.

These, in fact, are the "New Brahmans"—those who made the necessary changes in the traditional heritage of learning and teaching and adapted their way of life to the new era. The liberal education they received expanded their horizons in various ways. Some were attracted by ideas of liberty and equality, others by the movement for the emancipation of women, and yet others by study of the ways by which other subject countries had freed themselves from foreign domination. They read Mill, Spencer, Mazzini, and Garibaldi. It was inevitable that their lives should be changed. Yet they did not entirely abandon their heritage. Nothing demonstrates this more clearly than the tremendous popularity of Shivaji as a symbol of resistance to foreign rule in Maharashtra in the late nineteenth and twentieth centuries.

The intellectual ferment, which was the result of the introduction of so many new ideas, had as its counterpart a political movement whose vigor and importance made Maharashtra one of the most important regions of India in this period. Though the Indian National Congress had been organized in Bengal by a circular to the graduates of Calcutta University in 1885, Congressmen from western India soon came to predominate in its councils, and Maharashtra became the scene of the major political controversy of the years 1885–1915. This was the struggle between the Moderate and Extremist wings of the Congress. Their leaders were G. K. Gokhale and B. G. Tilak, respectively; both were Maharashtrians and both Chitpavan Brahmans. Tilak had been one of the founders and Gokhale a member of the famous Deccan Education Society of Poona (founded 1884), which operated a high school and college teaching Western subjects in the city. But Tilak resigned from the Society and turned his full attention to vernacular journalism and political agitation about 1890. The growing divergence of their views resulted in the formation of the two wings of the party by the mid-90's.

The Moderates, or Liberals as they were also known, called for the use of constitutional and parliamentary means only in the Congress' campaign to secure a larger voice in government and increased political rights for Indians. They advocated gradual progress toward a goal which the whole Congress defined in 1907 as *"swaraj,"* self-government or political independence. This was to be accompanied and even preceded by social reform, for the Moderates felt keenly the need to eradicate certain objectionable features of Hindu society.

The name of Tilak's group, the Extremists, refers to their methods. They advocated complete independence first, holding that any means, even extreme and violent ones, were justifiable by this goal. Social reform was to follow later. Tilak, however, unlike the Moderates, devoted much effort to building up a mass party, mainly through his skillful manipulation of traditional symbols in the vernacular press.

Most of the authors of the selections in this book were active adults or were growing up in this exciting period. Brahmans were thus among the first to attain eminence in the legal profession, as administrators, as educators in fields of Western learning, and as public figures and Western-style politicians. The "New Brahmans" introduced in this volume are members of three of the most numerous and important of the dozen or so Brahman castes of Maharashtra. Chitpavans belong to the coastal strip south of Bombay, although many have migrated to the Deccan plateau since the seventeenth century. Since the time of the *peshwas,* they have consistently held positions of eminence in many fields. Of the authors of the narratives in this volume, the Karves and Kolhatkar belong to this caste. Karhada Brahmans, numerically a small group, also live in the western coastal regions; Sardesai, the historian, belongs to this caste. Katagade, the author of *Pundalik,* is a member of a Brahman caste of the Deccan plateau spreading southward into present-day Mysore, the Deshasthas, as is Lilabai Patwardhan, although she married, with some opposition, a Chitpavan.

Selections from the writings of these individuals have been chosen to demonstrate how the winds of change were stubbornly penetrating the chinks of even the closely guarded Hindu home. Karve became a social reformer, defying caste tradition to marry a widow after the death of his first wife and taking steps to aid other widows by opening a school for them. The autobiography of his second wife, my mother, demonstrates the kind of life to which she would have been condemned as a young widow in a rural family if her brother had not held advanced views as a result of his Western education; and we see how the revolutionary step she took in marrying again as a Brahman widow changed the course of her life. Sardesai's account shows the gradual change in his outlook as he pursues his educational career, serves the Maharaja of Baroda, travels abroad, and finally devotes himself entirely to the study of Indian history, a field of study stimulated both by Western interest in India's past and by national consciousness. Katagade and Kolhatkar clearly show Tilak's appeal for the young, and the heightening of national consciousness brought to small towns, if not exactly to the countryside, by the penetration of the vernacular press. Lilabai Patwardhan shows us the "new style" of modified arranged marriage common in cities in the twentieth century, in which the age of marriage has risen to about what it is in the United States and in which the bride and groom, often both college-educated, exercise some choice in the selection of a marriage partner.

My selection of these particular works for translation into English has been, of course, somewhat arbitrary. I have attempted to choose from a very large literature not what was completely typical, but those works which I thought demonstrated best the changing trends in Indian society and culture in a period of rapid and significant changes. The autobiography is not a traditional form of Indian literature; in fact, poetry was greatly preferred to prose in traditional India. A few Moghul rulers wrote their memoirs, but before the nineteenth century the ordinary citizen would never have dreamed of it. The autobiography is, then, a "direct import" from the West. Some of these early autobiographies show a refreshing lack of sophistication in literary matters, so that what is revealed unconsciously is as important as what the author consciously chooses to tell us. I hope that these selections will be read with both levels in mind. I have included my wife's essay "Grandfather" as an example of recent Marathi prose style.

What Indians write in English is only a part, and a small part, of their total literary output. Much more of the vernacular literatures should receive the attention of Western readers than actually do so because of the language barriers separating the West from India and Indians from each other. Modern Indian languages have received scant attention in Western universities; and one of my objects in preparing these translations has been to alert the Western reader to the importance of materials available in the Indian vernaculars.

Although I have been speaking and writing English for the last fifty years, I can lay claim to no special literary excellence; and my Indian English may strike the reader as slightly unusual. I should like to thank Ellen E. McDonald for editing and annotating the selections and for writing brief introductions to each; and John J. Gumperz for suggesting the title, and for his advice and counsel. Most of all I should like to thank my wife, at whose suggestion I originally undertook these translations. This book owes as much to her as to me and is, in a sense, a joint venture.

The authors and/or publishers of the Marathi autobiographies have very kindly given me permission to publish translations of selected parts. I record here my thanks to: The Hingne Women's Education Association, for the autobiographies of my parents; Dr. D. S. Sardesai, brother of G. S. Sardesai; Shri Pundalikji Katagade; Shri Y. G. Joshi, for Mrs. Lilabai Patwardhan's autobiography; and C. C. Kolhatkar, for Chintaman Ganesh Kolhatkar's autobiography.

D. D. K.

D. K. KARVE, Social Reformer

INTRODUCTION

In the following three selections, members of the Karve family discuss their family life. Through the achievements of its members in the fields of education and social welfare this family has become almost a "national institution" in India. The story of their continuing intellectual and practical achievements begins with Maharshi Dhondo Keshav Karve (b. 1858), who died in November, 1962, at the age of 104, part of whose autobiography is translated here.

Before discussing Maharshi Karve's accomplishments in the field of women's—particularly widows'—education and in social reform, which commenced about 1890, we must indicate something of the significance of social reform in the context of Indian society and politics at the end of the last century. For social reform movements to occur at all indicated that remarkable changes in values were then coming about not only in Maharashtra but in many parts of India among the Western-educated. These changes were inspired largely by the philosophies of such thinkers as Rousseau, Locke, and Mill. Yet elements of these philosophies will not be easily recognizable in these pages, suggesting a creative assimilation of new ideas introduced into the Indian milieu more through Western education than through direct contact with Westerners.

This intellectual ferment grew up in the last quarter of the nineteenth century in urban educational centers in many parts of India. In Maharashtra, these were Bombay and Poona; and the proponents of the new ideas were a small but enthusiastic group of Western-educated young men, mainly Brahmans. Their reaction to Western influences took the form of a dual demand for political independence and social reform, and assumed important personal dimensions for the individuals affected by the movement. Not only did they dedicate their efforts to the creation of organizations which would embody their ideals and extend their reform efforts, but many proceeded to implement in their personal lives in a most literal sense the reforms they advocated for society as a whole, regardless of personal cost.

This demand for reform on two fronts, political and social, soon raised the question of which was to come first—social or political reform? The view of the Liberal wing of the Indian National Congress (founded 1885) was that social reform must precede political reform and that the medium of that reform must be education. This wing of the party was at the height of its political influence from 1885 to about 1907, roughly the period of Maharshi Karve's greatest activity in social reform. The Extremist wing, on the other hand, maintained that political independence must precede social reform, and this issue was the subject of hot public and private debate in these years.

Although Maharshi Karve never became associated with a political party, he agreed with the Liberals that education provided the most effective path to social reform, and he was prepared to put his views into effect at both the organizational and personal levels. He became an indefatigable organizer of reform associations for widow remarriage and educational institutions for women. His original determination to bring about change in the social status of widows broadened to become a lifelong concern with women's education.

The source of this interest in raising women's place in society is not made explicit here, but it was perhaps prompted indirectly by the uproar raised earlier in the century by the British over the custom of immolation of widows upon the pyres of their dead husbands which was practiced in some castes (*sati*). Throughout

England *sati* was condemned as inhuman and a sign of the moral inferiority of the Asiatic races. *Sati* may be seen as the logical extreme of social solutions for disposing of widows where caste customs did not permit them to remarry. Although *sati* had long since disappeared from India as a usual practice in any caste, Maharshi Karve's caste, the Chitpavan or Konkanastha Brahmans, did not sanction widow remarriage. Such husbandless women were deprived of both financial support and social standing and were often condemned to very unhappy lives as unpaid domestic servants of their in-laws. Real tragedies occurred when the widow was a child-bride—that is, when she had been betrothed at an early age but the marriage had never been consummated. In India she was considered unable to remarry. That the deplorable condition of such women was not only socially tolerated but actively supported could be taken as proof of the moral inferiority of Hindu religion by nineteenth-century John Bull. It was this imputation which Maharshi Karve set out to combat.

Having concluded that the prohibition on widow remarriage, which had all the force of a religious commandment, must be changed, in 1894 Maharshi Karve established the "Widow Marriage Association" both to aid widows wishing to remarry and to break down public opposition to such marriages. Turning to the problem of widows who could not or would not remarry, he took steps to make their position economically more tenable by educating them, establishing his first educational institution, the Hindu Widows' Home, in Poona in 1896. It has been suggested that segregating women and restricting their movement by the well-to-do in agrarian societies is a demonstration that the family can afford the loss of labor power involved in keeping its women at home and uneducated. In such a society, to educate women was socially revolutionary indeed. The final step was the establishment of the Indian Women's University in 1916.

The extent of the revolution in values for which Marashi Karve and his co-workers were in part responsible may be gauged by the fact that the "Widow Marriage Association" voted to disband, its services no longer required, on April 18, 1958, D. K. Karve's centenary. Both the Hindu Widows' Home and the Indian Women's University are now flourishing educational institutions of more than 2,000 enrollment each. The Home operates elementary schools, high schools, teachers' training institutes, and women's hostels in about a dozen cities of Maharashtra with about 2,500 enrollment in all its branches; and the University, now located in Bombay, has achieved statutory recognition from the Bombay (now Maharashtra) State Government and guides affiliated colleges and high schools for women in Poona, Bombay, Baroda, Ahmedabad, and Nagpur. The total enrollment in all branches is over 5,000.

After the death of his first wife in 1891, Maharshi Karve, who was also determined to practice what he advocated in personal life, decided to marry only a widow. By this time he had become a life member of the Deccan Education Society, a "secular missionary society" modeled on the Jesuits of young men of advanced views whose aim was to "cheapen and facilitate education" for the Indian public. This Society operated the Fergusson College in Poona, where life members of the Society agreed to teach for a minimum of twenty years. There Maharshi Karve was associated with such figures as the famous Maharashtrian Liberal, G. K. Gokhale. Despite such enlightened company, when in 1893 he married Anandibai, the widowed sister of his college friend Narharpant Joshi, it was to the accompaniment of loud public discussion, much of it critical.

In his efforts to make widows economically self-supporting if they were to become equal members of society—an unusual application which Maharshi Karve seems to have made of Spencer's "survival of the fittest" theory—the principle followed was that these schemes on the behalf of widows would meet with better public acceptance if traditional customs were flouted as little as possible in all other respects. To shield his educational enterprises from the public controversy surrounding the question of widow remarriage Maharshi Karve adopted the expedient of separating the second Mrs. D. K. Karve from his educational institutions as far as possible, and she pursued no public career, although she was well educated for the time. It is clear from portions of her autobiography translated here that as stepmother to a son by her husband's first marriage, Raghunath, as mother of three sons of her own, and as household manager for a large number of other dependents she was largely responsible for the success of her husband's enterprises.

Her sons fully justified her hopes for their success. The first, Shankar, practices medicine in Mombasa, Kenya. The youngest, Bhaskar, is secretary of the Hindu Widows' Home. The second, Dinakar (b. 1899), translator of the selections in this volume, was educated at Fergusson College, where he received the B.Sc. degree. He was awarded the Master of Science degree by the University of Bombay through its affiliate, the Indian Institute of Science in Bangalore, and the Ph.D. by the University of Leipzig, Germany, in 1924. He became professor of chemistry (1925–1946, 1957–1959) and the Principal at Fergusson College (1946–1957). After his retirement in 1959, he was for two years a member of the Bombay State Legislative Council, where he was also active in matters of educational policy. He is a frequent writer on educational and language reform in *The Economic Weekly* (Bombay) and various other Indian and Western journals.

India's best-known woman anthropologist, Dr. Irawati Karve, is Dinakar's wife and the author of the third selection, the essay "Grandfather." Born in 1905, she was educated in Poona and married there in 1926, after which she completed her education in Germany. She has been head of the Department of Sociology and Anthropology at the Deccan College Research Institute in Poona since 1939 and was guest lecturer at London University in 1951–52. Both she and her husband were Distinguished Visiting Scholars at the University of California, Berkeley, in 1959–60. Mrs. Karve is the author of *Kinship Organisation in India* (1953), *Hindu Society, An Interpretation* (1961), and of numerous other papers and monographs in the field of anthropology and is also well-known in literary circles in Maharashtra for her personal essays and articles in Marathi.

Maharshi Karve's autobiography, *Atmavritta (My Life Story)*, was first published in 1915 in Marathi, with a second edition in 1928 and a third, including a biographical account of the years 1928–1958 by N. M. Patwardhan, in 1958 (all published by Hingne Stri-Shikshan Samstha, Poona 4). The first selection in the present book includes portions from the original Marathi work and a conclusion taken from a condensed version in English published in India in 1936 under the title *Looking Back*.

His life story is followed by that of his second wife, Anandibai (1865–1950), who first set down her reminiscences in disconnected episodes which were edited by her youngest daughter-in-law, Kaveri Karve, into an autobiography which first appeared in 1944 (*Māzhe Purāna [My Story]*, ed. Kaveri Karve, published by Keshav Bhikaji Dhavale, Bombay 4). Irawati Karve's essay "Grandfather," which closes this section, was first published in Marathi in 1958.

E. M.

MY LIFE STORY

J. K. Karve

EARLY LIFE AND EDUCATION

Murud, at one time a fairly prosperous village, is my native place. It is situated on the western coast of India, about 90 miles south of Bombay in the Ratnagiri District. I cannot trace my ancestors beyond my great-grandfather Raghunath and his elder brother Keshav, who built an imposing house in Murud and donated liberally to the construction of the temple of the goddess in the center of the village.

My grandfather appears to have mismanaged the family property, and, although my father Keshav had faint memories of former riches, he grew up in very poor circumstances. He was married to my mother when he was thirteen and she was seven. In 1843, when he was nineteen, he separated legally from his two brothers.[1] He completed his elementary education[2] in the government school at Murud and, as there was no possibility of further education, took service as a manager for a Brahman land owner. He faithfully served his employer and later his sons for forty

---

[1] According to Hindu law, family property is jointly held by all males. All sons have an equal share in their father's property. Should the brothers wish to hold property independently, they divide the ancestral property and draw up a deed. Joint property-holding was and still is a fruitful source of family quarrels and the division of property and separation of brothers a common occurrence.

[2] In Marathi, the vernacular. British-sponsored vernacular elementary schools were established throughout the Bombay Presidency beginning in the 1820's and 1830's, but traditional schools supported by student fees continued to function.

years and received, besides food and clothing for himself, Rs. 25 per year, which was raised to Rs. 30 in the last few years.

My mother belonged to a family who lived about four miles from where my father worked. The first three children born to my parents soon died and only three, my elder brother, my younger sister, and myself, survived. As there was no school where my father worked, he arranged to send Mother and the three children to Murud, which was naturally very inconvenient for him, as he had to cook for himself and live like a bachelor. This was when my brother was nine and I was four. For the rest of his life Father never lived with us but visited us three or four times a year.

Our ancestral house was in ruins, but a small new one was built in the garden, which had fortunately not been sold. My father was a very frugal man and made it a point never to borrow money. The new house he built for us at Murud cost Rs. 400. As we could not afford to buy a cow, we could hardly get any milk when we first came to stay in Murud and had to accept the traditional free gift of buttermilk from the family of Father's employer.

Father died at the age of sixty when I was studying in the English fifth standard in Bombay at the age of twenty-one. He had begun to entertain some hopes about me, but unfortunately he did not live to see me established in life. Mother, however, lived long enough, first to suffer humiliation and persecution on my account, because I had married a widow, and later, when the edge of the humiliation had been blunted to some extent, to visit the women's educational institution I had founded in Poona and shed tears of joy. She died at the ripe old age of 80.

I was born on April 18, 1858, at the house of my mother's brother. Soon after we moved to Murud I began to attend the old type of school there, one that taught the three R's efficiently. It was a one-room school where the more advanced boys helped the beginners under the guidance of the teacher. School was held in the morning and again after the midday meal recess. After the religious songs, the first thing was usually to run our dry pens lightly over model sheets so as to improve our handwriting. Corporal punishment, often of a very harsh kind, was quite common in our school. Strokes of a cane on the palm, knuckles, or legs, sitting and standing up in quick succession for anything up to 100 times, or bending down and holding one's toes for several minutes were the usual forms of punishing mischievous pupils and also those who were particularly bad at their studies. We used smooth wooden boards spread with fine dust or sand and blunt sticks to write the alphabets, do sums, etc. In the upper classes, however, stone slates were used.

Even as a child I had a sweet voice and my pronunciation was very clear. In our house there was a tradition that every day part of a sacred legend was read.[3] At first my elder brother was in charge of this, but soon it devolved upon me. I used to finish the daily reading before I went back to school in the afternoon. This had become a routine in our house like the daily worship of the family gods. We thought that such reading was a means of acquiring merit. Occasionally I undertook to read in one single day from morning to evening some religious text in praise of God. For example, when my brother went up for his examination, I read aloud the whole of one such book on the first day of the examination in the hope that he would be successful.

When my boyhood friend went to Ratnagiri (the headquarters of our District and the town from which the District took its name) for his English education and others of my contemporaries left Murud to join the training institution for elementary teachers, I remained at home without companions. I was very short in stature and was too young to be admitted to the teacher-training school. Though some others, who were younger than

---

[3] He mentions *Harivijay* (Victory to God Hari [Shiva]), *Ramavijay* (Victory to Rama, an incarnation of Vishnu), *Shivlilamrit* (The Nectar of Shiva's Play), and *Laghu-Guru-Charitra* (The Story of Guru [the God Dattatreya]). These collections of legends about gods and supernatural figures are typical of traditional Marathi vernacular literature. The first three are by Shridhar (1678–1728), the most prolific of Marathi poets.

the minimum age but were tall and hefty, added a year or two to their age and secured admission, I was unable to follow that course. When these friends of mine came back to Murud in the long vacations, I went to them and carried on further studies with their help. Occasionally, they used to send me their examination question papers and I wrote out the answers at home and sent them back. But there was no chance for me to learn English.

In the rainy season, when all our ponds were full, most of the people in the village used to go for a swim. Usually a boy would be taught how to swim when he was about eight or nine years old. But I was terribly afraid of water. Ordinarily a good swimmer would enter first and the learner, with either a rope or floats made out of dried husks of coconuts or a dried hollow pumpkin tied around his waist, would be cautiously lowered into the water. Instead of this well-tried method, our neighbors decided to use a more drastic method on me. Instead of going to the pond, where there is shallow water near the bank and a novice can stand up and regain his breath, they took me to the well behind our house. It was early afternoon, and nobody was in a mood to enter the water so soon after the midday meal, so they plotted to throw me into the well alone. While I was protesting and crying from fright, they tied some coconut husks around my waist. One of them told me that he would follow me into the water, and then two of them caught my hands and threw me into the well. If a rope had been tied to my waist, I could have seized it, but in the circumstances I was so terrified that I did not even think of moving my arms and legs. When the people on the edge of the well saw that I was about to drown, one of them jumped in and pulled me out. This thoughtless procedure gave me such a fright that even a reference to swimming was enough to make me faint with terror. The next Sunday I hid myself in the dark attic of our house when all the others were ready to go for a swim. They searched for me everywhere but could not find me. I remained in that dark attic for several hours and came down only when I was sure that the swimmers had gone to their houses. For some weeks after that nobody bothered me about swimming. Later I learned to swim and lost my fear of water.

We had no mango tree in our orchard and so during the mango season we took a lantern and went late at night or very early in the morning to some of our neighbours' orchards and collected all the mangoes that had fallen down under the trees. Occasionally one of the owners detected us and scolded us, but we paid no attention. This kind of theft was not considered very wrong by the people of my village.

When I was seventeen I prepared to go up for the Second Grade Public Service Examination along with some others who were going up from Murud. The examination was held in September during the rainy season, and it was impossible to reach our District headquarters of Ratnagiri, as many of the creeks were impassable. We, therefore, decided to go to Bombay by a ship that was due to sail from a creek about six miles from Murud. The time of departure was fixed at midnight, and we all went to the ship in the evening with our kits and put up at a *dharmashala* on the bank of the creek. At about 9 p.m. a storm broke out and it began to rain heavily. The creek was soon flooded and it became impossible for the boat to sail. It was no use waiting there as the stormy weather continued till the next morning.

We then returned to Murud, although it was not at all easy to wade through the rushing waters of the creek near our village. It was clear that we could not reach Bombay in time for the examination. However, there were still four days before the examination was due to begin at another District headquarters, Satara, 110 miles away. There was a good road with proper bridges on rivers, if we could cover the first forty miles, in which there were several difficult streams to cross. Our guardians were naturally unwilling to let us go. However, by afternoon the rain cleared up a little and we pressed them so much that in the end we obtained their reluctant consent.

One of our friends had already returned to his village about three miles from Murud in disappointment. Hoping to take him with us, we left with our kits and proceeded to his house that evening, spending the night there. We had now only three days before us to cover the 110 miles. The rain had almost stopped, but our friend could not get permission to accompany us. So we started early the next morning, and our friend came a little way with us in order to see us off. We pressed him so warmly to accompany us, even without his kit, that he agreed to do so. We, therefore, marched off and halted at a village twelve miles off for bath and meals. Our friend's guardian, finding that he did not return even after an hour, concluded that he had accompanied us, hurriedly got together the necessary things for him, followed us, and caught up with us at our halting place just before we set off on our next march. Our friend thus got his kit and we all started with our kits tied behind our backs by long pieces of cloth over one shoulder and under the other arm with a firm knot in front.

Each of us was dressed in a *dhoti,* shirt, and short coat and wore thick leather sandals. The headdress was a square piece of broadcloth folded round the head, which also served as a covering at night. A rough woolen country blanket, carried over one shoulder during the day, served as a bed at night. When it rained, this blanket was folded lengthwise and used as a kind of raincoat and hood to protect the head, back and sides down to the knee. Each one also carried an umbrella. The kit contained a spare *dhoti* to be used as a bedsheet, a silk cloth to be worn at mealtime, a small drinking cup, a few books for study, and a decent supply of victuals that would not spoil for three or four days.

We stopped for the night in a village not far from the main road. After supper and a few hours rest, we started at 3 a.m. and reached the main town nearest our village at about 6 a.m., where we went to the house of a police officer from Murud. We had covered about 40 miles in the first 24 hours, though we were very tired and could not proceed without some food and rest. Our host did everything for us and suggested that we should hire a horse to carry our baggage so that we would be more at ease and walk faster with less fatigue. After our meal a horse was hired, and we started off on our journey at noon. It was a good metalled road, and free from the burden of our kits we walked briskly, especially in view of the fact that we still had to do 70 miles in 36 hours. At night we slept at a *dharmashala* and starting again at 3 a.m. we arrived in another good-sized town at noon. A well-to-do family there had a big hostel where Brahman travellers could have free meals. So we took our baths in a stream and ate there.

Satara was still 36 miles off and it was already afternoon. The examination was to start at 11 a.m. the next day. People in the town naturally began to discuss the matter, and it was pointed out that although Satara was 36 miles by the metalled road, it was only 24 miles by a foot trail. There was a valley through which one had to pass but we could cross this stretch before it was dark if we made haste. We at once prepared to start, but the owner of the horse was understandably very unwilling, as the animal was very tired and the valley was dangerous.

Nevertheless we pressed him, and with great reluctance he consented. The horse plodded slowly on, and we too were tired. Hope spurred us on; but what incentive was there for the poor animal? It was very nearly sunset and the horseman would not enter the foot trail near the valley. Again we pressed him and he yielded. After some distance, the horse began to stop every few minutes. We then beat it and after every lash it would move on for a few paces and stop again. We beat the unfortunate dumb creature very cruelly, but even that was of no use and ultimately the poor creature sat down and would not move in spite of all our efforts. It was pitch dark and we were in the middle of the valley. The path was very narrow, hardly four feet. On one side there was a high rock and on the other a deep chasm. Trees and shrubs shut out the sky. It was only very occasionally that we could get a faint glimpse of the stars. What were we to do? We could not wait there for morning because of the danger of wild beasts. The horseman was in a dilemma. To stay with his horse meant danger to his life; to abandon the animal and make an escape meant sure death for it. At last he decided to follow us until we reached the hilltop plateau at the end of the valley.

We gathered up our kits and moved very slowly and cautiously out of the valley and onto the high plain at dead of night, halting near some shepherds' huts to decide what to do next. The horseman flatly refused to go a step further. If we could have obtained another guide, we would have tried to move on, but that was out of the question at that time of the night. So we had to pass the night on the open rock, huddled shivering in the chill wind until dawn. We were very sorry for the horseman, for we had led him into trouble and probably caused the loss of his horse. Whether it fell a victim to some wild beast or died of fatigue or recovered and went with its master we had no means of knowing. We could not please him by paying him liberally, as we were all poor boys and had only seven or eight rupees apiece. With that we had to manage everything, including examination fee, hotel charges at Satara, and other miscellaneous items. We paid him only the full fare that had been settled for Satara and left him to curse us and his fate.

In the morning we were able to inquire our way from the passers-by, and there was no need for a guide. We had so far to go that it was certain we had no chance of reaching Satara in time, but we thought it best to proceed toward our destination, though late. We reached Satara at 5 p.m. and lodged with a gentleman from Murud who was employed in a government office, taking our meals at a nearby hotel. Hearing our story, he at once went to the chairman of the committee in charge of the examination. The usual practice was to register the candidates in the forenoon and set the essay paper in the afternoon. That year, however, the whole day had been taken up with registration of the candidates, and no essay had been set. The chairman told our host that he would be glad to register our names the next day before the setting of the first paper.

Delighted that all this struggle had not been in vain, we slept deeply that night and hopefully went to the examination hall. The names of all my friends were registered, but the members of the committee thought that I looked too young to be seventeen years of age and summarily rejected me. I protested that I had with me an extract from the school register and took it from my pocket to present to them. Since from my appearance one would judge me to be only about fifteen, they probably thought that I was trying to deceive them. They, therefore, did not care to read my certificate, informed me that they had no time to talk to me, and went about their business.

Oh! What a shock! With dejected heart I returned to our lodgings. I had already waited three years after completing my studies and now to wait for one more tiresome year! The thought was extremely depressing, and I do not know how I spent the few hours until my friends returned. They had been examined in mathematics; the answer books were to be read and the results declared in the morning, so that only those who received passing grades in that subject would be examined in other subjects. My friends went to the examination hall the next day to hear the result and all returned in dejection—they had all failed. Without staying in Satara even for sightseeing, we retraced our steps to our homes to resume our daily routine. Even to this day I have vivid memories of the adventurous trip and its tragic end.

FURTHER EDUCATION IN BOMBAY

Many undreamt-of things have occurred in my life to give an unexpected turn to my career. A young Murud resident who had failed the matriculation examination was induced to start an English class there about three months after I returned from Satara. As I was at loose ends, I joined this class, thus beginning to learn the English alphabet in my eighteenth year. The fee was one rupee per month, and about fifteen students joined the class. Since I was not sure I would be able to carry on with these studies, in the month of September I again appeared for the public service examination, even at the sacrifice of my English studies, and was successful. Postponing the idea of joining the teachers' training school, I continued with the English class. In less than two years we completed three high school standards and had to go to some larger town to continue our studies or give them up.

My younger sister was already married, and my elder brother had taken a job as a teacher and had begun to earn Rs. 5 per month. The responsibility of the family was thus reduced to some extent, and Father and Brother decided to send me to Ratnagiri, our District headquarters, for further studies. I attended the high school there for about six months but fell ill and had to return to Murud. Malarial fever would not leave me and as the rains started, steamer communication with Ratnagiri stopped. I was thus forced to remain at Murud. Just about this time there occurred a vacancy in the local Marathi school to which I requested the Headmaster to appoint me, but he was reluctant to do so because I would be leaving to resume my studies in five months. The salary of Rs. 5 a month would greatly aid my further studies, and in my anxiety to have the position I requested an educated member of a rich family of our village who had come home to recoup his health to put in a word for me. That did the trick and I had my first brief experience in the profession I had decided to follow. I had now decided to join several friends at the Robert Money School, a missionary high school in Bombay. This I did in November at the commencement of the next school year.

In Maharashtra there was and still is the custom in charitably inclined families, even of moderate means, of feeding promising but needy students several days of the week to help them with their studies. I could easily have gotten free board in this way. We discussed this matter in our family before I left for Bombay, and the consensus was that we should not lose our self-respect. I would get a scholarship and could earn something by giving tuitions.[4] Whatever I required in addition was to be borrowed.

When I was in the fifth English standard [5] an incident occurred which demonstrated how timid and shy I am by nature and how I lack presence of mind. Bimonthly examinations were held at the school, with scholarships awarded on the results. A few weeks after I joined the school, it became apparent to intelligent students in my class that I would be a competitor for a scholarship. Copywriting was then regarded as a special subject, to which one hundred marks were assigned. Students had to write one page of the copy book every week, and grades were assigned to these copies at the time of the examination on the basis of the marks of the previous weeks.

My handwriting was bad, and I received the mark F (fair) for the first three or four weeks. Knowing the importance of the subject I made serious attempts to improve my handwriting. I soon wrote a copy far better than my previous ones and received the mark G (good). Mr. Jackson, a very strict teacher, would examine our copy books and leave them on his table until the afternoon poetry lesson when he would return them to us. One bold rival of mine went to Mr. Jackson's table and surreptitiously examined the marks on the copy books. Finding the G on my book and thinking that I had found someone else to write a better hand for me, he brought the matter to Mr. Jackson's notice when we met for the poetry lesson.

Mr. Jackson wrathfully demanded to know who had written the copy. Terror-stricken, I quavered that I had written it. He concluded that I was dishonest, ordered a boy to fetch a cane, then commanded me to hold out my hand. Touching my fore-

---

[4] Private tutoring. Such terms as this and a few others noted hereafter as being specifically Indian or Indian English expressions are usually terms taken into the vernaculars from British English. In these cases we do not translate with American English equivalents.

[5] After completing four or more vernacular "standards" or grades, a student could join an English high school of seven standards. Standards I–III were spent mainly in learning English, which was used as the medium of instruction in Standards IV–VII.

head with the hand to blame my fate, I presented it to him, but
he noticed my movements and began to suspect that perhaps he
had judged too hastily. I was then sent to my classroom to write
a copy in the presence of the teacher. I was still very nervous, so
the copy I wrote was not as good as the one I had written at
home, but it was much better than the previous ones and showed
that I was not dishonest. If I had had the presence of mind and
the courage to offer to write another copy in class, a good deal
of trouble would have been saved.

When I found that I was progressing well with my studies,
I felt free to earn some money for my living expenses. An opportunity to do this presented itself that same year when a fellow
student asked me to coach his younger brother. I readily consented
without settling what payment I was to receive and began to
coach the boy one hour every day, expecting to earn at least two
rupees per month. When at the end of the month I received only
one rupee, I was greatly disappointed; but still that was the first
rupee I had earned by my own efforts and I valued it as such.
But I gave up that tuition from that day.

In Bombay I lived with a gentleman from our village who
was a teacher in a Bombay school; as he often received a number
of requests for coaching students, he used to let me take one of
them. This usually brought me two or three rupees per month.
One particular case I remember was that of an elderly gentleman
who asked me to read poetry with him for one hour every week.
Though he gave me only two annas a reading, this income of
half a rupee per month gave me great satisfaction.

From this time on I made it a practice to set aside one pice
in every rupee that I earned for charitable purposes. If I received
some unexpected payment or gift, I used to put the whole of it
into this "trust." I do not know how I came to think of this plan,
but I remember that I did this from the very moment I began to
receive my scholarship. I did not touch this "charity trust" until it
had accumulated to three rupees. Then came an opportunity to

use it. The owner of the boarding house in Bombay where I took my meals began to show symptoms of tuberculosis and had to close down his establishment and return to Murud. Before he went, he found it impossible to pay back five rupees which he had previously borrowed from me. When I went to Murud in the summer vacation, I visited his house to inquire about his health. He, his mother, and his wife were sitting in the front room with anxious faces and immediately inquired whether I had come to demand the return of my five rupees.

"Oh, no," I told them. "On the contrary I have brought three rupees with me as a present for you." With these words I handed over my "charity trust" to him and saw tears of gratitude fill his eyes. That was my first experience of the joy of giving.

About seven or eight months after I went to Bombay Father died after a short illness. During the monsoon season the coastal steamers suspend their services; if I had wanted to see him, I would have had to undertake a long journey on foot, so my brother and my mother did not write to me about his illness at all. Hence the news of his death came as a great shock, and I was particularly sad that I could not see him before his death.

This created a problem for the family. Brother was a teacher in the elementary school in a small town quite far from Murud, to which he had returned during Father's last illness. Father's death took place in August, and we carried on till the Diwali festival in October and November. Then, when I went to Murud during the vacation, a family council was held. It was decided that Brother should seek a transfer to Murud as soon as possible, look after our affairs there, and live with Mother, and that I should continue my English education. Brother had earned eleven rupees a month, but at Murud he received only seven rupees to start with and eight rupees later. However, he and Mother promised to send me at least four rupees per month by living very economically and I was to manage with that and anything I earned with scholarships and tuitions. If worse should come to worst, we could borrow some money from our maternal uncle.

At Murud, whenever we children had had to do the cook-ing,[6] I generally did the minor chores while my sister, assisted by my brother, looked after the major part of the work. At Bombay, the teacher with whom I was living, his brother and I decided to cook for ourselves in an effort to spend less money than we did by eating at the boarding house. That was when I had to do the work in real earnest. We took turns at it and I did my part conscientiously. Soon, however, my host brought his wife to Bombay and she took charge of the kitchen. I took my meals with them for some years.

I vividly remember one incident which took place about this time. A census was taken in India in 1881. Enumerators were to be paid at a generous rate of one rupee per day. Many temporary enumerators were required, and in an attempt to get an appoint-ment I went for an interview, but there was such a huge crowd that I decided it would be impossible for me to get into the room. There was of course no queue and in the general hubbub and confusion the bolder candidates jostled their way in.

I was on the point of going away in despair when a tall, well-built Jewish student in our school who had already pushed his way in and secured an appointment saw me standing in a corner. Directing me to follow him, he said a few words to a policeman and took me in through a side door. There, after reading a short passage in English and spelling a few words, I was appointed an enumerator. But for that fellow-student of mine, I could never have pushed my way in. Many times, when there was too big a crowd at the ticket window of a railway station, I have had to miss my train. The census enumeration work brought me twelve rupees, which was a great help to me.

I completed the high school course without difficulty and passed the matriculation examination successfully.

---

[6] When women in Brahman families have their menstrual periods they do no cooking because their touch is believed to be polluting. The husband, the children if they are old enough, or an older woman member of the house-hold must take over during this time.

College Education

Even after I learned of my success in the examination, I was uncertain about my chances of entering a college. It was only when I learned that I stood sixteenth in the list of successful candidates and that I had a good chance of securing a scholarship that I felt sure of further progress. The question of the choice of a college was solved by the Principal of the Wilson College,[7] who, we learned from the Principal of the Robert Money School, had offered scholarships to both my friend Joshi and me. It was also convenient for us to join the Wilson College, as it was only a few minutes' walk from our place.

Joshi was very intelligent. He stood third in the University list and secured a University scholarship in addition to the college scholarship. As he also came from a poor family and had to struggle with difficulties, he thought that I would make a suitable companion and invited me to read with him. When we were in the senior class in the high school, we had studied together in the evenings. Like me, he had begun to learn English late and was relatively advanced in age. He had decided to bring his younger brother to Bombay for his education and found it convenient and economical to have his wife there too and to run a small household with me as a paying guest. We hired cheap and rather inconvenient rooms and lived very economically, with the result that our individual monthly expenses including rent came to about six rupees.

We attended the Wilson College for one year but joined the government Elphinstone College for the next two years in order to take advantage of Principal Wordsworth's lectures. During the first year, I received a scholarship of eight rupees per month, of which the fees took five rupees. The next two years I did not get a scholarship, although I got a free studentship. Usually I had two tuitions during all the three years which brought me about

[7] A private college conducted by the Scottish Missionary Society, Free Church of Scotland.

fifteen rupees a month. Thus I was able not only to meet all my expenses but to pay off two hundred rupees which I had to borrow during my high school education. I passed all my examinations in the second class.[8]

My shy and retiring nature kept me confined to my studies. I did not make friends and did practically no reading outside the required texts. Joshi, however, was of a different nature. He would make friends with the clever students in the class and learn from them what extra reading they did. He would also visit teachers and professors to ask what extra books were worth reading. His companionship was very useful to me. Whenever we were tired of study or went for a walk we discussed the latest political and social questions, and I could get the benefit of his general reading and up-to-date information. He had a great liking for Herbert Spencer's works, and, impressed by the force of his arguments, I formed my agnostic tendencies during this period. He afterwards changed his views considerably, but I am almost where I stood then.

In Hindu society the usual joint family consists of a man and his wife, their sons and daughters-in-law, and the grandchildren. Persons living in such joint families have to adapt themselves to each other, often enduring considerable inconvenience and foregoing some of their personal freedom. But people usually do not mind it because all members in a family are closely related to each other. There are, however, no instances of communal households formed by persons quite unrelated to each other. This would be a new kind of joint family. In the first place, financial matters could be decided on the basis of a clear set of rules, thus removing one cause of friction in the ordinary joint family. Secondly, it could train us to tolerate minor differences of opinion and different ways of living.

Joshi had started married life soon after he graduated from high school, whereas I had started married life about six months

---

[8] That is, with a grade of B.

before I passed my high school matriculation examination.[9] But although he and I were living in the same flat in Bombay, both our wives had never been there at the same time. After we had both passed our B.A. examinations and started to earn, the question arose whether we should have separate establishments. I had visited Joshi's family at his village in summer vacations and had also become acquainted with a sister of his who lived in Bombay. Similarly he had visited my people at Murud in one vacation.

Now when we were thinking of bringing our wives to Bombay, Joshi suggested that we all live together as a joint family. I at once accepted the proposal and the new setup proved to be both convenient and economical. The two young wives divided the household work according to an agreed plan. Further, my wife's widowed sister, who later assisted me in the management of the "Widows' Home," also came to live with us and helped in the work. Joshi's younger brother, who had come to Bombay to study law, became a member with his wife. Shopping was entirely in charge of Joshi and his younger brother, as I was no good either at selecting the proper stuff or in bringing down the price that the shopkeeper first asked. Instead I undertook to keep the accounts and look after the financial side. Another friend, Mr. Kale, also joined this communal household for a couple of years, at first alone and then with his wife. Altogether were about twelve to fifteen persons.

Of course there was an occasional exchange of harsh words and some friction, but this never became very serious. We had a rather detailed set of rules. Thus, when there was a guest for less than three days, the host was not charged extra, but if someone was absent for less than three days, he did not get a remission either. For the year 1888 we had an average of 12.1 persons per

---

[9] The expression "starting married life" here means that they began to have normal sexual relations with their wives. Both were married earlier, but their wives had not attained puberty and remained in their parents' homes away from their husbands.

day and the average monthly expense per person was five rupees, one anna. This included rent and food expenses, but clothing and sundries were purchased independently by each family unit.

At the beginning of 1891 Joshi left Bombay. At the end of the same year I went to Poona to join the Fergusson College, and this experiment came to an end after seven years. I must confess that most of the credit for the success of this experiment in communal living must go to the women, who had to spend the whole day together, divide the household work, and suffer each other's peculiarities of behaviour. The men spent most of the day outside the house and did not have to put up with each other's constant company. Considering that in Bombay the rooms are small and privacy not a very easy thing to achieve, our wives deserve high praise for the result.

DOMESTIC LIFE

After passing the B.A. examination, I found it necessary to earn money and to put my family affairs on a sounder basis. Although for some time I served as a teacher in several high schools, I found that I could make more money by giving private tuitions. Mathematics was my special subject and I could easily earn about twenty or twenty-five rupees a month for an hour's tuition a day, so I kept two or three such tuitions and decided to read for my M.A. degree. However, I failed to get that degree and continued with my private tuitions.

According to the custom of those days I had been married at the age of fourteen when my wife was eight. Her family lived very near our home, and I had known her quite well. Although we had played together as children, we had to forget our relation as playmates after our marriage and behave as strangers who are too shy to speak to each other. We communicated when necessary through my sister. My marital life began under my parental roof at Murud when I was twenty, and our son was born just after I graduated from high school. I was living in Bombay most of the time while my wife and the child remained at Murud, where I used to visit them in the vacations. Both of them came to live with me about six months before I passed my B.A. examination.

My brother and mother were highly pleased with my success in life. I wished to make satisfactory arrangements so that the family affairs at home would proceed smoothly. For some time I sent monthly contributions, but in the end it seemed best to pay a lump sum, which could be profitably invested. Thus I saved Rs. 1500 and paid it to my brother on the understanding that there would be no further financial responsibility on me. He had his salary and the income from the ancestral estate, which had been somewhat improved by Father. I myself lived frugally so that my savings could be used for some public purpose.

The happiest times I spent with my first wife were when I went to Murud during the vacations. My parents were very considerate and treated me with great indulgence, for they were beginning to entertain hopes that I might achieve something to raise the status of the family. They allowed me to teach my wife and sister when I was there, and my brother carried on the work during my absence. This was in the eighties of the last century when education for women was not even dreamt of in the villages. After my wife came to live with me in Bombay, both of us were very busy, but whatever time we could spare was devoted to her education. My wife could read Marathi and learned a little English too. She had a mild disposition and never complained although the brunt of the work in the joint family fell upon her. She helped in the education of my son in the early stage, and I also engaged a private tutor instead of sending him to a school. Later I sent him to live in the family of a friend where he attended a regular school.

I was now regarded as belonging to the upper middle class and the people of Murud, including my mother and brother, expected that I would celebrate my son's thread ceremony[10] with some pomp, giving gifts to the priests and a feast for our acquaintances. Instead I persuaded my relatives to agree to a proposal that instead of spending money in this way, I should have the religious ceremony performed unostentatiously in a suburb of Bombay at the house of a friend and should instead make a donation of Rs. 200 to the Murud Fund,[11] the interest on which was to be spent annually for the education of girls. I persuaded another friend to do the same, and he contributed Rs. 100 to the Fund.

Although I did not believe in many of the old religious practices, I always pleased Mother by giving her money to be spent according to her ideas of religious and social duties in matters where she was concerned; thus it was easier to get her consent to my way of doing things, when it was contrary to her views.

It was very unfortunate that before I could give sufficient rest and comfort to my wife, she fell a victim to consumption. During this protracted illness she remained at Murud and I wrote her long letters in order to comfort her, to which she replied in a spirit of resignation. Only a few months before I left for Poona, she died at Murud. Again I found it impossible to be there because of monsoon rains. I spent only the bare minimum on her obsequies and gave Rs. 500 to the Murud Fund in her memory to be spent on English education and girls' education.

SECOND MARRIAGE

I was practically settled down in Bombay. I had reduced the number of my tuitions and joined a private high school with the idea of ultimately becoming a permanent teacher there. Nothing definite had been settled, however, when one morning I received

---

[10] The rite of investing boys of the upper or "twice born" castes with the sacred thread takes place when they are about eight years of age and signifies the commencement of their religious education.

[11] A fund which Maharshi Karve originally established.

a letter from Mr. Gokhale.[12] As he had been my classmate in the Elphinstone College, where we had both taken mathematics as our special subject, we were well acquainted. But during the seven years since our graduation we had not been in communication. His letter, therefore, surprised me considerably. Some years previously, a band of patriotic young men had started an association, a secular missionary society called the Deccan Education Society, whose object was to spread secondary and higher education. They had started first a high school and later a college in Poona.[13] Mr. Tilak,[14] who later became the great leader of the Indian National Congress, was the principal founder, and Mr. Gokhale joined the society a little later.

The letter from Gokhale stated that the life-members of the society wished me to join them and take over the teaching of

---

[12] G. K. Gokhale (1866–1915) and B. G. Tilak (see note 14) were Maharashtra's greatest nationalists in the last decade of the nineteenth century and early twentieth century, though they were of opposing political views. Gokhale, who during this period was a leading figure in the Moderate wing of the Indian National Congress and the leading Indian parliamentarian in India's British-dominated representative institutions, attempted to work through British-established political institutions for a larger measure of political independence and more representative institutions for India. At the same time, however, he stressed the importance of social reform in India's independence struggle and recognized the role of education in promoting social reform. He is the founder of the Servants of India Society, a lay missionary association for social reform and political education.

[13] The Fergusson College, named for Sir James Fergusson, then governor of Bombay, is today a highly respected educational institution in India.

[14] B. G. Tilak (1856–1920) began his career as a journalist and educator, then became leader of the Extremist wing of the Indian National Congress. Although he maintained that political independence must precede social reform and that even violent means are justifiable for this end, he also made strenuous and largely successful efforts to increase public knowledge of and pride in the Hindu national tradition and to further the growth of Maharashtrian regional culture. His two sedition trials (1897 and 1908) and subsequent prison terms, both the consequences of his anti-British agitation in the vernacular press, caused a great public outcry. Tilak was the first public figure known all over India to be jailed by the British government for political reasons, though jail-going later became a well-known side of the Congress' resistance to British rule. These activities made Tilak a great popular hero in Maharashtra, where he is still considered by many Maharashtrians the greatest figure in the independence struggle. He had left the Deccan Education Society before Maharshi Karve joined it.

mathematics in the College. It further asked me, if I was favourably inclined towards the idea, to come to Poona to talk things over. The College, which was admitting students only for the first two years' work, now intended to admit seniors also and required a teacher of mathematics. Professor Gokhale was to relinquish his mathematics post in order to do more work in history and political economy. It was this post which I was to take over from him.

I was not very diffident about my ability to teach the subject as I had already coached several students up to the B.A. standard, but I was a little nervous about handling large classes in the college. However, I decided to go to Poona and have a talk with Gokhale. It was then decided that I should have a two-year contract at Rs. 100 per month and that the question of my joining the society permanently should be considered at the end of this period. Thus my life in Bombay came unexpectedly to an end, and I took up my duties in Poona in November, 1891.

The Deccan Education Society had been founded, on a basis of self-sacrifice, in order to "cheapen and facilitate education." Young men with good qualifications were expected to join it as "life-members" agreeing to serve for a minimum period of twenty years on a relatively low salary. In the beginning they received Rs. 30 per month, later about Rs. 75. The higher salary offered to me was intended to compensate me to some extent for the loss I sustained when I moved from Bombay to Poona. But when I later became a life-member, I received the same remuneration as the others.

It was only a few months after the death of my wife, and I took the youngsters who were members of our communal family to Poona with me. My widowed sister-in-law continued to manage our household in Poona. My colleagues did not wait for the completion of the probationary period but asked me to become a life-member in April of the following year. This I readily accepted and threw in my lot with them. I continued to teach in the Fergusson College until my retirement in 1914, although long before that I had become deeply involved in my various social reform movements.

Whenever I thought of marrying again, the prospect of marrying a girl who was young enough to be my daughter frightened me. There was no possibility of marrying anyone older, because no girl remained unmarried beyond the age of twelve or thirteen in those days. Naturally the question of marrying a widow came to my mind.[15] I had thought about this matter even when I was a boy. Widow remarriage was quite unknown among the higher castes although one or two such marriages had taken place. I was only eleven years old when the first such marriage was celebrated in Bombay in 1869. We in Murud were especially interested because the bride belonged to our village. This event produced a great commotion in Maharashtra. In 1871, a public discussion among learned Brahmans was held in Poona to determine whether the marriage of widows had the sanction of the ancient Hindu lawbooks. The verdict was six to four against the marriage of widows, and the religious elder gave his final decision in accordance with that.

Another event brought the matter again into my thoughts. A friend and fellow student of mine from Murud took the lead in arranging the marriage of his young widowed sister. As the event took place at Jabalpur, several hundred miles from Poona and Bombay, it did not attract much attention, but it did leave an impression on my mind. A different kind of incident, which I remember very well, took place in Murud about the time when I appeared for the public service examination. An orthodox priest who lived not far from our house had a daughter whose husband had abandoned her. She was living in her father's house, wearing the red *kunku* mark on her forehead,[16] when somehow she fell victim to some unscrupulous man. She continued to live in the family until her condition could no longer be concealed but

---

[15] The term "widow" here refers to a girl whose husband had died before the marriage was consummated.

[16] All women who are not widows wear the red *kunku* mark on their foreheads in Maharashtra.

had to leave the house after that. The father was threatened with excommunication by the village council for having harboured a sinner and had to pay a heavy penalty. Some years later I met the woman in a place of pilgrimage in southern Maharashtra which incurably sick people, women in difficulties, and lunatics often seek out. The poor creature saw me while she was going round and round the temple counting her rounds on the beads of a rosary and turned her face away. The episode left an indelible impression on my mind.

Joshi and I often discussed the question of the marriage of widows; both of us were sympathetic about the subject. As long as my wife was living, the matter was of only academic interest. But after the death of my wife I thought deeply about the problem and came to the conclusion that if I were to marry again, it would be to a widow.

Now after I had been in Poona for some time, not only friends but my brother and mother also began to press me to give my consent to a second marriage. In those days marrying a widow meant being cut off from society, especially in the case of persons who had relatives living in the rural areas, which were very orthodox. My first task was, therefore, to persuade my brother and my mother. They were very good-natured and had a high regard for me. No doubt my marrying a widow would cause them great humiliation and they had to prepare themselves to face it. I also told them that if they did not give me their consent, I would prefer to remain a widower throughout my life. They were thus in a dilemma. They realised how strong my convictions were, but they also knew what they would have to endure in our village. Finally, however, they gave me permission to do what I thought right, provided however that I did not involve them in any way.

The next question was perhaps more difficult in the society in which I was living, namely, to find a suitable bride. Some friends had actually suggested some suitable widows as possibilities, but I was hesitant and could not make up my mind. The

question was solved in an unexpected manner. My friend Joshi
had a younger sister named Godu, who had been widowed at
the age of eight. She had lived in the family of her late husband
until she was about twenty-three, when Joshi brought her to
Bombay intending to educate her. She lived in our joint family
for a few months before she was admitted to the famous Pandita
Ramabai's[17] school as its first widow student. When the school
later moved from Bombay to Poona, Godubai[18] went with it. Her
head had been shaved according to the prevalent custom, and
as her parents were orthodox in their views, the idea of marrying
her never entered my mind.

About this time Joshi's father was in Poona on a short visit
and came to see me. To my surprise he asked me directly why I
had not married again. When I told him of my intention of
marrying a widow if at all, he remained silent for a few minutes
and then replied that, in that case, I did not have to go far to
seek a suitable bride. I replied that I understood what he had in
mind but asked whether he was serious. When he answered in
the affirmative, I requested him to see his daughter to ask whether
she was agreeable to the proposal.

Although the elder Mr. Joshi was an orthodox Brahman in
his day-to-day behaviour, he was in essence a liberal-minded person who attached great importance to sentiment and purity of
thought. One could really describe him as having very broad
human sympathies. He went to Godubai's school and reported
to me that she was willing to marry me. I also learned that the
head of the school had persuaded her not to submit to the barber
and she had let her hair grow. She was thus ready to marry me
as soon as convenient. Her father could not, of course, associate
himself openly with the marriage and went away to his village.

[17] This famous Sanskrit scholar was converted to Christianity in 1883. Her
school is now being conducted under the auspices of the Church Missionary Society.

[18] -*bai* in Maharashtra is a word meaning woman, attached to proper names;
it is also a term of address for married women in parts of North India.

My friends were ready to help in all the arrangements. It was the first marriage of a widow to be celebrated in Poona, and they wanted to make it an important event. The question of a house in which to celebrate the wedding would normally have been difficult but a householder whose widowed daughter had herself been married in Bombay some years back came forward and offered his house. We even secured the services of a very learned priest with advanced views in this matter, although a couple of my friends were prepared to recite the sacred verses and perform the religious ceremonies if it became necessary.

My second marriage was celebrated on March 11, 1893. It caused a great commotion all over Maharashtra. Personally it did not involve much change in my daily routine, but apart from newspaper comments, my brother and my mother had to bear a considerable amount of persecution and condemnation in our village.

CONSEQUENCES

In order to enable the reader to get some idea of the public opinion at the time, I would like to give short excerpts from a few of the newspapers in Maharashtra at the time:

Partially or Wholly Favourable

A learned and highly respected Brahman priest went to Poona especially to perform the ceremony. This is very remarkable, and the widow-marriage was probably the first to be celebrated in Poona.

If anyone who possesses natural sympathy for others, good education, self-respect, and determination has had to face the calamity of the death of his wife, he can follow the excellent example of Professor Karve.

A number of highly respected persons in society came to Poona especially to witness the marriage ceremony while many others sent congratulatory messages.

Professor Karve, instead of behaving as a learned fool, has shown real moral courage.

This has been an exceptionally good match.

Mr. Dhondo Keshav Karve, B.A., Konkanastha Brahman,[19] age 35, life-member of the Deccan Education Society, Professor of Mathematics, Fergusson College, was married to Godubai Joshi, age 24, a student in the Sharada Sadan. Godubai's first husband died very young and her elder brother, Narharpant Joshi, B.A., Ll.B., has given his consent to her marriage. Mr. Joshi and Mr. Karve are friends. From the time Mr. Karve lost his first wife, he decided to marry a widow and he deserves praise for carrying out his resolution. If child-widows are married in this way the reform may become popular. The reformers who only talk about reforms or write about them should remember that Mr. Karve is not a talker—he is a doer.[20]

The remarriage[21] which took place yesterday was, except for being a remarriage, in every way decent, and was performed according to the strict orthodox ritual. Whatever may be our opinion on the general question about the necessity of widow remarriages, we must say that if the thing is worth trying at all, it ought to be done in a way that will make it popular. Mr. Karve, though never known to be a blustering reformer, has set a practical example of moral courage which not a legion of would-be social reformers have shown in their whole conduct.[22]

Except that Mr. Karve's marriage was against the Hindu tradition, one can find nothing objectionable. No "Brahmo" priest was brought to conduct the rites.[23] They were conducted by a learned

---

[19] The coastal area south of Bombay from which Maharshi Karve came is known as the Konkan. "Konkanastha" is the adjective form. Like both Tilak and Gokhale, he belonged to the Chitpavan Brahman caste, the caste of the Peshwas, the hereditary prime ministers and *de facto* rulers of Maharashtra before the British conquest.

[20] This is from Tilak's Marathi newspaper, the *Kesari*.

[21] The usual term for widow-marriages in India.

[22] From Tilak's English-language weekly, the *Mahratta*.

[23] The Brahmo Samaj was a reform Hinduism movement originating in Bengal and spreading to Maharashtra under the name of Prarthana Samaj. It denounced idol worship and substituted instead its own austere ritual. This movement has been likened to Protestant reform sects in Christianity and in fact shows considerable Christian influence.

shastri well versed in the ancient sacred books. Messrs. Karve and Joshi have, through their courage, put the reformists of the previous generation to shame.

It should not be assumed that we are totally against widow-remarriage. Under the calamities mentioned by the law books, a woman can marry again if she wishes.[24] But there should be some limitations according to the ancient law books.

If our religion really prohibits the marriage of widows, then this marriage and the persons who went through it shall have to be condemned on religious grounds. But looking at it from a purely rational point of view, we may say that Dhondopant[25] has set a very good example to his contemporaries. If at all there is any room for criticising the marriage, it is very small indeed.

(The last remark of an orthodox person, proud of the ancient tradition, in an imaginary conversation between him and a reformer); "If you are asserting that the ancient law-books approve widow-re-marriage, I shall certainly not agree with you. But if you are repre-senting Professor Karve's action as an attempt to alleviate the miseries of Hindu widows, then we shall say that you ought to be ashamed by the extraordinary courage shown by him and he deserves every praise. If people like him come forward and do what they preach, it will not be long before others follow them."

On the whole, looking at the marriage of Dhondopant and Godubai from the social and ethical point of view, we think that it will be a great help to the advocates of widow-remarriage and this marriage will be considered an important stage in the history of social reform.

Even if it is a widow's marriage, if it is performed with the correct ritual and in the traditional manner, it may gain the support of some and ultimately become accepted.

---

[24] Contradictions may be found in the many ancient Hindu law books. Although one of them states that in case a woman's husband is dead, lost, impotent, or licentious, she may marry again, the tradition has been for Brahman widows not to do so.

[25] *-pant* is an honorific suffix traditionally denoting a Brahman, Dhondo is his personal name.

How the authors of our religious books could sanction a system by which women, for no fault of theirs, were condemned to life-long sorrow, we do not know. And if the ancient law-givers left them no way out, we ought now to provide a way out for them. Marriage for widows is a much better arrangement than certain other evils current in our society.

Critical and Disapproving

The bride and groom in this marriage are: 28 year old child-widow Godubai Joshi, whose hair had been cut off according to the "wicked" custom, but who, since she began to attend the school of Pandita Ramabai, received the "clear light" in her heart and has now adorned her body by allowing her hair to grow; and Professor D. K. Karve of the Fergusson College.[26]

It cannot be argued that a widow's marriage has any special importance or significance. It is quite clear that nothing will be gained by this marriage.

Professor Karve's health is very ordinary, one can almost say, very weak. Therefore, we think he did wrong in marrying for a second time when the first marriage had come to an end and also because there was a son who, according to the Hindu tradition, could perform the necessary rituals for the dead ancestors on both sides.

This marriage can neither be called a *pat* or a remarriage. In fact, only these funny reformers can praise the moral courage of somebody who becomes the slave of his passions and does something which has never been done before in his family.

We are sorry that we have to give him some praise for his moral courage; but we think even greater praise is due to him for his total ignorance of the Hindu religious tradition.

In this affair of a widow giving herself away, there has been no caste-mixture and so the progeny cannot be called cross-breed. But it would have been better if instead of taking pity on a woman who had already spent 10 or 15 years as a widow and got used to it, he had bestowed his favours on one who had only recently become a

---

[26] Sarcastic.

widow, for that would have removed the stigma of previous acquaintance between the bride and groom.

If you ask us what the result of this widow marriage will be,
the answer is that a new caste of half-breeds will be formed. These
new half-breeds cannot stand comparison even with the servants of
the old mixed castes. They can only be compared to the converted
Christians of Goa.[27]

Women's education has progressed, "jewels" like Pandita Ramabai have come forward, women have begun to feel that they should
have the same rights as the men; therefore, we must say that it is
good that the custom of widow-marriage has come into vogue. The
elders of our religion are now of no use, so at least a few leaders
should come together and think about this matter.

This marriage is, among the Hindus, just like those that take
place in other castes. A true Brahman born of the seed of a Brahman
would never perpetrate such a deed.

Of course "Aunt" Pandita Ramabai would be pleased with this
action of her disciple, and the reformers will also be rejoicing. Is not
this act of "reform" the limit?

But public agitation did not end with newspaper comments.
According to my usual practice of spending at least some part
of the annual summer vacation at my native village, I decided to
go there with my wife. I had resolved to submit to whatever
treatment the people there would give me. Without letting anyone know our exact programme, we suddenly arrived there one
evening and occupied a room on the outside of our house but
attached to it. The news spread among the Brahman population
of the tiny village like wildfire. Everybody began to discuss what
steps should be taken against me, and a meeting of the Brahman
caste-council was called the next day, to which every adult
Brahman in the village was invited by means of criers. We were
careful not to wound the feelings of the orthodox people by

---

[27] These were held in contempt by Hindus.

any action of ours. My wife cooked food for us in the outer room, and we did not enter the house.

In the meeting of the caste-council, although there were a few people who were not so totally against me, particularly those who were in service outside and had come to Murud in the holidays, nobody had the courage to speak up for me. Finally the meeting passed the following resolutions:

1. No person should sit on the same carpet with me.

2. No one should attend a meeting where I was present.

3. My brother should be excommunicated if I entered his compound again.

It was understood that nobody would touch either my wife or me or take food with us. Of course I knew a number of people in Murud who at least spoke with me though they would not sit on the same carpet with me. My wife, however, was in a much more desperate position. She knew nobody there, and occasionally some mischievous woman would come near and ask nasty questions to wound her feelings. During our short stay, I could not even speak with my mother or sister. There was no lack of voluntary detectives who kept a watch in order to find out if any food was passed to us from the house.

Finally after a few days we moved to a nearby town, where a friend of mine, grieved at the way we had been treated in Murud, invited us to spend a few days at his house. Both he and his wife welcomed us cordially, and the only restriction they observed was that at meal time my wife and I sat side by side at right angles to my host. In this way after about a fortnight we returned to Poona.

Next year, I went to Murud alone and lived in a vacant house about a furlong from our house. My niece, who was about eight years of age, brought food for me. My brother was able to see me, but my mother and sister came only once at midnight. It took about ten years before the people of Murud were pacified and I was allowed to enter my own house and live with my people.

I now[28] mix freely with people there, though many still refuse to dine with me.

In Poona I had not to encounter such direct and personal opposition. My landlord made no objection to our continuing in the same house, though later, when I wanted to change to a more suitable location, I had considerable difficulty in finding a house. Several times, however, people I had known previously or distant relatives came to visit us and indulged in abusive and violent language about the way I was destroying the great Hindu religious tradition. On all such occasions I either remained silent or at the most tried to put in a mild defence, both of which were usually without any effect on the excited person. Thus on one occasion my wife's younger sister's father-in-law came to see us, ordered us to sit in front of him, and then lectured to us for a full ninety minutes using the most offensive language imaginable. I tried to say that we did what our consciences told us but I could not get in a single word. Ultimately when he had blown off all his pent-up wrath, he went away with a last wish that he might never have to see our black faces again!

One of the ways in which the lives of people who had acted against the traditional way was made difficult was by rumours, either that the husband and wife could not get on well together and were thinking of separating, or that in the first instance the marriage had become necessary because of secret intimacy before the marriage, and so on. We were no exception to this and had our normal share of these. Once when Joshi came to Poona and we two had some legal business at the Registrar's office, people said that at first he tried to patch up our differences and that now a deed of separation was being drawn up and registered! But gradually society settled down to a more tolerant attitude towards us, and we began to live a normal social life.

---

[28] 1915.

FAMILY LIFE IN POONA

Neither of my two wives nor I was keen on fine food, a big house, or showy clothes. I do not remember any time when we were not about ten or twelve persons in the household, and so we were never in a position to spend much on these items. Experience has taught me that the pleasure the good things in life, like food and clothes and ornaments, bring is superficial and deceptive and that real happiness comes from actions in which there is less of worldly selfishness. Anandibai[29] and I had both grown up in the school of nature where hard work was the usual rule. What little time was left from the daily routine, we spent in each other's company and were happy to enjoy these short intervals of domestic bliss. Soon after our marriage I brought two young girls who were related to me and their husbands to live with us so that they could be educated. These, and my son Raghunath, made up our household.

About a year after our marriage Anandibai was expecting her first child. My first wife's sister, who had managed the household before my second marriage, had departed when I married a widow and there was no possibility of getting other help.[30] My wife herself suggested a way out of the difficulty, and I at once gave my consent. We decided to have the delivery in a women's hospital in Poona conducted by a Christian mission. Anandibai had a very strong constitution and carried on her usual household duties, even grinding food grains and pounding rice, up to an advanced stage of her pregnancy. She walked to the hospital, about a mile and a half from our home, and then gave birth to a son. On the eleventh day she and the baby came home

---

[29] This was Godubai's new name. According to Maharashtrian custom, the bride's name is changed during the marriage ceremony.

[30] At that time women usually gave birth at home, while some older woman relative looked after the household. At present most women in cities go to maternity hospitals for the delivery and return after ten or eleven days.

and on the twelfth day came the usual ceremony of naming the baby and having its ears pierced.[31] Now both my wife and I were opposed to this custom and decided not to follow it. But in order not to shock the neighbours who had gathered together, my wife told them that she was afraid that the baby would cry too much and merely touched his ears with a gold earring. None of our three sons had his earlobes pierced.

At the time of the second child's birth a year and a half later, I was out of Poona making propaganda and collecting subscriptions for the association for encouraging widow-marriages which I had established some time before. As Anandibai thought that her delivery would be without complications, she decided not to go to the hospital and made arrangements with a nurse. Unfortunately the child died a short time after its birth. This was one of the occasions when my public activities caused me to neglect some of my obligations to my family, and I was very sad about it.

After our marriage Anandibai's education virtually stopped, as, with so many persons in the household, she had to spend most of her time looking after them. For some time she tried to finish the elementary teachers' course but eventually found it impossible. Then we decided, when the eldest child was about three-and-a-half years old, that as a provision for any future need Anandibai should become a qualified nurse and midwife. Since the number of persons in the house had been reduced to three, this seemed the best opportunity. So she and the child went to Nagpur[32] where a year's course in nursing and midwifery had started. My son, a nephew, and I shifted to a house on the Fergusson College campus and, as a measure of economy, decided to cook for ourselves and do all the household work. The plan proved successful and Anandibai returned after a year with her diploma.

I must mention here one very happy incident. My father-in-

---

[31] This is a universal custom among Hindus. Non-Hindus, particularly Muslims, are often referred to by a term meaning "without the pierced earlobe."

[32] About three hundred miles northeast of Poona.

law, who in spite of his liberal and humanistic attitudes was a deeply religious man, once came to Poona. Because of the feelings among orthodox people about our marriage he did not stay with us but came for a visit. While we were talking, our little son came in. Beholding him, the old man said, "Oh, God, how could anyone have seen this manifestation of Yours? Your ways are inscrutable." With tears of joy rolling from his eyes, he embraced his little grandson tightly. It was his devout belief that God manifests Himself in every human being.

Social Activities

Soon after my second marriage I decided to undertake systematic work to break down the social barriers against marriages of widows. With that object I organised an association with the help of friends under the name of "Widow Marriage Association," not only to carry on propaganda through the press and by means of lecture tours, but also to render all possible help to widows intending to marry again. I worked enthusiastically for this organisation for a number of years, but gradually I came to the realisation that the problem of the improvement of the condition of widows had to be attacked from another side also, namely their education.

My contact with the public had revealed to me the fact that it would take a long time before public opinion could be prepared for the cause of widow-marriage and that it was very hard to break down deep-rooted prejudices in the matter of a woman's life-long loyalty to her husband. The best way to advance the cause was, I thought, to educate widows. That would make them economically independent and would enable them to think for themselves. Otherwise they would continue to be the domestic slaves either of their families by birth or of their families by marriage. Once they were freed from this bondage by education, they would be able to take any decision which they thought to be in their own interest.

At first I considered extending the scope of the Widow Marriage Association to include the education of widows, but on
mature reflection I changed my plan. If started under the auspices
of the Widow Marriage Association, the new project would bear
public suspicion that its object was to get widows married off
rather than to educate them. So I decided to start a separate
organisation, and the Hindu Widows' Home was started with
the help of friends and sympathisers in June, 1896. At first it was
just a hostel for widows in a couple of rooms adjacent to my
house; the widows attended the women's training college in
Poona. During the next couple of years I utilised all my vacations
for tours in different parts of Maharashtra and collected a sum
of nearly Rs. 10,000, of which my own savings of Rs. 1,000 formed
the starting point.

I had all along thought it necessary to have the Widows'
Home move out of the city so that it might have its own buildings
and grounds. For some time my efforts to secure a suitable site
did not succeed. Every year the civic life of Poona was disturbed
by the plague epidemic, and both my family and the inmates of
the Home had to move to a small farmhouse owned by a friend
of mine a couple of miles out of Poona. This man also owned a
considerable area of land near this farmhouse, part of which he
offered to me as a gift for a permanent location for the Home.
In addition he gave a cash donation to name a room in the new
building after his deceased daughter. I at once accepted this offer,
and we had a mud hut constructed there and soon moved the
Home into it.

The place was approachable from Poona only by a foot path
by the side of the irrigation canal and had not even a cart track
for communication with the city. This put two difficult problems
before me. Firstly, I had to keep my wife and children in the city
as the hut was too small to accommodate everybody. Secondly,
as the Home could not be left unguarded and unsupervised at
night, I had to walk there every evening after my work at
Fergusson College and return to the city in the morning. The

internal management of the Home was entrusted to my first wife's sister. Food grains and various other necessities for the Home had to be carried by human carriers, so every day I did my bit by carrying bags on my shoulder or strapped to my back.

Those were trying days for us all. The open space round the temporary hut was covered with thorny bushes, trees, and pointed stones, and the girls had to go through them to fetch water from the canal, about a furlong off. The roof was not rainproof and we had to cover ourselves with mats in order to keep dry when it rained. During the rains, the path was full of mud; but for almost two years I went there every evening with very few breaks. The real hardship was when either my wife or one of the children was ill and I had to leave them at night and go to the Widows' Home, my adopted child, which was so dear to me.

Soon, however, I was fortunate in getting enthusiastic and reliable colleagues to look after the internal management of the Home and I could then devote my attention to the collection of subscriptions and propaganda. In the years following, more permanent buildings were put up, the number of inmates grew rapidly, and a usable car road was constructed from the city. Then for some years I moved my family there, and the oldest boy and I went to the city every day in a bullock cart. Later still, when any day-to-day supervision on my part became unnecessary, I moved back to the city again so that the daily trip in the bullock cart would not be necessary.

The Custom of Shaving the Heads of Brahman Widows

I feel that more work has been done for promoting women's education and encouraging widow-marriage than for abolishing the custom of cutting a woman's hair when her husband dies. Often it happens that a particular reform which is not thought essential for the progress of society does not receive much attention.

It is true that women who become widows are not all subjected to this disfigurement, but the attitude of people living in
the rural areas is still not so liberal about this matter as that of
people living in cities. The custom is still fairly general in the
villages.[33] Once a widow's hair has been cut off, the course of her
life is usually settled. Then any idea of taking education or marrying again is permanently given up. She becomes a sort of unpaid
domestic help in the house of her late husband's family or that
of her parents or brothers. It is easier for a woman who has not
undergone this humiliation to make up her mind to join a school
for further education or to marry again. In fact, orthodox society
considers the growing of hair by a shaved widow much more
objectionable than her education.

However objectionable or disgusting a thing, constant association makes one get used to it. That these unfortunate women
have to submit to the barber at frequent intervals should be considered respectable, and that those who consider this custom to
be uncivilised should be unable to organise social opinion against
it is a shameful state of affairs. I would like to suggest that those
widows who are convinced about the savage nature of this custom should take courage and face the disapproval of society by
not submitting to it. I am sure that if a few older widows of, say,
fifty or sixty years of age would come forward and set an example,
it would surely have a desirable effect. It is true that this abomina-
ble practice does not have any immediate evil consequences for
society at large, but I do think it is a sign of our moral weakness.

As I have mentioned, the custom is slowly dying out in the
cities, but it is still prevalent in the villages. In this context I
well remember an incident that took place about fifteen or twenty
years ago in my part of the country. The question of social reform was frequently discussed in a family of my acquaintance,
and a woman member of the family heard these discussions. Her
husband used to say that it was barbaric to compel a widow to

---

[33] This was written in 1915. It is no longer true.

shave her head every few weeks throughout her life. The woman had also come to accept this view.

As ill luck would have it, the man died, and his wife, in order to satisfy the traditional attitude of the kin-group, cut off her hair to be cremated with his body according to the old custom. But she refused to submit to the frequent shaving of her head later on. Her sons were all well educated and in good positions, but none of them would stand by her; and when she remained firm, they asked her to live alone as they feared that they would be excommunicated if she lived in their house. In the end she went to live all by herself in a rented room but would not yield to what she considered an inhuman custom.

Once when I was in that village during a vacation trip, she managed to send word to me, and I went and spoke a few words of encouragement to her. That fear of social disapprobation should make some people behave in this manner to their own kin is a revealing commentary on the tyranny of social customs. I was in a way happy to learn that after her death nobody insisted on cutting her hair before her body was cremated.

The Hindu Widows' Home has helped in a small way to fight this evil tradition. When, ten or twelve years back, the first case of a shaved widow growing her hair occurred there, my second wife's widowed sister, who had joined me as a worker in the institute, was deeply shocked. But when other women workers in the Home favoured the woman's plan, she was allowed to carry it through. More than half a dozen women followed her example.

After some years, my sister-in-law herself took this step, to the great surprise of all. When, after great deliberation, she decided to let her hair grow, she told me that if by her action the institution was likely to suffer a setback in its educational work, she would give up her idea. Although I knew that a few orthodox people might be turned against the Home, I felt that my sister-in-law must not be deterred by that consideration, and

I told her to go ahead. Some people even spread the rumour that the step was merely a preliminary to a second marriage. One such gentleman wrote to me and asked point blank if that was so. In his opinion, apparently, there could be no other reason for a woman in her forties, who had spent more than a dozen years in the service of the institution and who had a twenty-five-year-old son, to refuse to have her head shaved every few weeks!

LATER DEVELOPMENTS

When the Hindu Widows' Home had progressed for some years, I began to entertain the idea of extending its scope to admit unmarried girls with the ultimate object of organising an institution of women's education which would deal comprehensively with the problem. Then too I had found that in many towns there were no schools for girls beyond the elementary level; and even when parents wished to educate their daughters, they had no means of doing so. The practice of allowing girls to attend boys' schools, which has become slightly more common at present, was vehemently opposed at that time. Also I hoped that if parents from other towns could confidently send their unmarried daughters to a reliable school and let them carry on with their schooling, the age of marriage would naturally rise.

I found, however, that the governing body of the Widows' Home was reluctant to let me expand the scope of the institution's activities, and I was therefore forced to start a separate residential school for unmarried girls. This was located for the first few years in the city of Poona but later moved to a site adjoining that of the Widows' Home. Later still, I succeeded in persuading the governing bodies of the two institutions to amalgamate; at last a single institution for women's education came into existence at Hingne near Poona.

Some years after this, I conceived the idea of starting a women's university, which was the last stage in the development of my ideas about the advancement of Indian women. In it I wished to introduce three major innovations: 1) the use of the mother tongue as the language of instruction;[34] 2) the study of such subjects as child psychology, human physiology, and home science, especially necessary for women; 3) greater option in the subjects of study so as to make it possible for women to avoid difficult subjects like mathematics and physical sciences.

This institution, the Indian Women's University, was started in 1916, at first as a branch of the Widows' Home, but later in its own buildings nearer Poona. Four years later it received a munificent donation from a great industrialist in Bombay city and expanded its jurisdiction to many other parts of the country.

During 1929–1930 I undertook a tour round the world, partly to inform people in other countries of our work and also, if possible, to get financial assistance. I visited Europe, the U.S.A., Japan, the Philippines and Hong Kong and was gratified by the response I received.

A couple of years later I also visited Kenya, Uganda, and Tanganyika in East Africa, where there is a large and prosperous Indian community, and made collections for my institutions. One of my sons, who is a private medical practitioner and has settled in Mombasa, naturally rendered every help, and the tour was a great success.

For the last several years I have been leading a retired life, leaving the management and expansion of my institutions to the younger workers who have taken over. I come from a long-lived and healthy stock and have fortunately had no serious illness. I am happy to live with my son, daughter-in-law, and their children.

---

[34] Instead of English.

AUTOBIOGRAPHY

cAnandibai Karve

The family of Pavaskar Joshi[1] was considered rather well-to-do in our village in Ratnagiri District. My grandfather had seen very good days, but he had also experienced poverty in his old age. No children from his first marriage survived, and he married again when he was in his fifties, paying 500 rupees to the bride's father. She was only about eight or nine years of age, as in those days no girl remained unmarried above that age. Nobody thought anything of such marriages then, nearly a hundred and fifty years ago. Even when I was young, such marriages of young girls to aged widowers were quite common. As soon as the girl had her first flux, the older women in the house sent her to her husband's bedroom and her married life began.

My father Balkrishna was the eldest of seven children, four sons and three daughters. When he was about eighteen years of age, while my grandfather was very old and weak and my grandmother had a ten-days-old child, the house burned down with all that it contained. With great difficulty the occupants were saved. My father, who had gone to a neighboring village to collect the land revenue, returned and erected a temporary structure. This shock proved too much for my grandfather and he soon died. All the family responsibility, therefore, fell on my father as the eldest son.

---

[1] Joshi, meaning astrologer, is a very common surname. In order to distinguish it from others, a family often attaches the name of the original village to which it belonged, in this case Pavas, to its name. The suffix -kar means "belonging to."

Father had a very quiet and steady temperament. He used to do everything only after due deliberation, whereas Mother worked very hard but was of an excitable nature. She brought us all up very strictly. She had eleven children, of whom I was the seventh. Only three sons and four daughters lived to grow up; the other four died young. Father died at the age of ninety-six; Mother died when she was seventy-five.

Father had some agricultural land and also did a little buying and selling. A small village had been given to our family as a grant by some former king, but the land in it was so poor that we hardly got anything out of it. Father also earned a little as a house priest but made it a rule never to officiate at funerals or rituals for dead ancestors.

I never saw Father get angry. Of course there was hardly any occasion for it. Mother used to work in the house from early morning till late in the evening. We three older children helped her in the house, and the brothers also worked in the field and the orchard near the house. Once, when Mother had asked me to prepare some vegetable dish, I lighted a fire in the wrong hearth, not knowing that it was where Mother kept her gold ornaments in a brass box. When she came in to see how I was getting along, she at once saw to her horror what I had done, gave me two or three hefty slaps on the back, and pulled out first the burning pieces of wood and then the jewel box. The ornaments, of course, were all twisted and melted; had not Father saved me and assured Mother that he would have the ornaments remade, I would have been punished again.

When I was about six years of age, my younger sister and I had an attack of smallpox, which I survived but she did not. Then another sister was born and was named Varanashi. But later, my mother saw the dead daughter in a dream and heard the words, "Mother, the new daughter is myself." After that Varanashi was called Krishni, the name of the sister who had died. For a long time after my smallpox attack, I was very weak, all my hair was gone, and the skin all over my body kept peeling

off. My grandmother looked after me during all this time. Father
was very fond of me and used to carry me around on his back.
He used to call me Godubaya.[2]

On the whole, we grew up in very poor circumstances. We
did not have white sugar in those days. A small quantity was
kept in a glass bottle in case it should be needed for medicinal
purposes. We had raw sugar, of course. It was supposed to be bad
for a Brahman to sell milk or milk products. He could give it
or buttermilk prepared from it to the poor, but he could not
sell it for money. When I was very young, I had an attack of
measles and needed milk, but no Brahman in the village would
sell it. So Father purchased a buffalo. It was the usual small
breed common to our parts and gave only four pounds a day.
But Mother somehow managed to provide a little milk and
buttermilk to the whole family. She made *ghi* from the butter,
and Father sold it surreptitiously to get money to buy fodder for
the buffalo. We hardly ever remember having eaten butter or *ghi*
at home. Also, because of the work in the house, we got almost no
time to play.

In her later years, Mother became very short-tempered and
was very harsh on everybody. The grinding poverty and the in-
terminable work made her very peevish and she often used to
beat us, particularly the younger children.

I remember one occasion when I was asked to look after my
baby sister. After all, I was not very old and I forgot to look after
her while I was engrossed in some play. Mother in a rage put a
wooden plank on the baby and threatened to stand on it, saying,
"I think it would be better if I killed her. Then you would not
have to look after her." I at once ran shouting to her, snatched
the baby up, and promised to look after her. Of course I now
realise that the large family, the anxiety about providing adequate
food and the strain of frequent babies and nursing must have
all told on her and made her so short-tempered.

---

[2] Godu was her name, -baya a suffix of endearment and one of the terms
for "sister." Later in her life almost everyone called her just Baya.

A young graduate student named Natu was a neighbour of my eldest married sister and her husband in Bombay. He was married to a cousin of mine (my father's sisters' daughter), but, as ill luck would have it, the young wife died of smallpox soon after she went to live with him. He was about twenty years of age, and my sister decided that I should be married to him. I was then about eight years old, but that was not considered unusual in those days.

My father, who had started from our village on a pilgrimage to Banaras, was prevailed upon by a friend of his in Poona to go instead to Bombay and visit my sister. When she made this proposal, he thought it a very good match. His pilgrimage was given up, and he returned to Devrukh, our village. There, the young man's father visited our house in order to see me. Apparently he was satisfied with me, and the marriage was fixed. As our family was very poor and the Natus were quite well off, the bridegroom's family was to spend everything for the ceremony. Even the usual custom of celebrating the wedding at the bride's house was modified, and my parents, my two brothers, and my younger sister went in *dolis* to Makhjan, about twenty miles from our village, where the Natu family had its house and farm. My father spent only about twenty-five rupees for my wedding. My name Godu was changed to Yashoda, but as the name of the eldest daughter-in-law is not usually uttered by her parents-in-law, they addressed me as "Girl." Most of the ornaments which I wore at the time of the wedding belonged to my husband's sister; and I soon realised that although my husband's family were well provided with farm produce like milk and vegetables and food grains, money in cash and, therefore, the things money can buy were in short supply.

I was married in the Hindu month of Vaishakh (about May) and was sent to my parents-in-law during Shravan (about August) for the usual celebrations of the Tuesdays in that month, when newly married girls carry out various religious and traditional observances. My mother's mother, who had been living with us for a long time, came with me as a kind of protector.[3] She belonged to a family in Devrukh, and we discovered later that she had also been given in marriage to the Natus of Makhjan. Actually this was against tradition. My mother was a Natu by birth and ordinarily I, as her daughter, should not have been given in marriage into the Natu family, as that kind of marriage is supposed to bring ill luck.

But my mother's mother had become a widow very early and had gone to live with her parents in Devrukh. She had had no contact with the Natu family, and when my mother was married, she had come to live with us. It was only when she accompanied me to my husband's house that we discovered that she had also been married in the same family. While I was still in my father-in-law's family, a letter came saying that my husband was ill in Bombay and my father-in-law went there to look after him. Unfortunately, however, he died there after a short illness and I became a widow within four months of my marriage. Some people said this was because I had been given in marriage into the family of my mother's father.

My mother's mother and I were now the two widows in my parental house. We had to sit in a corner. Of course as an eight-year-old girl I was so used to running about and playing that one can imagine how difficult this confinement to the house must have been. Because my hair had not yet been cut off, my touch was polluting, so my grandmother told me not to touch the water, not to play with my younger sister, not to go to Mother, not to fondle the baby. But this only irritated me and I would intentionally touch things. Then Grandmother would scold me. After my bath, when I wanted to put *kunku* on my forehead, my grandmother would stop me from doing it. And when I asked why, both she and Mother would wipe the tears from their eyes. I could not understand that either.

---

[3] It is customary, when a young bride goes to her husband's house, to send an older relative with her on the first few visits.

Father was the one who was most affected. He felt that this was the punishment meted out to him because he had not carried out his original intention of making the Banaras pilgrimage. So he decided to go to Banaras. By Diwali, he had made all the arrangements and left for Banaras, leaving Mother, me, my sister, two brothers, and our aged grandmother at home. How difficult Mother found it to take care of all of us, I still remember. Father had left enough rice to last us during his absence and just ten anans in cash. The buffalo was due to calve. Mother herself was with child but had not told Father about it. Because she realised he was going on a pilgrimage in order to expiate his lapse and to forget his grief, she decided to try to forget her own troubles and face the situation.

Mother had to do all the farm work, burning the field, sowing, transplanting, and a hundred other things. Just then the bullocks came down with hoof and mouth disease and so the ploughing had to be done by day labourers with Mother supervising. One day, while she was drawing water from the well, one of the ropes snapped. She exerted herself too much in pulling up the attached pots full of water and began to have pains. Soon after, she gave birth to a premature girl baby. Then the buffalo calved, but it would let only Mother milk it, and Mother was in bed with a two-day-old baby. So she wrapped herself in a blanket and milked the buffalo. As the touch of a woman in childbed is polluting, that milk could not be used for an offering to the gods, although we used it for other purposes in the house. Altogether Mother had a very hard time of it.

On the fifth day after the delivery Father returned from his pilgrimage and took over all the work. On the twelfth day the new baby was named "Kashi," the traditional name for Banaras. I was about nine years old and helped Grandmother in the housework. I swept the house, scrubbed the cooking pots, made preparations for the worship of the household gods, and looked after my younger sisters and brothers. It was heavy work, particularly because Mother was still very weak and could not get about.

Shortly after, Grandmother died and Father performed all the necessary religious rites.

Father appeared to have got over his grief over my widowhood and I also tried to hide my sorrow so that Mother should not think of it. Some time later, my parents-in-law wrote a letter asking me to come and live with them. They wrote, "We consider that she is now in the place of our son, so please send her." Mother was not very happy about it. But I thought that one mouth less to feed would bring some relief to Father and consented to go. I was about eleven years old then. Father bought me a new *sari* and I went to Makhjan.

My parents-in-law were quite well-to-do. They had a two-storied house. My father-in-law was a government revenue official in the village, and, although there was not much cash, there was enough and to spare of farm produce. My mother-in-law was a very good woman and treated me like a daughter. I had seen my parents get work done by day labourers in our orchard and field, and I soon began to supervise similar work in my new home.

My mother-in-law had in all twenty children. Out of these the first two lived, the next fourteen died, and the last three lived. (My husband, the eldest, died when he was twenty.) These younger children also behaved lovingly to me and treated me like a sister.

From our fields we got rice and other food grains, some fruits, and a lot of raw sugar from sugar cane. I did all the minor chores in the house, preparation for the worship of the house gods, cleaning the courtyard, and sprinkling a mixture of water and cowdung over it, and so on.

We had no well. Our water supply came from an irrigation channel passing through our compound; and I had to get up at 4 o'clock in the morning to fill all the pots with water, as otherwise it became muddy because of the cattle and human beings who crossed through it. Sometimes I got very weary of all this work and thought about my parental home and cried. But I also knew that there was no relief possible. Mother had warned me that she would never consent to take me back if I quarrelled with my mother-in-law. According to her, the mother-in-law was the mother for a married girl.

Sometime during the first year, my husband's brother's wife gave birth to a baby, and I had to do much more work even than before. The next year, when I was twelve, I was looking after all the cattle, milking the cows and buffaloes, feeding the bullocks, cooking breakfast for the farmhands and more. I went daily to the fields to supervise the farmhands' work and to pluck some green grass in the bean patch for the calves; and when I came home, I had to wash clothes and clean the dinner plates too. Thus I was busy from early morning till late in the evening. About Diwali, I was allowed to visit my parents for a month every year.

My mother-in-law always sent a lot of food with me when I went, because she knew that my people were not very well off. I must say that one rarely met such considerate and kind people as my parents-in-law. The thought that I should go to school or even learn something at home never occurred to anybody. Once when I brought back a little book on elementary arithmetic, my mother-in-law angrily took it away from me. It was universally considered improper for a woman to learn to read and write or calculate.

As I gradually grew into womanhood in my father-in-law's house, I realised that I was allowed to do all the work outside the house, but not in the house. A widow whose hair had not been cut off was supposed to pollute by her touch the food, water, the house gods, etc. I retained my hair until I was twenty-one, but afterwards, when my mother-in-law became old and weak, there was difficulty about the housework. Occasionally when she was ill, my father-in-law had to cook, and she did not like it. She began to drop hints that I should remove this difficulty by consenting to have my hair cut. The house priest also gave me sermons, informing me that every drop of water that fell from a widow's hair when she bathed gave her dead husband the life of a worm and he remained in Hell. I could well imagine how long he would thus be languishing there.

Although my mother-in-law loved me, she had loved my husband dearly; and since she honestly believed that only cutting off my hair would enable him to go to Heaven, she did her best to persuade me. I had heard of widows who had refused to have their hair cut being subjected to physical violence, bound by ropes, starved or shut up behind closed doors, and I feared that if I did not consent, I would also have to suffer such ill-treatment. On the other hand, the very idea of having my head shaved was horrible in the extreme.

Finally, however, I did agree. Only I insisted that I would not go to a sacred place of pilgrimage as was the custom but would have the thing over with in the house. And one day I had to sit in front of a barber and have my head shaved. When my husband died, I was so young that I hardly realised what it meant. Later, too, except for a few things like not wearing *kunku* or not being allowed to touch food in the house, I had no hardships to face. But it was when I lost my hair and had to wear a red *sari*[4] that I realised for the first time what it was to be a widow. I spent days and days with tears constantly filling my eyes, but there was no way out. And that was not all. The ordeal had to be repeated every month, and even now I feel for the unfortunate young woman that I was.

From that time, I was supposed to live the life of an ascetic, observing several fasts a month, keeping various vows restricting what I could eat and showing special piety in the worship of God. I had to be careful when I went out because the sight of

---

[4] Widows in Maharashtra whose heads had been shaved were allowed to wear only plain red *saris* or red ones with a small border or design in yellow or white. Older widows wore only white. This varies from region to region of India.

a widow was supposed to bring ill luck. People used to tell me, "You must have sinned in your last birth. And this is the punishment meted out to you. Now, if you behave well and worship God devotedly in this birth, He will reward you in the next birth." But such philosophy never satisfied me.

When I visited my parents' house at Diwali, my brother Narharpant,[5] who was being educated in Bombay, also came home on vacation. He was keen on educating me, but Mother refused to allow it. She thought that my way of life was the best and should not be changed. Moreover, when I came to Devrukh, she found jobs for me like sewing clothes for my sisters and she was unwilling to give up this help. But later, because Narharpant wanted somebody to cook for him in Bombay when his wife died, I did go there.

At that time my brother and his friend Mr. Karve were living in a communal household. There were thirteen or fourteen persons there, and my brother's wife and Mr. Karve's wife cooked for them. But when my brother's wife died, Mr. Karve's wife found it difficult to cook for so many people, and that is why I was sent to help. That I went there at all was pure accident. Normally I would have been at Makhjan, where I could not have been spared because my mother-in-law suffered from asthma and I was the only woman there to look after the household work. But because my elder sister had been very ill at Devrukh, I was allowed to visit her. My brother sent a letter from Bombay just while I was at Devrukh, and I went directly from there to Bombay. From that day, my contact with my parents-in-law ended and I never again went to Makhjan. I do not know whether they tried to get me back and what my father told them, but in any case I lost all contact with the Natu family. Much later, after I married again, my first husband's brother paid me a visit.

---

[5] His full name was Narhar (personal name) Balkrishna (father's name) Joshi (surname); *-pant* is the traditional Brahman honorific suffix. He is the "Joshi" referred to in D. K. Karve's autobiography.

In Bombay, I learned the multiplication table up to ten and
the Marathi alphabet. Then the announcement of the opening
of Pandita Ramabai's Sharada Sadan[6] appeared in the papers, and
Dada (the name I called my brother Narharpant) asked me
whether I would attend the school. But the announcement gave
twenty as the maximum age, and I was twenty-four. But Dada
went and saw Ramabai, and luckily she consented. On the 11th
of March, 1889, the Sharada Sadan opened in Bombay. I was its
first student.

At first I was a day student. As my brother's son was too
young to be left at home, I put him in a perambulator and
walked to the school. A servant from the school used to come
daily to fetch me and to help push the perambulator. I began to
wear a pair of *jodas* and to carry an umbrella as protection against
the sun. Widows, particularly those with shaved heads, were
not supposed to have footwear and people often peeped out of
windows and from balconies at my untraditional behaviour in
wearing shoes and carrying an umbrella. However, I must say
that I was not very happy in Bombay. The family lived on the
fourth floor and the rooms were small. The humid, warm climate
of Bombay was very exhausting. I had to cook for over a dozen
people either in the morning or in the evening. In my parents'
house or in the house of my parents-in-law we hardly ever ate
bread; preparing rice is easy by comparison.[7] But in Bombay,
bread had to be prepared every day. Going to school was becoming very difficult for me. Pandita Ramabai invited me to come to
live in the school, but my brother refused to agree to this.

My brother Dada was a very violent man. Once, because our

---

[6] The name means "Home of Wisdom." The home was opened with funds
Pandita Ramabai secured from the publication of a book, *The High-Caste Hindu
Woman,* and lecture tours in America in 1886–1888, and was supported by the
Ramabai Association of Boston.

[7] To make bread in most parts of India, unleavened dough must be
kneaded and shaped into individual tortilla-like pieces and baked on a circular
iron plate over a charcoal or dung fire. The point here is that each piece must
be prepared and baked separately and means much more work and time than
cooking rice.

youngest brother did not get good grades in school, he beat the youngster mercilessly with a stick. When I went to rescue him, I also got a stroke. Then I applied some turmeric to the weals on the boy's body but, when Dada discovered this, he beat me again. Then I really began to think that it would have been better if I had not come to Bombay.

In this way about three months passed. Planning to send home my youngest brother and then go to live in the Sharada Sadan, I had him write secretly to Father to ask him and Mother to come to Bombay. They did come, but instead of supporting my plan, they tried to persuade me to return to Devrukh. Fortunately I thought of appealing to Pandita Ramabai and, to my great relief, she rose to the occasion. She offered fifty rupees a year to my father so that he could engage a servant to help in the work at home, on condition that I be allowed to reside in the school and carry on my studies.

This was agreed and I went over to the school as a resident student. For some time Mother remained in Bombay with my brother to help in the work of the joint family in my place. In order to repay the money Pandita Ramabai had paid my father, I used to look after her small daughter. She also persuaded me to let my hair grow so that I did not have to bear the humiliating experience of sitting before a barber every month. I took all kinds of precautions to keep this matter secret, tying the end of my *sari* tightly over my head with a safety pin under the chin so that nobody would see my hair. I even went to Devrukh in the vacations, but nobody discovered my secret. Of course I had to wash the hair at night when nobody was about.

The number of students in the Sharada Sadan was very small, and since I was the oldest I became Pandita Ramabai's favorite. She often told me how difficult her life had been. Although she had become Christian, the school was conducted on strictly secular principles with a number of respected Indian leaders of different religions on the governing board. About twenty months after the school started in Bombay, Pandita Ramabai decided that

Bombay was not a very suitable place for such a school and shifted it to Poona.

The other students in the Sadan were much younger and had gone to regular schools. I had never had any schooling before this, and since I was the oldest many duties were assigned to me. Thus I had to milk the cow, look after guests, and cook for Brahman visitors because they would not eat food cooked by other castes. My study therefore was not very satisfactory and I was weak in most subjects. Still I managed to complete six Marathi standards and learned English of the first three standards. My stay in Pandita Ramabai's Sharada Sadan taught me a number of things, particularly feelings of compassion to widows, orphans, and other such helpless humans. I also learned to do hard work and never to waste time in useless things.

Once Father came to Poona to pay me a visit in the Sharada Sadan and stayed with Mr. Karve, whom he knew through Mr. Karve's friendship with Narharpant, my eldest brother. Mr. Karve was a professor in the Fergusson College now. Father asked Mr. Karve whether he was considering marrying again, and Mr. Karve replied that if he married at all, he wanted to marry a widow.

Next day Father came to see me. He spoke to me about marriage and persuaded me that this was the best course. With some hesitation I gave my consent. When Mr. Karve learnt about this, he requested Father to get the consent of his mother and brother too. My father at first agreed but later decided that if people realised that he had helped in bringing about this match, he would be excommunicated and would have to suffer a number of disabilities. So he went back to Devrukh and left Mr. Karve to take further steps.

In a few days Mr. Karve came to see me in the Sharada Sadan and made me an offer of marriage, explaining at the same time that he was a poor man and that we would have to face persecution from society. I accepted his offer, and he went away to his village to get his mother and elder brother to consent to this step. When he declared that he would either marry a widow or not marry at all, they gave him the freedom to do what his conscience dictated.

Pandita Ramabai was not very pleased about my plan to remarry. She thought Mr. Karve's small stature a sign of bad health and also drew my attention to the fact, which of course I knew already, that he had a twelve-year-old son. But when she saw that I had made up my mind, she persuaded Mr. Karve to assign a life policy worth Rs. 3,000 to me and had the document drawn up.

Even now, I am surprised at the progressive nature of my father. No ordinary Brahman father in those days would ever have thought of even tolerating the marriage of his widowed daughter, let alone persuading her to follow that course. Even in our house, where everybody feared the pollution of the shadow of the Untouchable Mahars, my father used to allow them to come up to our porch and often gave them buttermilk. In the first few years of my widowhood, he allowed me to make all the preparations for the worship of the house gods. He used to say, "The God who allowed you to become a widow must allow you to do all this." Altogether, he was exceptionally reformist and liberal for his times.

My marriage was celebrated with orthodox religious rites by a learned priest on March 11, 1893. That was also the anniversary of the Sharada Sadan, which had been started on that day four years back; and Pandita Ramabai held a big reception there, which all the students attended. My name was changed to Anandibai.

I never uttered my husband's name, Dhondo,[8] not because I believed in the superstition that if a wife utters her husband's

---

[8] Dhondo means "stone." When a woman loses a number of children by death, she may give her living children uncomplimentary names in the belief that the god of death can be persuaded to avoid such children. Thus D. K. Karve's elder brother was named Bhiku, "beggar."

name his life is shortened, but because I did not like the name.
So I always used "Karve" whenever I had occasion to refer to
him.[9]

After I began my married life, I went once or twice to the
Sharada Sadan as a young bride would go to her parents' house.
But very soon the institution gave up its secular policy and became openly a Christian missionary institution. Most Hindus removed their wards from it and it moved to a place about twenty
miles from Poona. Once or twice Ramabai tried indirectly to get
us converted, but when she found that we had no inclination for
it, she gave up her attempts.

My marriage created great commotion in society. All kinds
of rumours were started about us. Some people said we were
cousins, because when Karve and my brother were living in a
joint family in Bombay, I had stayed there. My great fear was
that if my children did not grow up to be good and intelligent,
then orthodox people would say that it was the natural result of
such behaviour against the ancient tradition. Very few people
in Maharashtra were sympathetic to us at that time. Once the
Principal of Fergusson College invited us to dinner and his wife
presented me with a coconut and food grains as is usual for a
newly married woman. This was quite exceptional, and when
we were walking back to our house people peeped out of their
windows and doors to see what a remarried couple[10] looked like!
During the first few months, when Karve went to the College
and I was alone at home, I used to feel very lonely. I was also
fearful that somebody might do physical violence to him, because he had violated tradition.

I well remember our first trip to Murud, the village in the
Konkan where the Karves had their house. We were treated as

---

[9] Traditionally, a Hindu woman did not utter her husband's first name,
referring to him instead in an indirect fashion, as "Sir," "Mr. . . . ," or just
"they," the respectful plural used in referring to elders. Anandibai thus observes
the tradition in a somewhat less than traditionally respectful spirit.

[10] That is, couples where the wife had been a widow.

outcastes and were not allowed to enter the house where my mother-in-law and her son lived for fear that they would be excommunicated. We stayed in an outbuilding where cattle had once been kept. My new mother-in-law was a very kind-hearted woman and treated me with consideration, but the neighbours were just terrible. I lighted the fire in our little room so that people would think we were cooking our own food, but my mother-in-law managed to send food to us secretly.

Most of the neighbours merely pointed at us or smiled when they passed the house, but one or two women actually insulted me by their offensive remarks. I remember one of them who asked whether I was pregnant when I married. I had had enough, so I told her it was so (though of course it was not), and the child was my husband's. Then she really had something to talk about! I also remember that one friend of my husband's was very cordial to us. He invited us to dinner, and both he and his wife gave us presents. Even his old mother lovingly combed my hair and tied it into a knot.

After I returned to Poona, our family grew by the addition of several young relatives of my husband's and mine until there were seven members. I again began to attend school, wishing to finish high school if possible. Here again people in Poona thought it funny for a grown married woman to attend school and made remarks about me within my hearing, but I never paid any attention to them.

About four months after my marriage I became pregnant. I was already advanced in age at the time of my marriage and I believed that every woman should have at least two or three children. About this time, our home had become a boarding house for a number of children of remarried couples. We had a scheme under which such couples who were living in small towns and not in a position to send their children to a residential school in the city could accommodate them in our house, where they were financed by other remarried persons in better circumstances. Thus we had four such students, and with the original four of our relatives we made quite a big group.

I had made arrangements in the mission hospital through Pandita Ramabai for my delivery. In order to save the bother of calling for a carriage at night, I asked two of the students to accompany me to the hospital in the evening and return home in the morning. As it happened, it was in the morning that I felt my time had come; and after walking to the hospital in the company of one of the students, I gave birth to a son. Pandita Ramabai had wanted me to have a daughter and was a little disappointed.

On the twelfth day, the boy was given the name Shankar; and, as neither my husband nor I liked the traditional piercing of the ears, I merely touched the child's ears with a gold earring and applied a little *kunku*.

About a year and a half after the birth of my first child, my second child, also a son, was born. As my first delivery had been normal, I decided not to go to the hospital and called a nurse to our house. Unfortunately, however, the child died soon after its birth. My husband was out of Poona at that time and was very sorry to learn about this sad event.

Soon after this, my widowed younger sister came to live with me, bringing her son for his education. My husband suggested that she should go to the girls' school, and, when our son was a little older, I also began to attend school. But this time I went to live in the school dormitory as they allowed me to bring my child with me. He became a great favourite with all the teachers and students. One friend used to call Shankar "Gladstone," because my name Anandi means "glad" and my husband's name Dhondo means "stone."

When Shankar was two and a half years old, the first plague epidemic started in Poona.[11] So my child and I went to Berar, and later my husband and the children and my sister all came too. We lived in a rented house till the epidemic in Poona sub-

---

[11] About the end of 1896.

sided. There we heard that a new one-year midwife's course was being started at Nagpur, and my husband sent an application in my name. Soon after we returned to Poona, I learned that I had been admitted and so I went to Nagpur with my son. My knowledge of English and Hindi was extremely limited, and I had great difficulty in following the lectures, but somehow I managed to complete the course and get the certificate.

Although my husband started the Hindu Widows' Home Association in 1896, the actual work of the institution did not begin until 1899 in a rented house in Poona. The house was spacious, with an inner courtyard. Our family lived in one part and the girls in the institution in the other. Before this, the girls who had been admitted had lived in the dormitory of the local school for girls.

Even after the institution opened in 1899, only the newly admitted students lived in the rented house while the others continued to live in the school dormitory. My husband used to teach them in the morning and evening, and they often completed two or three grades during a year. However, we were greatly bothered by the annual visit of the plague epidemic, and soon the Home shifted into a temporary structure at Hingne about three miles out of the Poona city limits.

After that I did not have much direct connection with the institution, which was managed by the men and women workers who joined my husband in his work. Also, my husband was of the opinion that people were not so opposed to the education of widows but were adamant against their marriage. He was, therefore, very particular to see that nobody should have grounds to charge that the widows in the institution were influenced or persuaded to marry again. If I had been allowed to participate in the management, such a charge might easily have been made and could well have retarded the progress and popularity of the movement for widows' education.

For many years, after the shifting of the Home to Hingne,

Karve used to walk there every evening after his college work, often with provisions and supplies, remaining there for the night and returning in the morning because he did not wish to leave the inmates and the women workers alone at night without some responsible man in residence. Often I used to resent this but later I realised the necessity.

Then for some years, we tried the experiment of living there. We arranged for a bullock cart to take my husband and children to school in Poona every day and bring them back. One day, when a new driver was driving the cart, he lost control of the bullock and the cart overturned. My eldest son broke his arm, and my husband received some bruises. Some time later, Shankar had an attack of typhoid which lasted several weeks. My youngest son was born at Hingne, but he also did not thrive in the place. Ultimately we decided to shift again to the city. By this time one or two men workers who could live at Hingne had joined my husband, and it was not necesary for him to be there every evening.

While at Hingne, although I used to take care of such duties as checking purchases and buying corn or firewood from the villagers, I took no part in the internal management of the Home. The atmosphere there was intentionally kept traditional and orthodox; I was not allowed to touch the water used in cooking and drinking and I also took my meals separately from the inmates.

During the whole of my married life, I have sheltered and raised so many poor orphans and helpless widows that it would be impossible to count them. Some of them have done fairly well in life; others died. Some of the widows who came to me for shelter had been driven away by their parents or their husband's people and could not join the Widows' Home because there someone had to sign the admission form as guardian. But I admitted these unfortunate women into my home and tried to help them.

For some I found suitable husbands, others learned some useful occupation, and so on.

My own children were never very happy about the number of outsiders I had in our family, partly because I could not give these orphans the same standard of food and clothing as I gave my own children. My sons would sometimes protest that this double standard in the house was making them feel unhappy and guilty. I, on the other hand, thought that these poor creatures, who would otherwise have starved, were glad to get at least the coarse food and old, repaired clothes which was all that I could give them. If I had treated these orphans as I did my own children, I would not have been able to help even one tenth the number of them that I actually did. These children helped me in my household work, and I could manage without engaging domestic help. I often went to friends and asked for old clothes or other assistance for them.

Sometimes my husband's attitude to money exasperated me. Soon after our marriage he gave his life insurance policy of Rs. 5,000 to the Widows' Home. I always thought that if he were to die while the children were still young, I would have a hard time of it raising them. Then, some years after the Widows' Home opened, Karve decided to give up his service in the Fergusson College and devote himself full time to the new institution. He had only a few more years to serve to be entitled to a retirement pension and to a life insurance policy of Rs. 3,000 taken out by the College. So I opposed his proposal vehemently and fortunately succeeded in persuading him to continue at the Fergusson College for the necessary minimum period. In this way he has been getting a small pension since 1915.

Even though Karve's salary from the Fergusson College was not very large, still he would spend some of it for charity or to help some poor relatives. The amount I got to run the household was very meagre. I used to supplement it by working as a midwife in my spare time. Sometimes a well-to-do person would place his son or daughter with me as a paying boarder. One girl was a ward of my husband, the daughter of a rich man in Bombay who had died, naming my husband as trustee for the minor girl. The trustee was to get Rs. 400 per year as his remuneration, and the girl's expenses were to be paid out of the estate. This girl remained in my house for a number of years and meant a considerable financial relief to me.

My greatest anxiety was that if my sons did not turn out well, people would say that children of such marriages could not possibly turn out well. I looked to their studies and told them that their father would educate them only up to their twentieth year. After that they would have to shift for themselves, so they should study hard. Fortunately all three sons have made good in life.

The good atmosphere in a family is dependent solely on the loving relations between husband and wife. My husband used to be away very often on account of his work for the institutions he had founded and I had to see to all the usual affairs of the family—the children's food, illnesses, studies, the family budget, and so on. I had the impression that he approved of what I did—at least he never said he did not. But on the whole he was a man of very few words. I had known that right from the time when I lived with my brother in their joint establishment.

Whether with me or with the children, my husband behaved in a reserved and calculating way. Of course I never mentioned to anybody else that he behaved so to me. My policy was never to let Karve know how his sons behaved to me and never to let the sons know how Karve behaved to me. Sometimes I got angry at his behaviour, but I kept it to myself.

Although formerly he never had time to talk with me much, when after an illness[12] he went to stay with my second son Dinu[13] and his wife, he used to come every day to visit me in my little

---

[12] About 1940.
[13] Familiar short form of Dinakar.

cottage in the compound of the Women's College and spend an hour talking over old times and old friends. I did not want to go and stay with my son, as I was not willing to give up my freedom. But I was too old to look after my husband, particularly after his illness, so he went to live with our son and daughter-in-law while I continued to live alone.

My husband is a kind of universal friend. He never criticises others and so even those who worked in the Widows' Home and left on account of some difference of opinion still maintain friendly relations with him. But my nature is different. If I see that something is not properly done or that somebody is not doing his duty, I will openly criticise and so many people are offended. Karve's is a one-track mind and he often does not even notice things which others would see immediately. For example, when he came to ask me about marriage, he thought that he would have to wait several months before my hair could grow again. He did not notice that although I had covered my head with the end of my *sari,* I had allowed my hair to grow.

One of his traits, namely not being fastidious about food, proved a great boon to me. He would eat with relish whatever I gave him. If rice or bread was left over from the morning meal, he would insist on eating it in the evening not only out of careful management but because he *liked* it! I never in my whole life remember hearing him say that a particular dish was not to his liking or that I had not prepared it well. The only thing he disliked was *ghi,* and he protested vehemently when I tried to make him eat some by mixing it with rice or vegetables.

Sometimes in fun I tell him that although people call him Maharshi, some of the credit is due to me. For if I had not managed the family affairs and set him free to carry out his public activities, he could not have achieved so much. But that is merely in the lighter vein. I consider myself fortunate that I could give him some help in his great work.

GRANDFATHER

Irawati Karve

"I am enjoying myself thoroughly. I am getting the utmost joy out of life." He paused for a moment and continued, "I am enjoying life." Somebody was interviewing Grandfather, and he was speaking in his usual clear voice. I could hear everything in the next room. "Grandfather" is my father-in-law. There is hardly any occasion for me to speak to him, almost never to address him directly. When I came into the family, the children of my oldest sister-in-law called him Grandfather, and I came to use the same term when speaking of him. I have been in the family for over thirty years; for at least fifteen of those years he has lived in our house. And still I have not been able to understand him. Some words or actions of his still shock or surprise me.

Even now. How sincerely he was saying that he was helping himself to life's good things, and there I sat, listening to him in bewildered surprise! I am 52, and he is almost 100. I cannot say that my life has been full of sorrow or unpleasantness; but neither can I say that I will be able, in the future, deliberately to search after life's pleasures. Looking back on the path that I have walked, I see important milestones. Some are happy events; others are equally painful ones. Many loved ones are gone forever. Not that I am daily shedding tears for them, but their memory would make it impossible for me to give myself up unreservedly to the joys of life. One recalls the words in *Venisamhar:*[1]

---

[1] A Sanskrit play.

"Gandhari[2] has given birth not to a hundred sons but to a hundred sorrows." These words seem to me to hold the essence of life and love. During the hundred years of Grandfather's life many loved ones and valued colleagues have gone, never to return. His parents, two wives, sons, grandchildren, and many fellow-workers are no more. My mother-in-law and my eldest brother-in-law died only a few years ago. Does he never think of them?

On the day my eldest brother-in-law, his first son, died, many local friends came throughout the day to pay condolence visits. One gentleman came early in the morning and Grandfather spoke a few words with him: "After all, he was pretty advanced in age and was also in bad health. A man has got to die one day." The visitor was naturally shocked to hear these words, but they made me feel rather queer too. His attitude to his family is like that of a tree under which cattle rest during the hot part of the day. They sit in the cool shade for a time and then go away. Others take their place. That is his family. He is in the family, but he has hardly any real contacts with it.

One of my daughters, his granddaughter, lives in Phaltan. When last year he completed ninety-nine years, some friends there went to her and asked her to give her reminiscences about him. She said, "What can I tell you? I can really think of nothing. When I was very young, Grandfather used to visit us occasionally, but I can never recall his having spoken with me. When I was a little older, all I remember is, 'Grandfather, tea is ready; Grandfather, dinner is served; Grandfather, there's somebody to see you.' I don't remember having said anything else to him."

I do not think his other grandchildren could tell any other tale. We daughters-in-law had the same experience. I have asked his sons and they also do not appear to have had long conversations with him. He is just not a talkative person. Not that he hates to

---

[2] The queen in the epic *Mahabharata* who gave birth to a hundred sons, all of whom died in a great battle.

speak, but I do not ever remember him discussing domestic affairs in the family circle. He was a member of many committees of the Women's University, but I don't recall that he took an active part in the discussions. My mother-in-law used to say, "Most of the day he was not at home and if after supper I started some domestic topic (a bother for Grandfather!), he would turn his face to the wall and go to sleep. What could one do about it? However you bothered him, he would not say a word, but would do exactly as he wanted." "Exactly as he wanted . . ."—that is his peculiarity. One reads in his autobiography that once he got an idea, he would think it over for days and months. Once he came to a definite conclusion, he would translate it into action. It was then, and not before, that others came to know his ideas.

It was after he had started the Widows' Home at Hingne. Grandfather was a professor in the Fergusson College at that time. One fine day, without consulting anybody, he assigned his life policy for Rs. 5,000 to the Home. My mother-in-law used to say about it, "When as a Hindu widow, I married again, I lost all contact with my parents' home and my first husband's family. My second husband's people treated me as an outcast. I already had Shankar, my first son. The usual means of livelihood for a Brahman widow, serving as a cook, was closed to me. If unfortunately I had been widowed a second time, there was nothing else for me to do but commit suicide. I cried, quarrelled with him, abused him, but he would not budge. Then I realised that *I* had to be the one to look after my children, and I did that as best I could."

Yes. She was the one to care for the children. Grandfather used to give her forty-five rupees out of his salary of one hundred. The cost of living was not very high in those days, but I don't think he ever seriously thought whether the husband and wife, three sons, and one or two others could manage on that sum. It is best left to one's imagination how Mother-in-law managed everything in the cheapest possible way and still saved a little out of her meagre monthly allowance. Grandfather was very frequently away from home, but the children had to live with their mother all the time and there was a real feeling of resentment against her. They often recall, "We never had the courage to take any of our friends to our house"; or, "I got my first jacket when I was in the B.A. class"; or, "I have often helped Mother to wash the cooking utensils." When the sons and daughters-in-law celebrated the old couple's golden wedding anniversary, Mother-in-law said, "He has not purchased one new *sari* for me during the last fifty years!"

Grandfather had decided to educate his sons as far as the B.A. degree (as he was a life-member of the Deccan Education Society, his children had no fees to pay) and then they were to shift for themselves. The second son (mother-in-law's first son) became a doctor, and whatever extra was spent for his medical study in Bombay he paid back after beginning practice in East Africa. The third son stood first in the B.Sc. examination, got a scholarship, and passed his M.Sc. He then wanted to go to Europe for further studies—but where was the money to come from? Grandfather would not ask anybody. Groceries for the Widow's Home were purchased at that time from a shop near the market owned by a shopkeeper named Adhav. Mother-in-law went to him and asked for a loan of three thousand rupees. That good soul gave the money without the slightest hesitation, trusting her word. But then she insisted that Grandfather should write a regular promissory note! Of course my husband spent much more for his education in Germany. He returned Rs. 5,500 to his father, and this money was utilized to send the third son to England.

My mother-in-law occasionally used to recall all these things, and her eyes would fill with tears. Grandfather would remain silent for a long time and then say, "Everything has now turned out well; why are you shedding tears now?"

Her first son was my mother-in-law's favourite. He was fair-complexioned like her father's people; the other two sons were dark like the Karves. He was intelligent and pushing and did well in life. But the main reason was that he was the first child

after her widow-remarriage. She was naturally very fond of him
—but he had gone out to Africa. She used to ask, "Could you
not have practiced here in India?" and pat came the reply, "We
never had what we could call a home. It was more like a *dharmashala*. So for fear that my place in Poona would become another's, I went out to Africa." My mother-in-law's house was in
reality like that, but was she alone responsible for it? But she
used to feel it and make such occasional remarks which naturally
brought forth a retort. Grandfather never said a word and nobody
said a word to him. Shankar came to India for a holiday once in
five or ten years. When Mother-in-law heard about it she was
terribly excited. "Shankar is coming; he must stay with me. I
won't allow him to stay with any of you," she used to insist. Then
she made all kinds of preparations. Of course Shankar got bored
after staying with her for a couple of days and shifted to one or
the other of his brothers. But still the old lady was very happy
while he was in Poona. With the approach of the day of his departure, she became very uneasy and her eyes filled with tears.
"Shankar, I won't see you again," she would say again and again.
Shankar could hardly control his emotion. "My mother's grief
kills all the joy of seeing you all," he would say. We found it
depressing too. Grandfather was the only one who was unmoved.
—"Oh, Shankar, have you come? Well, Shankar, is it time for
you to go back now?"—That was all. Cattle taking shelter under
the shade of a tree . . .

Grandfather's behaviour was the same towards everybody.
But Appa (Grandfather's son by his first wife) used to tell us that
Grandfather was a strict disciplinarian with him. He had to shave
his head and wear the usual orthodox tuft of hair on the back of
his head until he went to college. He was not permitted to see
dramatic performances—and the fun of it was that all the sons,
but particularly Appa and Shankar, were very fond of concerts
and dramas. Naturally they had to attend them on the sly. These
two felt the need to seek freedom from this strict regime; and,

possibly as a reaction against the extra economy in their youth, both of them were rather free with their money. Remembering his own boyhood, Shankar did not deny anything to his sons. Naturally Mother-in-law was very angry about her son's extravagance; and as he paid no attention to her, his wife had to face the mother-in-law's wrath. When Mother-in-law came on a visit, there was an air of apprehension as to what remark she would pass. Even ordinary items of expenditure she considered quite unnecessary. One word led to another and feelings were embittered.

Grandfather was quite the opposite. He did not say a word about it. Naturally he was very popular among the daughters-in-law. If we gave a dish full of pieces of mangoes to Grandfather, he would eat them with great relish. He took tea and whatever one gave him with it. He never asked if it was proper time for tea, how many times the others had already had tea that morning, whether the food had been prepared at home or purchased in the bazaar. It just never occurred to him.

I believe he has never gone to a shop and bought an *anna* worth of anything in his long life. He has travelled all over the world, visited all parts of India collecting subscriptions for his institutions, but I think he probably never bought his railway ticket. Somebody purchased his ticket, and he paid the money.

He was very particular about his dress. He used to wear a particular kind of *dhoti,* turban, and coat, but somebody else had to do the work of buying the cloth, giving it to the tailor, and getting it back. As far back as my memory goes, it was either Mother-in-law or one of the sons. Once he asked Appa to buy a blanket. I think he was to go out on a long trip, and all the blankets in the house were old and threadbare, patched up again and again. So it was decided to buy a new one. Appa bought a new two-coloured blanket for his father; the price was sixty rupees. Grandfather got a monthly pension of seventy rupees. He quietly paid the sixty rupees and made a note never to ask his

eldest son to buy anything for him again. Mother-in-law was very
angry about it. That blanket was a standing joke in our family,
but Grandfather never said a word.

Of course Appa would have paid for the blanket; so would
any of the other sons, but Grandfather never took a pice from
his sons for himself. Even if he wanted a postage stamp, he would
pay for it. He himself and others have written about it, but I
have always failed to understand it. I said to myself, for fifty
years the old man never bothered to find out what his wife was
wearing, from whom she obtained what supplies. What kind of
nonacceptance is this? [3]

Mother-in-law went to town every day. Sometimes she collected subscriptions for the institution, sometimes she sold copies
of Grandfather's autobiography, sometimes she asked for money
or clothes or corn for the orphans she always had in the house,
sometimes she also asked for something for herself. Soon after my
marriage, I started my new household and Mother-in-law came
to stay with us, as she found our house more convenient for her
expeditions into the city. Once she brought something with her
when she returned from the city and asked me to serve it at
dinnertime along with what I had cooked. That was our first
clash. I told her, "I would eat whatever poor stuff I prepared at
home, but you go round and ask for things. I shall not eat any
of that and shall not give it to my husband." That was the last
time Mother-in-law brought anything to my house. None of the
daughters-in-law approved of this habit of the old lady's, but
Grandfather used to eat anything that was placed before him.
Whether it was purchased out of the monthly allowance of forty-
five rupees he gave her, or whether somebody had given it to her,
was a question he never cared to bother about.

At first, I could find no explanation for this attitude of Grand-

---

[3] *Aparigraha,* nonacceptance of favours from others, is one of the methods
for disengaging oneself from attachment to material things and desires prescribed
by an ancient doctrine. Release from *maya,* the illusion that the things of this
world are real, and absorption into *Brahman,* the absolute, is the goal of most
schools of traditional Hindu philosophy.

father's, but now, after fifteen years with him, I think I can offer an explanation. I cannot say that this is the right one, but I think it is in keeping with his character. Of course Grandfather never used the word nonacceptance, which I have used. His principle in life can be stated thus: never to accept anything for himself from others; and, secondly, to do what he feels is right—without saying a word about what others are doing. The "anything" he refuses to accept is money. If anybody gives him money, it goes straight to the Widows' Home. An Indian Prince once gave him an annual pension of five hundred rupees. It was meant for him personally, but he always gave it to the institution. He was there only to put his signature to the receipt. He gladly accepts, however, if any gift in kind is given to him, such as a piece of apparel or something to eat or a motor-ride. He never feels that he should not accept it or that it is necessary to return the favour on some future occasion. He never takes things to extremes. Big-sounding words like "renunciation" are beyond him. He will not take a cent for himself, but if some other offering is given with a feeling of love, he does not refuse.

Also, whatever rules of life he has are for himself only. He does not strive to convert others to his way of thinking. As long as he could, he used to take long walks both morning and evening. But I have never heard him preach about it to anybody. Naturally, Mother-in-law and the sons did what they liked. Grandfather never insisted that they should adopt any particular rules of behaviour. He lives his own life according to his own lights and does not bother about or even know about what others are doing.

I believe he has never had the feeling of being obliged by others if he accepted things other than money. When he travelled about getting subscriptions for the Home, he always stayed with people, used their cars when available, and so on but never thought that this indebted him in any way. His attitude was that people did all these things for the institution and this was only proper. He was the guest of his different hosts because he was working for the institution. He could not possibly repay these obligations directly or indirectly out of his meagre salary; the idea never occurred to him. Payment out of the institution's funds would have been improper. But sometimes people became accustomed to the idea of taking favours from others.

Grandfather was once very ill and had to stay for over a month in a nursing home in Poona conducted by a famous surgeon. He was treated there with great consideration and was given medical treatment, food, and nursing. When he came home to convalesce, the surgeon was asked to submit his bill, but he would accept nothing. Ultimately, on being pressed, he agreed to accept repayment only for the expenses for medicines and injections. This was paid by the sons. When Grandfather had completely recovered, we told him all this. He said, "I have no balance in my bank account now, but I will pay back the money in the course of the next few months." We all protested vehemently that he would have said nothing if the surgeon had refused to take anything. "You would not have minded if the surgeon had placed you under obligation—actually, even as it is, he has given you his services free. But you are refusing to accept this little service from your sons who owe you everything and who are trying to do their duty on this rare occasion. Do you think this is fair?" He had to confess that we were right. But that year, he gave me twenty rupees as a *Diwali* present and told me to buy a piece of cloth for a blouse for myself and sweets for the children. When he saw my hesitation, he declared, "Don't think this is a repayment of a debt, it is just a *Diwali* gift." What could I say in reply? I had to accept it. That year, all five daughters-in-law (wives of the four sons and a nephew's wife) and the grandchildren received a *Diwali* gift from him for the first and last time!

I do not remember that Grandfather ever gave sweets to a child or took one on his lap. Even when he is eating something and there is a dish full of it before him, it never occurs to him to give some to a child who is standing by looking expectantly at him. He has no liking or attraction for children. My eldest brother-in-law, Appa, was exactly like him. Of course Grandfather never ill-treats a child, never loses his temper with any child. Only he never cares to fondle a child. If a bold child makes advances, he will be pleasant. But there will be no caressing. Grandfather and his eldest son, who are quite indifferent to children, are quite exceptional in my experience. Mother-in-law occasionally said too that Grandfather did not want children. How far this was true and how much imagination was mixed with it, I do not know. One thing is true, that Grandfather never gets angry with anybody, so that he is very popular with the grandchildren, as with the other members of the family.

Grandfather is really a very timid individual. It seems rather strange to make such a statement about him when one recalls that he married a widow in the teeth of the opposition of society and faced the wrath of his friends and relatives. But in spite of all this, it is quite true that he is by nature a very timid person. He is not capable of facing up to people in controversies, of carrying on debates, of putting forward his point of view forcefully. Usually he remains silent. Occasionally he may write about his views, but he is not inclined to take part in verbal controversies.

Tempers rose and the atmosphere became quite hot in several meetings of the Women's University, but Grandfather merely listened to people and kept mum. One of his women colleagues had to face a queer charge of defalcation of twenty-six thousand rupees of the University's money. The charge was patently false, as was proved after examination of the account books of the previous ten years. The framers of the charge and the motives that prompted them were also discovered later. During that episode, the lady concerned and one of her colleagues went on day and night checking account books and preparing the defense, with the occasional help of my husband. Grandfather was in the Syndicate of the Women's University. We told him that we would look after the legal and technical side but that he should just say that on the basis of his long association with the lady concerned, he did not think she would ever be guilty of such a thing. We told him that his silence would lead to all kinds of speculation. But no, he never spoke out. The lady had not been like other widows who had come to the Home. She had been a student of the Girls' High School in Poona and would normally have joined the Fergusson College. But her father persuaded her to join the Women's University because he was fired by the idealism behind the institution, and the Women's University had used her coming as a propaganda item. She had devoted her life to the service of the institution, but Grandfather would not stand up in her defence.

This was not a solitary example. Whenever any of his colleagues who had helped to develop the institution had to face criticism for anything, he remained aloof. When he collected subscriptions, he always let somebody else take the lead. Another colleague of his has described an incident in which Grandfather was insulted and snubbed by some rich man. He at once turned to his companion and scolded him for having exposed him to the situation! Various other fellow workers had similar experiences. Everyone had to defend himself without aid from Grandfather, in his institutions as in his family life.

If the sister of his friend Narharpant Joshi had not been a widow, I do not think he would have gone about making inquiries for a suitable bride. He was mentally prepared to marry a widow, but to engage in the matter-of-fact business of making inquiries with friends would, I think, have been beyond him. When Mother-in-law came to live with us, there was always some friction between us. But Grandfather never paid any attention. This was not due to selfishness or indifference, but to extreme timidity and lack of boldness. He has described a revealing incident in his autobiography: when he was at school, the headmaster was once about to give him corporal punishment for an offence he had not committed. He merely put his hand to his forehead to bemoan his fate and held it out to receive the strokes of the cane. This led the headmaster to pause and investigate the matter further; ultimately Grandfather was proved innocent. But he could never boldly stand up and declare his innocence. This contrast between a naturally timid person and his achievements, which invoked harsh treatment at the hands of society and required great moral strength to bear, is an intriguing one to me.

Grandfather was never very talkative, even in the family circle. But his most usual activity was collecting subscriptions. That is also a very interesting juxtaposition. But it must be remembered that he usually never went about alone and that when he met people, he said very little beyond stating the object of his visit. But he spoke very well and with great sincerity from the platform.

Grandfather and his eldest son, who was also not inclined to talk much at home, cannot be characterised as haters of men. But they are incapable of making advances or asking questions, of trying to understand people's attitudes or putting themselves in other people's positions. They are not prepared to lose their hearts even for a moment. There is deep satisfaction and joy in this feeling of oneness with others, but there is also the risk of sharing the grief of others. They do not like the disturbances created by strong emotions and passions in the steady and peaceful flow of life—they desire no uncontrollable flood of joy and no heart-tearing stab of pain or anger. That is why their contacts with men are guarded and wary. Their feeling of compassion for the unfortunate is intellectual rather than emotional. This attitude may perhaps achieve more, but a person living with them sometimes doubts whether they are real human beings or only shadows.

Grandfather used to walk miles and miles, but I doubt if he ever paid any attention to his surroundings. He did make occasional remarks about the weather and the roads being dusty or muddy. But the deep blue sky or the approaching storm clouds, the green splendour of nature or the parched, thirsty fields, the exquisite view from the hill near Poona, sometimes blocked out by dust storms—all this appeared never to touch him. He never enjoyed natural beauty, trees and shrubs, the sky, the animals. His mind was completely occupied with man and his fate in a particular social setting. But even in that there was a certain aloofness.

His life has always run in a rather narrow groove. Both amusement and work are confined within narrow lines. Formerly he used to play some very simple card games during the long vacations but he disliked anybody who played so as to create difficulties for other players. His grandchildren and daughters-in-law soon got bored with these simple card games. For some years past, he has given up cards.

His sole amusement now is reading. He reads almost everything in Marathi except modern poetry and mystery stories. I think formerly he was not very fond of novels. In English he confines himself to serious writing and does not care for plays, novels, poetry, travel books and the like. When he comes across any such book in our house, he turns to the title page and puts it away. Formerly he did not read books on sociology and anthropology, but now he reads them all the time. No book on my table remains long there before Grandfather takes it to read. He can never sit down with just one book but must have a heap of a dozen or so. Many of them are so technical and dry that even I find it difficult to follow them. I think he does not understand all that he reads now. He reads about a page or so of a technical book, puts it down and starts another and another, but if he finds an easy book in Marathi, he enjoys reading it immensely. When he is reading an article by some humorous writer, provided there is no poetry (!) in it, everyone can hear his hearty loud laughter. I suspect that the reason why he never liked stories, novels, and poems was his desire not to be touched by strong human emotions and passions.

Even his procedure in the starting and developing of institutions was confined within certain well-defined limits. After he started an institution, he handed it over to some carefully chosen colleagues who looked to the internal management. He was never interested in day-to-day routine administration. The idea of dominating an institution as the boss never attracted him. If he thought his colleagues guilty of extravagance, he would sometimes say a word or two, but never intervened even when his colleagues had violent differences of opinion and seemed ready to fall upon each other. In the University administration, he was quite uninterested in such academic matters as subjects of study or curriculum planning. His insistence was on proper keeping of accounts. He was always particular about circulars to annual subscribers and would make inquiries about how many new ones were registered and how many old ones had dropped out. He never doubted the capacity of his colleagues to run the institutions efficiently. Just as he never bothered about how his sons were running their lives, he was also unconcerned about the internal management of his institutions. He concentrated on the work of collecting subscriptions.

Now, after retirement, he goes to his institutions only on ceremonial occasions, never inquiring about how this or that is being managed. He has been fortunate in attracting a band of selfless and able colleagues, and his institutions have prospered. But if he had not had this aloofness or disinclination to enter into controversies and quarrels, and if he had taken a leading part in the unfortunate differences in the Women's University, it is probable that an amicable settlement would have been reached and the headquarters of the University would have been transferred to Bombay without the bitterness and animosity that actually resulted.

That is the stream of Grandfather's life. He treads the narrow path. He shuns formality and pretence. He takes a decision and sticks to it. This reminds me of an incident that happened some thirty years back. After I received my M.A., Dinu (my husband) decided to send me to Germany for further studies. He informed Grandfather about the plan, but Grandfather did not approve. What was the point in further studies! It would be very expensive; I could easily get a job in the Women's University without it.

But Dinu would not hear of it. He was confident of getting the
necessary finances. After that Grandfather left Poona, and we
went ahead with our preparations. When the date of my departure
was fixed, Dinu wrote a letter to his father telling him the date
of departure and asking for his blessings. Grandfather promptly
sent a reply saying that he had already stated that he was not in
favour of the plan. No blessings—nothing more. For a long time
after that, I was rather bitter about this episode, especially as he
had enthusiastically sponsored further education in foreign countries for some other women who were not particularly good at
their studies in India.

But I think I have come to understand his line of reasoning
and have forgotten my anger. Once he has stated that he does
not approve of a certain course of action, he will not, for the
sake of form, give his blessings. Of course it is impossible for him
to show his disapproval by angry words, but it is equally impossible for him to pretend what he does not believe and to speak
words of blessing. Further, the other women whom he en-
couraged to undertake studies in foreign countries were graduates of or workers in his Women's University. His heart, which
is insulated against humans, is given unstintingly to his institutions, especially the Widows' Home at Hingne. He loves his
institutions ardently and his indifference disappears like magic.
Mother-in-law loved her sons, their wives, and children, and
always used to utter words of praise for them, even going to the
length of saying they were superior to others. Grandfather had
the same feelings for his institutions. In his autobiography, he
has made a comparison of the achievements of women graduates
of the Women's University and those of other Universities with a
list of names, dates, and so on. He has come to the conclusion that
the Women's University graduates were doing considerable social
service, and others were not. Many of the former were widows,
their degrees had no recognition from Government, and it was a
moral responsibility on the institution to enable them to earn
their livelihood. So they were helped to start girls' schools in dif-

ferent towns in Maharashtra, and the institution and Grandfather killed two birds with one stone. But it is clear that the kind of comparison which Grandfather made was unfair, and it led to considerable feelings of resentment in the minds of women graduates of statutory Universities.

Once you have a feeling of love, you cannot apply reasoning and logic to the matter. I am rather tall by Indian standards and Mother-in-law used to say, "She is like a *dipmal* (a stone pillar with protruding pieces for oil lamps)." My daughter Jai is also tall, but then Mother-in-law would say, "Oh, how slim and tall is my Dinu's daughter." Grandfather's attitude to his institutions is exactly like that. He used to say that women must not be sub-jected to the strain of learning through English, or of learning mathematics and sciences; they should concentrate on subjects particularly suited to them, and that is why he started the Women's University. Some of the graduates of this University went to foreign countries with the help of scholarships to under-take further studies. Grandfather was highly pleased about this. He never worried that they would be subjected to the strain of learning through a foreign language. On the contrary, the fact that graduates of the Women's University were the equals of other graduates was used as propaganda material! There is no logic about love and loyalty, and it is no wonder that Grand-father behaved like this about his institutions, which are his sole passion. About his institutions he is not an impersonal shadow, but very much a human being with strong feelings.

Even among the institutions he has started there are degrees of affection. As long as the University's headquarters were in Poona and the Principal of the only college in Poona as well as the Registrar of the University were life-members of the Widows' Home, Grandfather probably did not consider the two as separate entities. The Widows' Home was the mother of the University, and he expected the two to remain united for ever. In fact, the University seat had to be shifted to Bombay; and, while the wife of the principal benefactor was trying to bring this about, the workers at the Widows' Home were trying to keep it in Poona. In this controversy Grandfather could not remain neutral, and his love for the Widows' Home proved more powerful. Everybody had to go through a long period of bitter quarrels, and Grandfather did not give a lead in these matters. Though many of those who passed through the trial suffered a great deal of worry and anxiety, Grandfather came through unaffected and continued to occupy his position of honour.

His first and foremost love is the Widows' Home at Hingne. If, on reading a letter, Grandfather appears particularly pleased, my youngest daughter immediately concludes that there must be an offer of a substantial donation to the Hingne institution in it. If somebody from outside Poona comes to visit him, he never misses the opportunity even now to tell the visitor to go and see the excellent work being done at Hingne. His devotion is neither proud nor offensive. Many social workers think that the institution where they are working would not go on with equal efficiency if they were to retire from active work and so they try to dominate the administrative machinery. They do not allow anybody else to occupy any important position, trying to do everything themselves. Grandfather never took that attitude and so all his colleagues have put in their best efforts. Neither his colleagues nor the members of his family were dwarfed under the shade of his greatness.

Many great men consciously develop some peculiarities of behaviour. Not caring for things of the body is usually considered a sign of greatness. Grandfather does not make any special effort to satisfy the needs of the body, but he also does not look down on the good things of life. Many sagelike men in India honestly think that reading and writing should provide sufficient joy for the body whereas all other things that give joy are a sin, but Grandfather is an exception. He never pursues the joys of the body, never begs for them, never feels that he has missed something valuable. But if he gets something that gives joy, he tastes it with great relish. He has no craving for alcohol; in fact, he is not even conscious that there is such a thing in this world. But his son once gave him a bottle of wine so that he could take a glass before retiring at night. He sipped it with evident enjoyment, nodding his head and saying, "Very nice!" When the bottle was finished, he forgot all about it. He does not eat meat, but he likes a crisp omelet with onions in it. He likes to drink chicken soup or beef tea, but when the supply of cubes is exhausted, he forgets that also. He does not like wheat *chapatis* or anything prepared with a lot of *ghi*. But when he is dining out, he eats whatever is served to him. Once he went to dine at the house of one of his adopted daughters. When I casually asked him in the evening what he had eaten, he told me, "Oh, she knew I did not like things prepared in *ghi* and still she made *shira* with a lot of *ghi,* and I had to eat it!"

In the days of rationing we made it a rule to buy nothing in the black market, but to eat only what we got on our cards. Only occasionally I gave some of my wheat ration to some friends and took some *bajri* (millet) in exchange. Grandfather ate red milo, maize, and parboiled rice without the slightest complaint. What little sugar we got was so divided that Grandfather got a little more than his share, but we never purchased any extra sugar on the black market. All the usual sweets were prepared with raw sugar, and he ate everything without protest. When rationing was discontinued and we began to get enough sugar, he again began to eat sweets made with refined sugar. Many people are fond of describing at great length the hardships they had to suffer during rationing. But Grandfather took everything philosophically.

By the time he reached 70, he had lost a number of teeth and those that remained did not articulate. Naturally he found great difficulty in chewing his food. His sons asked him to have the remaining teeth pulled out and get a denture. He liked the idea, but Mother-in-law would not hear of it. She put forward a series of arguments. She said, "When people lose their teeth, God evidently intends them not to eat food which requires chewing." But Grandfather was not prepared to believe that God made confidential communications about His plans to her. He told her, "We are born naked, but we do wear clothes later, or we use glasses when our eyes fail us." Then she said, "But pulling out healthy teeth is a dangerous job. You will lose a terrible lot of blood." To which he replied, "Oh, I am not worried about that." Then she put forward what she thought was an unanswerable argument. She said, "Now you are spending a couple of hundred rupees for a denture at the age of seventy. Suppose something happens to you, who can use it? Your clothes or your sandals may be of use to somebody but you should not spend so much money for a denture."

Grandfather would normally have appreciated this argument, but the absence of teeth was not only an inconvenience to him, it was an inconvenience to others; and he was very particular about not causing the slightest inconvenience to others. He did not say anything to Mother-in-law, and she got the impression that he had allowed himself to be persuaded. Then one day he went to stay with his eldest son in Bombay and came back after some days with a new denture. Mother-in-law was very angry and gave a long lecture, but he kept mum.

Now he can eat everything that others eat. He has never thought of adopting queer rules of conduct, advertising them, and thereby making himself a thorough nuisance to everybody concerned. He likes the real poor man's food: *bhakri* of *jowar* or *bajri,* garlic chutney, and sweet oil are his favourites even now. Vegetable prepared from *ambadi* leaves or raw jack-fruit with boiled oil and garlic poured over it is a special treat to him. He relishes what the average person relishes. Naturally he has his likes and dislikes like everyone else, but he never makes a fetish of such matters. He never classifies foods as creating good or bad moods in people. He treats all eatables alike. They become one with him when he eats them; they take on his qualities and not the other way around.[4] When some food faddists hear from him that he drinks tea or coffee several times a day, they are very disappointed.

What applies to enjoyment of food also applies to other types of enjoyment. He enjoyed family life without any reservations. Some Mahatmas have referred to the sexuality of their wives in order to emphasize their greatness; some have extolled celibacy, and some have put unnatural restrictions on their colleagues and disciples. Grandfather lived a full life but not even the severest critic could point to the slightest improper conduct with regard to women. He spent his life in an institution for women, especially widows, but never took any personal service from any of the inmates. He never crossed the sharp line of propriety, never thought that he was doing anything special, and never advertised the fact.

He appreciates beauty. He has never been a great conversationalist, but he often talks to himself loudly and clearly; and one can get to know his thoughts. Sometimes I feel a little guilty for listening in on something hidden in his heart which is now being revealed to me. But I never make an attempt to listen, and what comes to my ears is so innocent and childlike that I realise that he has nothing to hide. His reserved nature is not the result of an attempt to hide something from people. It is just his character. The other day a recent issue of *Vanyajati,* a magazine dealing with primitives in India, was lying on my table and according to his usual custom he took it to read, along with some other books. As it was on the top of the heap he picked it up first and looked at a picture of a beautiful primitive girl. Observing it carefully, he muttered, "Fine, fine!"

He is very fond of good music and drama. I do not remember

---

[4] Concern about food is omnipresent in India, a land of severe ritual restrictions on what may be eaten by the orthodox on the one hand and of food faddists on the other. The author refers here to some theories and practices of food faddists.

his ever having bought a ticket for a concert or a play. But if
someone took him along he went readily enough and sat until
the last notes or the final curtain. He does that even now.

His innocence is childlike. His peculiar self-centered nature
is also that of a child. The only difference is that real children
get angry and excited and this child is entirely contented and
happy. If occasionally we bring home pineapples or mangoes or
similar fruits which everybody likes and give everyone a dishful
of pieces, Grandfather eats his share with the utmost pleasure and
then innocently asks, "Was that all my share?" Then either Dinu
or I give him some more from our dish. He honestly thinks that
he never asks for anything more than his fair share but eats just
what he should get.

Grandfather is very orderly in his habits. His clothes are
always carefully folded and kept in their proper place in the
wardrobe. Nowadays, he does not notice if they are soiled, and
it is Dinu's job to send them to the laundry. Many old people,
especially after they retire, are very careless about their appearance and dress. In fact, some public workers think it is a sign
of greatness to be slovenly in their dress. Grandfather has never
been like that. His dress is plain but neat. If a button comes off
his shirt or coat, he always asks someone to sew it on. He wears
long-sleeved shirts; so that he does not have to bother with cuff-
links, the tailor sews on a small piece of white tape at the ends
of the cuffs. Sometimes this piece of white tape comes off, but
Grandfather never uses such a shirt; he insists on getting it
properly mended. When he goes out, he has an ankle-long *dhoti,*
a long coat, and cap, formerly a turban.

He always gets ready about a quarter of an hour before an
engagement. Some two years back he was to go out for some
public function at 9 p.m. As usual, he put on his going-out dress
and was ready at 8:45. The people who were to take him out
did not turn up until 9:30, and by then he had taken off his coat,
changed into his housedress, and sat down in the living room.
Then the organisers came with the car. I was very angry for

this inordinate delay, but he merely said, "Wait. I will change and come with you." He had on a clean white pyjama, his usual dress in the house, and I said that he need not change into a *dhoti*. But that did not meet with his approval. He went into his room and came out properly dressed.

Only the other day, on my return from one of my tours, I saw in the sitting room a new pair of flannel trousers. On inquiry I learned that Dinu had had it made for Grandfather and the tailor had delivered it only that morning. The next day Grandfather had to attend some public function. It was February and quite cold, so I asked him to wear not his usual *dhoti* but the woolen trousers instead. He liked the idea and was quite pleased with the brand new trousers. After his bath he put on the trousers and I handed him the coat from his wardrobe. The coat was of grey wool while the trousers were brown. He took the coat, looked at it and asked, "How can I wear this coat with this pair of trousers? Will the colours match?" Even when I told him that they matched well, he was still not quite reassured. It was only when my youngest brother-in-law told him that the two colours did go well together that he was persuaded to put on the coat. Dinu was out of Poona when all this happened. On his return I told him about the incident, and he got the tailor to make a new pair of trousers of the same colour as the coat.

If the barber does not come every two weeks, he remarks that his hair needs trimming and that the barber should be called. Of course he forgets things often now, and, if the barber comes only a week after the last visit, Grandfather dutifully sits for a haircut. He never forgets to take his sandals off before treading on the carpet, but he must put them on before he steps onto the stone floor.

Formerly, Grandfather was very hard up for money on his pension of only seventy rupees, after paying thirty-five rupees to Mother-in-law, which she claimed with great insistence. Since the time he came to live with us, he has insisted on paying twenty-five rupees to us—a part of his policy of nonacceptance of favours from others. After this only a few rupees are left to him for his personal expenses, and formerly he had to be very economical. I have said above that he had not paid much attention to his family, but there was one exception. About twenty-five years ago he gave a thousand rupees to his eldest son because the other sons had received similar sums for their education. The son immediately invested it in publishing a new edition of his book on birth control. Some years later, when Appa was again in financial difficulties, particularly on account of his wife's long illness, Grandfather came to know about it, as we all discussed it openly. But peculiarly, he thought it necessary to do something about it. Fearing that if he handed over the money to his oldest son, it would be spent immediately, he kept a sum with his youngest son, who was secretary of the Widows' Home, with instructions to hand it over to Appa in case of need.

Since Mother-in-law's death, Grandfather has had practically no expenses. A joint account has been opened in his name and Dinu's, and money is continuously being credited to it. Grandfather never inquires how much money has accumulated. If occasionally we suggest that he might give a donation to some deserving cause, he at once consents. I think these last few years are the only ones in his life when he has not kept detailed accounts of his income and expenditure. We get decent clothes made for him and spend his own money for them. Even then his account shows a respectable balance. Every year he asks Dinu to pay a few hundred rupees to various charities. He does insist on keeping some petty cash with him and personally pays the barber and hands out a coin to our servant when he has to replenish his stock of *supari*. That is the only remnant of his earlier habit.

His behaviour is that of a happy person. His speech is agreeable, and his laugh is the sweetest and frankest that one could hear. He can never be stiff or formal. His natural behaviour is so attractive that one is charmed. Very often I try to persuade my mother to come and stay with us. When my mother-in-law was alive, she used to remark on seeing my mother, "Well, Bhagirathibai, you have come to stay, it appears. I suppose it is going to be a long visit!" After this greeting, it was very difficult to persuade my mother to stay for any length of time. Now when my mother comes, Grandfather says, "Oh, is that you, Bhagirathibai? It has been such a long time!" Mother is so pleased with this and says to me, "He recognised me! It is only four months that I have been away, and he said that I have been away a long time!"

Although Grandfather never gave me his blessing in a formal manner, I think of two occasions in particular. On the day after my marriage, the Karves gave a big dinner party. During the ceremony, relations on both sides had behaved so foolishly and with such lack of understanding that I was very angry about everything. My peace of mind had been completely shattered. People were reciting poems during the dinner and according to the custom Grandfather gave the last recital. In my excitement, I never bothered to hear what the others were reciting but Grandfather's clear, sweet voice and enunciation immediately caught my attention. He was slowly reciting the verse:

> *The dearest friend, the entire kinship,*
> *All desires, great treasure, life itself,*
> *To the woman the husband, to the man the wife,*
> *Let this be understood by the young couple.*

How clear were his words, like some carving on stone; and as each nectar-filled line fell on my ears, it was engraved on my heart. I became quiet and peaceful and entered into the Karve family with this great blessing.

The second occasion occurred only five or six years ago. We had all gone with Grandfather to spend the *Diwali* holidays at my brother's house in Hyderabad. On the day before the principal festival we sat up late finishing the decorations and watching the children setting off fireworks. There was no point in getting up early on account of the holidays, but my brother and Grandfather got up before six and had their early tea, and Grandfather put on warm clothes and took a turn in the garden. This was the first day of the Hindu year, and I awakened to his footsteps outside the window. And then came to my ears the clear words of the verse he was reciting: "Do not allow the lamp of knowledge in your heart to be extinguished." These words, uttered on that auspicious morning, have also been engraved on my heart and showed me the true path in this phase of my life. His first blessing had lighted the first part of my life, and I am hoping that this new beacon will light the second part.

Only recently I was trying to explain to an American friend what is meant by *sthitapradnya,* "a wise one." After about an hour, he asked me, "That is all very well, but have you ever seen or met such a person?" And at once I answered, "Not only seen or met; I am living with one in my family. But I am so ignorant that I could not distinguish whether the signs indicated a self-centered egoist or a wise sage."

How fortunate I am that I am the daughter-in-law of such a man! And how still more fortunate that I was not his wife!

II. G. S. SARDESAI, Historian

INTRODUCTION

In the following short selection, Rao Bahadur Govind Sakh-aram Sardesai (1865–1960), probably Maharashtra's best-known historian in the West, recalls his boyhood. The facts of his life and official career may be summarized briefly enough, for his real achievements were reserved rather for the study of history. Of Karhada rather than Chitpavan Braham stock, he was raised, as was Maharshi Karve, in the Ratnagiri District of the Konkan coastal area, a district which produced a disproportionate share of India's famous men during the last quarter of the nineteenth and first quarter of the twentieth century. Despite considerable finan-cial difficulty, he managed to obtain a college education. After fail-ing in his first attempt at the B.A. in 1887, he secured the degree in the following year and was hired as clerk and personal reader to the Maharaja of Baroda. He continued in Baroda service for thirty-seven years, eventually becoming chief tutor of the palace school. In 1925 he retired, very much against the wishes of the Maharaja, to concentrate upon his beloved studies in history.

Sardesai might have remained just another member of the flourishing regional school of Maharashtrian historians writing in Marathi had it not been for the influence of his lifelong friend and correspondent, Sir Jadunath Sarkar, the Bengali "doyen of Indian historians" and India's first great moderate na-tional historian. Their association broadened the interests of both. Their fifty-year correspondence, lasting from 1907 until Sarkar's

death in 1958, reveals a compulsion about work, much of it
drudgery, with a passion for "getting the facts" in the sphere
of political and military history. Both men displayed a proprietary
air toward the Mughal-Maratha period, which was their specialty,
and believed that they were alone in "putting things in proper
order."

Sardesai had begun in the mid-1890's with translations into
Marathi of, significantly, Seely's *Expansion of England* and
Machiavelli's *The Prince*. These were followed by nine volumes
of Maharashtrian history in Marathi, *Marathi Riyasat* (1901–
1932). After retirement from Baroda service came fifteen years of
arduous editorial labors in selecting and publishing both indigenous and British documents in Maratha history. Forty-five
volumes of selections from the collected papers of the Peshwas,
the last rulers of the Maratha state before the British conquest in
1818, appeared in 1930–1934. Seven volumes of complementary
English documents from British residencies in areas under the
Peshwas' control before 1818 followed in the years 1936–1940.
During all this time Sarkar constantly urged him to revise the
Marathi Riyasat and publish it in English. This he did, the *New
History of the Marathas* appearing in three volumes in 1946–1948.
This work and its Marathi counterpart established India's claim
to an indigenous Hindu historical tradition and Maharashtra's
claim to a regional history of splendor and importance. The *New
History* remains the standard work in English on the political
history of the Maratha empire.

Through these writings Sardesai became a sort of hinge between the Western historical tradition and a flourishing regional
culture. To Maharashtra he presented through translations and in
his own work models of Western political theory and Western-
style political history. For the West he has thrown light on an important Indian political system and by his use of indigenous
documentary sources combatted a popular Western belief that
"India has no history."

His autobiography, *Majh Sansarayatra* (*The Pilgrimage of My Life*), from which the following selections are taken, was published by K. B. Dhavale in Bombay in 1956.

E.M.

THE PILGRIMAGE OF MY LIFE

G. S. Sardesai

My father was a collector of revenue from the cowherds who used to graze their cattle in the region south of Bombay on the slopes of the Western Ghats. In those days, revenue was not collected on the basis of the area of the fields and the nature of the crops, but on the number of cattle owned by each cowherd. The collector had to go out into the subregions, counting the cows and buffaloes and exacting payment from the owner. Every year, this office was auctioned off and the highest bidder was appointed collector. Once he had paid the amount of his bid into the Government treasury, he was allowed to keep whatever surplus he could collect from the cattle owners. But that required a lot of travelling about, and often the cowherds hid their cattle in inaccessible places when they saw the revenue collector coming. At times they did not hesitate to attack the collector or to incite a vicious beast to attack him. Originally it was my father's maternal uncle who was the collector; later my father became his assistant.

I remember accompanying my father on these expeditions when I was a boy and enjoying the open-air life, the rich food with milk, butter, *ghi,* fine rice, and other delicacies. We had a number of servants with us, but as none of them was a Brahman, my father had to cook for himself. The midday meal was usually on the banks of a small stream under the shade of a tree, and the evening meal was in the cattle shed of some cowherd. Every morning my father would collect the cowherds in that region, note down their names and the number of cattle they possessed, fix the fee they had to pay, and then go on to the next halting station.

This life kept him away from home most of the time, and nobody bothered about his marriage until he was twenty-five years of age. Finally through the help of some mutual friends his marriage with the daughter of a nearby priest was arranged. My mother was then about ten or eleven years of age. About five years later, when she was sixteen, I was born, the eldest son of my parents, in 1865. At that time my mother and my father's mother were looking after our house and the surrounding fields and orchards, while my father was out collecting revenue from the cowherds.

I well remember this small house in Govil where I spent my childhood. Later, we all worked and helped to make it into a very beautiful place, but at that time there was jungle all round. There was a small well near the house, which was nothing more than a hut with walls made of branches of trees plastered with mud. There were many snakes; and jackals, panthers, and wolves were plentiful. Gradually my father cleared the forest, put in fields for planting, built a small dam to divert the water of a nearby stream into the backyard, planted fruit and flower trees and created a fine orchard. My mother and grandmother supervised the farmhands and I went with the cattle when they were let out to graze. Many years later when my brothers and I were well set up in life we built a solid two-storied house on the site of the original hut. It was only in 1945, when none of us or our children wanted to live there, that we sold off the whole estate and the house.

My mother came of a family of priests named Athalye. My father's people were householders.[1] The difference in the status

---

[1] Among Brahmans, there are two distinct groups, those who officiate as priests and those who do not. The latter are called householders (*grihastha*) and have a higher status than priests. Nonpriestly Brahmans today follow such varied occupations as farming, clerical work, teaching, medicine, and law.

of the two types of Brahmans is not considered very important now, but in those days everyone was aware of it. My mother was the only daughter and eldest child of her parents. Her four brothers have been of great help to me and my family in later life. In fact the Sardesai and Athalye families have retained their friendly relations to this day; and we all feel great affection for each one of this very large group, which now comprises several hundred persons if one counts all the children.

My grandmother was a very skillful manager of the house and a fine cook. My mother, on the other hand, was equally efficient in looking after the farm and the fields, supervising the farmhands, and getting everything done at the proper time. In this way, even though my father was usually away from home, the affairs of our family were carried on quite satisfactorily.

In those days of my childhood, schooling was not considered important, and even Brahmans never had any ambition beyond a clerkship in a government office. Father taught me the Modi script[2] to prepare me eventually for the career of a clerk. Paper was such a rare commodity that my father kept a few sheets in his portfolio and carefully cut narrow strips which were used to write invitations for important ceremonies like marriages or thread ceremonies or for giving receipts for money. I learned the alphabet with a wooden slab on which dust or fine sand was spread, and a piece of straw or a bamboo splinter would serve as a pen.

The first seven years of my life were spent either following my mother or grandmother in the fields or watching the cattle grazing in the meadows. My thread ceremony was celebrated with great pomp in 1872. My father at first had wanted to invite at least one hundred Brahmans to the ceremonial feast but instead

---

[2] *Modi* was the cursive script formerly used in writing the Marathi language. With the advent of printing it has gradually lost out to *Devanagari,* the old Sanskrit script which is now used in writing Hindi and Marathi by hand, and for printing. India, especially before British rule, had many special scripts— scripts for business, scripts for religious sects, and scripts for some of the major regional languages.

he invited about two hundred cowherds among whom he worked and they went away fully satisfied after a sumptuous feast in the Brahman style.

After this my grandmother took me to a nearby village, made arrangements for my stay with one of her relatives, and enrolled me in the elementary school there. The village was about six miles from our house, and I occasionally went home on holidays. But the year and a half that I spent there was not a very happy period, particularly because we got nothing to eat until noon. Tea was almost unknown then, and we got no milk either. We had school from seven to eleven in the morning and then again from two to six. There was no clock in the school, and the working hours were only approximate.

After eighteen months there I was enrolled in a school only two miles from home. There arrangements were made for me to stay with a family on payment of about eight pounds of rice per month. This town was a very interesting place, with a river where one could swim, many rice fields, and a population which actively carried on such social activities as public worship in the temple, religious discourses, and dramas. I still have vivid memories of such activities in the five years (1874–1879) I spent in this little town. The old gentleman and his wife with whom I lived treated me with great kindness and taught me not only many Sanskrit verses and hymns but also how to make baskets and mats from bamboo and ropes from the fibres of a kind of flax that grew in that region. Doing useful work with one's hands is a great thing and I feel that I benefitted greatly by this.

During this time, our family's fortunes gradually declined. When the number of persons in the family was small, we could manage on my father's income; but the number of children went on ever increasing, and things became difficult. The little hut became inadequate, and Father added a sort of veranda at right angles to it. Unfortunately, however, while he was away on his work and I was at school, the whole structure with all that it contained completely burned down the night of June 5, 1876.

My grandmother, my mother, and the younger children could save only themselves. When I heard about it the next day I went to Govil and saw the smouldering ruins of the house, the stored grain and straw and everything else that we had possessed. Although my father built a new home with my granduncle's help, that marked the decline of our fortunes.

The year 1877 was the year of the great famine in the whole country. The system of cattle fees was abolished the same year, and revenue was now collected on land area and the nature of crops as in other parts of the country. Father thus lost his job and also began to suffer from ill health. There were days when we had no food in the house and had to borrow from the neighbours. My father tried various other enterprises, bidding for the toll station on the main road and buying and selling forest produce, but he did not succeed in anything. The debt piled up from a few hundred rupees at the start to some thousand rupees, and it was only when my brothers and I began to earn that we could pay it off.

In the month of May, 1879, after I had passed the fifth grade of the elementary school, I got an opportunity to join the English school at Ratnagiri. My maternal uncle was a clerk with a lawyer in that town, and he helped me to live there and study. After about a year, I began to get a small scholarship and exemption from fees and could thus continue my studies without burdening my father. The high school at Ratnagiri was one of the best in all Bombay province and one of its students topped the list of successful students in the University entrance examination every year for several years. In 1881, Tilak and his colleagues started the New English School in Poona and also began to publish the *Kesari,* a weekly which criticized the government for its anti-Indian policies. This paper we avidly read in the Ratnagiri high school, and there were animated discussions about current problems.

During the last year I was at the Ratnagiri high school we

had two very good teachers who gave us excellent tuition. One of them, Moro Waman Kirtane, soon became my father-in-law. When he found that I was not yet married, he approached my father and proposed that I should marry his daughter. Father told him that although he approved of the girl, he could not take the responsibility of feeding one more mouth when he had difficulty maintaining his already large family. But Mr. Kirtane made an extraordinary offer. He said, "I will keep my daughter with me after her marriage until your son is able to earn his living, and I shall also pay the expenses of his college education."

This silenced all objections, and my marriage was celebrated on February 29, 1884. The eldest daughter-in-law, considered to be Lakshmi,[3] thus came into my ancestral home when I was nineteen years of age. The same year I passed the final examination of the high school and prepared to join college. I planned to live in my father-in-law's house, for he had been transferred to Poona after a year at Ratnagiri, and to join the Fergusson College, which was to open that year.

In Poona I was never very happy. Ratnagiri was a small place, and my Konkan dialect was thought funny in Poona. The people there were more sophisticated, and I felt shy in my father-in-law's house. In the college I was not one of the group of students who had known each other and the professors, who until the previous year had been their high school teachers. Thus I did not mix very well. Fortunately I did not remain in Poona very long. Very soon my father-in-law was transferred to Sholapur, and I decided to continue my studies in Bombay.

So in September, 1885, after one semester in Poona, I joined the Government Elphinstone College and went to live with Mr. Bapusaheb Athalye, whom I had got to know in Ratnagiri and who was now practising as a lawyer in Bombay. I managed to carry on with the help of an occasional scholarship, concession in fees, and some private tuition or whatever other work I could

---

[3] The goddess of prosperity.

find. My father-in-law was not in a position to pay for my education, and I was glad that I did not have to depend on him. In 1887 I failed in the final B.A. examination but passed it at the second attempt in 1888.

Just about that time the Maharaja of Baroda inquired of Bapusaheb whether he could recommend some young man to serve as a personal reader and clerk to look after his private correspondence. Bapusaheb mentioned my name and said that I would be available after my B.A. examination was over. I learned the result of the examination on the 24th of December and immediately went to Baroda. In the meanwhile, however, the Maharaja had proceeded to Mahabaleshwar[4] with his son, who had been ill. The Maharaja's brother, who was his secretary, appointed me as personal reader and clerk to the Maharaja on Rs. 70 a month from January 1, 1889, and ordered me to Mahabaleshwar to join duty.

In my very first meeting with the Maharaja, he began to dictate to me a long and complicated statement about land measurement, temple lands, and other matters about which he had been having discussions with his officers. It went on and on until I had taken down at least twenty or twenty-five sheets. Apparently he was not displeased with my work and so began the next chapter of my life. I was to continue in the personal service of the Maharaja for thirty-six years.

The greatest benefit I received through my service with the Maharaja was the very extensive travelling I did with him and for him in India and in Europe. I met hundreds of interesting people and saw many new scenes and countries. My first trip to Europe was in 1892. I went again in 1900, the year of the great Paris exhibition, and also lived with the prince for five months in Oxford. Then I went a third time in 1905 and a fourth time

---

[4] Mahabaleshwar, a hill station about two hundred miles south of Bombay and 4,500 feet above sea level in the Sahyadri range of the Western Ghats, was formerly the hot-season capital of Bombay Presidency under British rule.

in 1911 for the coronation ceremony of King George V. I spent weeks and months in London, Paris, Rome, Switzerland, Scotland.

On my first trip, I still had the traditional long tuft of hair at the back of my head, which all orthodox Brahmans are supposed to have, but soon after I reached St. Moritz, the Maharaja's brother cut it off. On my return to India my father took me to our ancestral house in Govil and made me undergo a purification ceremony which involved shaving my head, a sacred bath, offerings in the sacred fire, and feeding of Brahmans. This was because I had undertaken a sea voyage, which is considered polluting by Brahmans, and naturally I had eaten food prepared by people of other castes and other religions. I did not go through this purifying ritual after my other trips, however; and although for several years I remained a vegetarian, later on I also began to eat nonvegetarian food occasionally.

During all this period, I read hundreds of books on history, philosophy, essays, and biographies and in a way prepared the ground for my later studies in Indian history.

Maharaja Sayajirao gradually began to appreciate my work and delegated more and more duties to me. I served as tutor to his children and grandchildren, as the chief accountant of his household, and as his personal secretary. By 1925, I had become more and more eager to devote the remaining part of my life to my historical studies, but the Maharaja would not hear of it. He insisted that I continue in his service, pointing out that the old Hindu tradition laid on the servant the duty of always obeying and serving his master. But I would not give in and retired from service against his will. This independence so angered him that he issued orders to reduce my pension by 50 per cent; and it was only several years later when his grandson became the Maharaja that I began to receive my full pension. But the loss of several thousand rupees in the intervening period could not be made good.

How Society Has Changed
in the Ninety Years of My Life

My thread ceremony was celebrated when I was seven years of age. The priest taught me the daily prayers and gave me the usual instructions about behavior, like putting the sacred thread over the right ear when relieving myself, taking a bath if I accidentally touched a person of the lowest caste, never eating anything without first taking a bath in the morning and putting on the sacred cloth,[5] and so on. But today most of the younger generation do not even know what a sacred cloth looks like or how a sacred thread is worn. Rules such as that one should not hear the voice of a menstruating woman while taking meals, or that relatives of a dead person are not to be touched for some days, or that a woman in childbed is to be considered polluting are no longer observed.[6] In my youth, there were no sewing machines and the women used to sew their bodices and men's vestlike apparel by hand. Every fortnight or so, the barber used to come to the house on a day that was considered auspicious, and then the whole of the head, except the traditional tuft, had to be shaved clean. A look at his crude instruments made us so nervous that bribes of brown sugar had to be offered to get us to sit before the barber. He bent the boy's head, held it firmly between his knees, and then went about his business with complete disregard of the tears the boy was copiously shedding. The ordeal never ended without quantities of blood flowing from the cuts and gashes caused by the none-too-sharp instruments.

---

[5] Garments made of silk or wool, considered ritually pure textiles, were worn by Brahmans at mealtimes, a custom still observed among the orthodox.

[6] These ritual precautions applied mainly to Brahmans. Although ritual practices vary with the region of India and the religious sect and caste of the Brahman, the most potent sources of pollution are blood and bodily effluvia, such as hair and nail parings, and death, as well as contact with a person permanently polluted by reason of his hereditary caste occupation. That is why Sardesai mentions menstruating women and relatives of the dead as persons to be avoided.

My wife Lakshmibai, renamed Mai, was born on July 7, 1874, and died at Kamshet near Poona, where I have been living since my retirement, on February 26, 1943. She was not very highly educated, but she was in the habit of writing down her thoughts and various incidents in her life. I only discovered after her death how voluminous her writings were. I have thought that if a selection of these papers is appended to this story of my life, they may throw some light on my domestic life.

Excerpts from Mai's Diary

August 10, 1910. I do not think my childhood was particularly happy. I used to be rather peevish and found it difficult to play with other children. I was also rather weak and often sat by myself or cried. I was married at the age of ten, and my grandmother used to say that my husband's people were poor in comparison to my parental house. Very soon I had to go to my parents-in-law; and as there was nobody who could accompany me, a poor student who lived in my father's house as a kind of dependent went with me. I did not know how a newly married daughter-in-law was expected to behave and was often scolded by my mother-in-law and her daughter. Sometimes I became very sad. My mother-in-law had her moods, and she often used very sharp words to me.

When my husband took service[7] at Baroda, I went there at the age of seventeen. One of my husband's cousins who had become a widow in her childhood came to live with us and also my father-in-law and three brothers-in-law.

For some years after I moved to Baroda, I continued to have very bad health due to my weak digestion. Up to about six months after the birth of my first son I was ill very frequently. Since then, however, I have improved very much and have never been seriously ill since. Now my second son is seven years of age. On the whole I am quite happy, because I did not have too many chil-

---

[7] The Indian term for "to be employed." (See D. K. Karve, note 4.)

dren and have servants to look after the household duties. I must say, I am not very fond of learning, and although my husband is very insistent that I should increase my knowledge by reading and should learn the English language, I never could bring myself to put in the necessary effort.

Whenever my husband goes with the Maharaja to Europe, I go to my father-in-law's house in the Konkan. Usually I spend three or four months every year there. This time, however, the Maharaja did not take my husband with him, so he took leave for three months and stayed in Bombay to finish the work on his history volume. My husband's younger brother was living in a suburb of Bombay at that time, and the thread ceremonies of my two sons were celebrated at his house.

In Baroda, there is always much to do. Many friends come or are invited for meals, my husband is busy with his reading and writing, and he also makes me read books. Often he dictates to me or makes me read things out to him. Then I also reply to all the domestic correspondence. Occasionally we go out for a ride in a carriage or for a walk. My sons are living with my brother-in-law for their schooling.

Sometimes we have differences of opinion, and my husband gets very angry. At such moments I feel that a woman's life is so useless and dependent. I keep on brooding over such incidents and I do not easily forget them. My nature is such that I do not speak out my mind openly, and tears begin to flow at the slightest provocation.

My husband is very angry because I do not learn English. But I just can not get enough time and energy for it.

October 18, 1910. When we returned from our short trip to Bombay, I brought back Minakshi, the daughter of my second brother-in-law, who lost his wife soon after the child's birth, together with my younger son and another related child. Minakshi is not a very healthy child and she is not taking to bottle feeding very readily. She requires almost constant attendance. This is of some advantage to me because I can resist my husband's continuous insistence that I go through a nursing course and become a qualified nurse. I dislike this idea intensely but have found it difficult to resist him. We have had a number of rather angry discussions about this, and I was afraid he would force me to join the nursing class. But the little motherless niece who had to be looked after saved me from a very disagreeable proposition.

I should like to mention here a rather unpleasant episode. My husband thinks that I should wear my *sari* according to the new fashion without one end tucked up behind at the back.[8] He thinks that that is the really respectable way. But I am not at all enthusiastic about this idea and find it very difficult to change to a new fashion after all these years. But I am afraid he is not going to yield on this point, and I am really nervous as to how I shall carry it off in front of the servants.

Two days ago we had a violent quarrel about this. He said there was bound to be awkwardness when any new custom was introduced. I stood up for my old fashioned nine-yard *sari* and the old way of wearing it. But he gave the example of Gujarati women who wear a shorter *sari* and do not keep the front part tucked up at the back. Also, he said, it was lighter, easier to wash, cheaper to buy, and so on. Finally I had to give in.

Then a few days later my mother-in-law came to stay with us for some time. But she was so angry at my new way of wearing the *sari* that she said she would leave because she could not stand this new-fangled idea. I remained silent, but my husband said if

---

[8] This conflict illustrates in small the kind of conflict going on all over India at the time. The home in India is traditionally separate and private, protected from the outside world to a degree it is not in the West. So seemingly superficial and trivial a matter as a change in the style of women's dress thus brought currents from the outside immediately into the home, burdening the *sari* with what were, to the traditional wife, new and alarmingly secular implications. The natural defense was to declare a change in the style of wearing the *sari* to be the sin of breaking the religious tradition. Sardesai, a pragmatist who has learned to eschew tradition when it is inconvenient to him, advances "rational" arguments to his wife on behalf of the new fashion. But note the outcome of the argument.

she had to go, she could. Even though the morning meal was ready, she started to go without touching the food. I bowed down in the traditional manner with folded hands and paid my respects to her, gave her money for the journey, asked one of the servants to go with her to the station, and she went away.

Some days later, I gradually gave up wearing the *sari* in the new way and took up my old dress. Apparently my husband either did not notice it or decided not to say anything.

III. C. G. KOLHATKAR, Actor

INTRODUCTION

"Bahurupi" means a man of many disguises, an actor who plays many parts. That is the story of Chintaman Ganesh Kolhatkar (1891–1959), the leading figure of the Marathi stage; fittingly, that is the title of his autobiography.

Drama and the stage have held a peculiar interest for Maharashtrians, as many of the individuals in this volume acknowledge. For the modern stage in this region has its roots in a flourishing tradition of folk performances referred to in this volume as *kirtans* or *hari-kirtans*. *Kirtans* themselves arose from performances of vernacular religious poetry and songs composed between the twelfth and the seventeenth centuries in Maharashtra. This era has come to be called the *bhakti* period, or age of religious devotion. This country-wide movement, proceeding from south to north in medieval India, held that the devotion of anyone, regardless of caste origin, to a personal God was a valid "path" to salvation, in reaction to many centuries of emphasis on the other two "paths" of traditional religious philosophy, works (*karma*), and knowledge (*jnana*). This movement was of great importance in laying the basis of modern Indian culture through its emphasis on communication across caste lines and in its popularity across regional barriers. Those regions with a vigorous *bhakti* tradition have been among the first to develop a vernacular literature. Maharashtra was one such fortunate region.

In Maharashtra the proponents of the *bhakti* movement are known as saint-poets. By adopting the vernacular as the medium by which to express their views rather than the not-generally-intelligible Sanskrit or Prakrit, these poets obtained a hearing by all members of the population, not merely the literate. As religious figures who had shed the many restrictions which prevented communication in ordinary social life with most people outside kin and village groups, they were able to propound their message without regard to their own social origin or those of their hearers. The *kirtan* in Maharashtra, the musical and religious discourse, became the medium by which the religious reform sects which grew up about the saint-poets propagated their views in public or semi-public performances.

It was not lost upon some early-nineteenth-century nationalists that the saint-poets, who were already associated with religious reform, could also be made to symbolize the demand for new modes of behavior in less strictly religious aspects of life. Moreover, their methods could be adopted for the propagation of ideas of nationalism and social and political change. The strong tradition of religious "theater" in Maharashtra thus combined with the new nationalism in "nationalist *hari-kirtans*" to become a new method of public communication and transmission of nationalist ideas.

This was not the only aspect of the modern Marathi stage, for near at hand lay rich historical sources of the Maratha empire and the whole vast corpus of Hindu mythology which could be utilised in dramas which would instill a new cultural consciousness and national pride. This was a development which could be expected to appeal to Western-educated urban groups most affected by nationalism. The influence of English theatrical literature upon the Marathi stage is evident in Kolhatkar's account, in which translations of Shakespearean plays figure largely; but here too selectivity was exercised in translation in accord with the new values of nationalism. Thus Othello in Indian garb could become a sympathetic figure to Indians attempting to rid themselves of "white" British domination.

Kolhatkar, like Madhavrao Patwardhan (see pages 287–300

below), is not known outside Maharashtra, and for the same reason. The deliberate choice of the vernacular rather than English as the medium of communication, although it enhanced regional patriotism, also walled off its users from other parts of India in the absence of an all-India vernacular. As most of Kolhatkar's roles were in historical and mythological plays and the drama of "social consciousness," his appeal was mainly to the urban middle class within Maharashtra. One of his most popular roles was that of a father who attempts to marry his young and beautiful daughter to a very old man in consideration of financial gain—a plot sure to be of interest in a time of changing marriage practices.

Although Kolhatkar's rather peripheral early involvement with nationalist activities led him into difficulties with the British government, as he relates here, he seemed to subordinate this interest to his acting career, for as he grew older he took no active part in politics. A distaste for formal education led to an inauspicious experiment with farming, which he describes below. Thereafter he joined a touring theater and became a great success in his chosen work, receiving in 1957 a medal of recognition from the President of India, and a stole woven of gold thread in honor of his position on the Marathi stage.

Bahurupi was first published in 1957 by H. V. Mote, Bombay 14.

E.M.

BAHURUPI

C. G. Kolhatkar

The time is about nine or ten at night. There is torrential rain in the month of Shravan. The wind is making a whistling noise as it rushes through hills and valleys, through bushes and trees. The shrill cries of insects mingle with the noise of the storm; the clouds hurrying across the sky make it almost impossible to say whether it is the light or the dark half of the month.[1] Instead of stars piercing the darkness of the sky, the glowworms, intermittently flashing their lights, draw the eye.

In Satara,[2] in a large house with two inner patios, two oil lamps are burning in a narrow hall off the front patio. A court is being held there. It is like that which Yama, the god of death, holds to fix the punishment of the dead for their life on earth. In the chair in the centre a white officer is presiding. Three or four of his black helpers are sitting on other chairs near him, showing the proper degree of respect. Like Chitragupta,[3] one or two clerks are playing with the papers in front of them. Four

[1] Determined by the waxing and waning of the moon in the Indian lunar calendar.

[2] Satara, in southern Maharashtra, is the old capital of the main branch of the pre-British royal house of Maharashtra, the house of Shivaji (1627?–1680), the founder of the Maratha empire. Shivaji's line soon became *rois fainéants* and their hereditary prime ministers, the *peshwas,* the real power in Maharashtra. After the British conquest in 1818, the current holder of the Maharaja's title was settled at Satara as the ruler of a small princely state. The state was annexed to British India in 1848 when the ruler died without heir. The Raja of Satara mentioned on page 137 is an indirect heir holding the title but in fact merely a wealthy landowner.

[3] The minor god in charge of records of the good and bad deeds of men.

or five black-shirts[4] are standing like the assistants of Yama round a young man who is clad only in a loincloth. In spite of the damp cold of Satara in August, the young man is sweating profusely. His face is anxious but somewhat determined. From the expressions and attitudes of the representatives of Yama, they appear to have had a discussion prior to this scene. Suddenly one of the officers of Yama gets up, comes to the youth and asks him threateningly, "What! You know nothing about this plot?"

Young man: No. I know nothing.

Officer (snatching the whip out of a constable's hand): Do you see what this is? This whip will peel your hide. Do you know that? (It is an unfailing instrument made out of the skin of dead cattle to put the stamp of victory on the skin of one's own brothers.)

The young man hesitates a little. The eyes of Yama himself and those of all his assistants are glued on his face. This slight hesitation gives these stone-hearted torturers a ray of hope. The officer cries, "Speak up! Tell us exactly what you know."

Young man: Really, I know absolutely nothing.

Even before the word "nothing" is out of the lips of the youth, the crack of the whip and the question of the officer, "Nothing?" fall on his ears. The glowworms in the blackness appear to have momentarily lighted up in chorus before his eyes; he blinks. For a second he is utterly confused. He cannot feel on his body any trace of the advances which the whip appears to have made in his direction. There is peace for a little time . . . he feels over his body with his hands, risks opening his eyes just a little and thinks, it must have been a crack in empty space to frighten me. He tries to gather his strength, to take hold of himself. It seems to him that Yama is conversing with his Chitragupta and his officers, and then the black devil standing near him takes his former seat. It is not his imagination. All this is actually happening; he realises it gradually. The officer who had whispered with Yama now begins to question him:

---

[4] Police constables.

Officer: Were you not a frequent visitor at Mr. Mutalik's house?

Youth: Yes.

Officer: Who took you to that house?

Youth: Bhusari.

Officer: Where did you get to know Bhusari?

Youth: Here.

Officer: Yes, but who introduced him to you?

Youth: I think it was Hinge and Narayan Mehendale.

Officer: Oh, they did! Why? Why did they introduce you two?

Youth: I think for the drama. In my house we had organized a drama club. We were planning to stage a play named *Tukaram.*[5] At that time Bhusari and I spent a lot of time together. He was also fond of acting in plays like me and wanted to get a part in the play.

Officer: But what has all that to do with Mr. Mutalik?

Youth: I did not go to the Mutaliks' at that time. Last April when the play *Zunzarrao*[6] was selected to be performed at the annual social gathering of the New English School, I was to play the title role. It was then that Bhusari took me to Mr. Mutalik.

Officer: But why to Mr. Mutalik?

Youth: Because Mr. Nanasaheb Mutalik had taken a prominent part when the students of the Deccan College in Poona had performed that play only a short time before. In fact, he had acted in the play and Bhusari told me that Mr. Mutalik had received high praise for his acting. So he suggested that if I got some hints from Mr. Mutalik, I could also make a success of my role. I liked this idea and that is why Bhusari took me to Mr. Mutalik.

At a sign from Yama, two or three officers gather round the youth. They have some discussion. The young man hears it, but

---

[5] A famous seventeenth-century saint-poet of Maharashtra.
[6] The Marathi adaptation of Othello.

he is ignorant of English and can understand nothing. But he does hear the name of the play *Rashtroddhar*[7] in their conversation, and he is a little taken aback, because that was the book that had been found when his house was searched. This play deals with the time of Shivaji.[8] But the British Government has banned the play and also confiscated the copies of the book. Naturally the young man is confused. At the suggestion of the white officer, the youth is asked, "Can you recite some of the speeches relating to your part in *Zunzarrao*?"

Youth (eagerly): Oh! Yes!

This reply appears to produce a change in the *saheb's* expression. He gestures to the youth to proceed. On the strength of the slightly more friendly expression on his face, the young man takes courage and asks with fitting humility, "But please allow me to put on my clothes. I won't be able to recite my speeches in this semi-nude condition." The *saheb* at once consents. The young man quickly puts on his clothes and stands like a wrestler ready to meet his adversary in the arena. Then he begins to recite Zunzarrao's third-act soliloquy.

The young man has a powerful and ringing voice. Moreover, this speech, like others he had recited in many plays, has a polish from long and faithful practice. The silent night, the agitated mind of the actor, all have the desired effect on the court of Yama, and the young man does not fail to see it. He heaves a slight sigh of satisfaction. The *saheb* has been tasting in his imagination the thrill of the Othello he knew. The young man is not a professional actor, but by practice he has attained to the excellence of a professional actor. The *saheb,* like a spectator looking at a play without buying a ticket, says in Hindi, "Anything more?"

The youth is waiting for this. His nervousness is gone; he is

---

[7] That is, *Rescue of the Nation*—obviously a political drama.

[8] The play was clearly considered to have contemporary political significance rather than purely historical interest by the British. Note that Shivaji, the hero of 17th-century resistance to Moghul rule, is being used as a symbol of 19th-century resistance to the British.

absorbed by the spirit of the play. He has won the first wrestling
match in the tournament. He begins another of Zunzarrao's
speeches, "If, unknown to me, the whole army had enjoyed her,
I would have lived in happiness and joy . . ." and, with his voice
rising to a new pitch, he closes the speech, "Zunzarrao, there ends
your life as a soldier." This so deeply affects him that with the
last word, he breaks down and falls to the floor. At that moment
the Yama in the *saheb* is dead and the man in him awakes; he
cries, "Very good! Very good!" and claps his hands.

It has been an exhibition of an artist's art with all his soul
poured into it.

Tonight my mind goes back to that first black night in my
life. After my release from the court of Yama, I rushed straight
to the one sure place of refuge, my mother's side. She stroked my
back with her hand, embraced me and said, "You should go to
sleep now. I will sing your favourite lullaby." With this, she began to pat me with her hand and sing the song of Abhimanyu.
It is a matter of great satisfaction that one does not know the
moment when one falls asleep. I thought my patron deity came
to me in a dream and said, "This great night in your life contained the very essence of your life. The night is the begetter of
many things, good and bad. This night is the herald of important
things in your life. Not only this night, but your good fortune is
linked with nights."

Today I realise how true the prediction of my goddess has
been.

My grandfather was the second of five brothers. In accordance with the tradition of the times, as soon as he had received
the usual education for a practical life, he had to carry the burden
of supporting the family, for he was a very clever and able man.
He carried out this responsibility and in so doing earned himself
great credit for fifty or sixty years. He then became a *sanyasi*.

His youngest brother Mahadev was also a very clever and

intelligent boy who finished his education in the ancient Sanskrit books very early. Then he went to Poona, studied astronomy and logic, and, at the special request of the educational officer of Bombay State, took up the study of English, which he soon mastered. He then became an Education Inspector and filled this post in a very creditable manner. It was thanks to this man's ability that our family came up in the social and economic scale. His most important work is his translation of Shakespeare's *Othello*. It was the first play in English to be translated into Marathi, and it was from this translation that the stage version, *Zunzarrao,* was adapted.

Thus, for about fifty years before my birth, music, literature, drama, and public speaking were cultivated in our family. Mahadev left this world in middle age. That poverty and adversity are the generators of ambition and ability was amply demonstrated by his six nephews. As Mahadev had no son, he adopted his brother's son Waman, who in the course of time rose to a very high position in the service of the state. Two other nephews also became well-known in Government service. Among the remaining three nephews, my eldest uncle followed his father in shouldering the responsibility of the whole joint family. He worked as a revenue officer and magistrate in some Indian princely state for some time. My father took to the profession of newspaper editor and publisher, and my youngest uncle became a contractor.

My father, Ganesh Narayan Kolhatkar,[9] studied English under the supervision of his uncle Mahadev. After holding various jobs in and about Bombay under the *sahebs,* he found it impossible to be as submissive as necessary and sent in his resignation, deciding to make newspapering his profession. Looking about, he saw that the province of Berar in northeastern Maharashtra had no newspaper and selected that as the field of his activity.

---

[9] Ganesh (personal name) Narayan (father's name) Kolhatkar (family name).

As his health was soon affected by the hot climate of Berar, my father later decided to move to Satara. There he started his own press and a newspaper called the *Maharashtra-Mitra* in 1867. While carrying on these ventures he took service in Baroda as the chief of police. Once while in pursuit of some robbers, he fell from his horse and was hurt. It was this injury that ultimately contributed to his death many years later.

It was while he was in Baroda service that the famous revolutionary Vasudev Balwant Phadke stayed with him incognito for some time. In Vasudev's obituary notice in the *Maharashtra-Mitra* my father later wrote, "He was famous after 1879. We regret that circumstances make it impossible for us to write anything in his praise." [10] Baroda service was no place for my father and he returned to Satara, starting a companion humorous paper in 1873. In this city of Satara I was born on March 12, 1891.

At the time of my birth, my father was a respected newspaper editor, an able councillor of the Municipality, a conciliator, and leading citizen in Satara. He was of an imposing stature with a strong build and bushy moustaches, and he looked somewhat unapproachable. He dressed in the old tradition with a long coat, a turban and a red-bordered folded cloth round his shoulders. In the cold season he also used flannel double-breasted waistcoats or short vests with Kashmir embroidery. [11] He had his food prepared according to traditional rituals and liked highly spiced and fried dishes. Every morning after his bath he would perform the daily worship, read the *Gita* [12] and put a spot of

---

[10] Vasudev Balwant Phadke (1845–1883), a Chitpavan Brahman, led a peasant revolt in 1879 which fed on the suffering and discontent produced by the worst Deccan famine in recent history (1876–1879). He was arrested in July, 1879, and transported for life to the penal colony at Aden, where he died in 1883. Under the circumstances no newspaper dared print anything laudatory about him.

[11] Curiously, a stock description of a rather unsympathetic character in modern Indian literature.

[12] The *Gita* or *Bhagawad-Gita*, regarded by many as the core of the Indian epic, the *Mahabharata*, is one of the most sacred texts of Hinduism. Its "activist" philosophy has received much attention from political and social reformers

saffron-coloured sandal-paste on his forehead. He chewed fragrant tobacco in ripe betel leaves and often used perfumed oils and scents. Besides reading and writing for the newspapers, he also attended to the work of the Municipality and the Local Board at home.

Father showed the curious effects of service in a princely state and the comfortable middle class life of Bombay on the habits of a comparatively simple boy whose early years were spent in a small rural town. He used to like musical concerts and dance performances. Altogether he was an appreciator of good things in life but also a very strict disciplinarian.

The house was spacious and had two floors, as the press was also accommodated in one part of it. There was a small garden in back, containing mostly fragrant plants—roses, jasmines, chrysanthemums, and so on.

The *Maharashtra-Mitra* was thoroughly nationalist in its outlook. Although my father was quite friendly with government officials, including the District Officer, and used to meet with them often, he was many times warned by Government for some of his criticisms. He was adept at critical and stinging articles, which were very discerning and often entertaining. In the "Imaginary Conversation between a Hindu and an Englishman," he wrote:[13]

---

seeking to relate their activities and beliefs in modern times to those sanctioned by tradition. It embodies the sermon of the god Krishna, disguised as the charioteer of the warrior Arjuna, persuading him that he must carry through his duty, however repugnant, of fighting his cousins in a great battle.

[13] This is intended to demonstrate the lengths to which the Indian press was driven to criticise the government while avoiding prosecution and closing down of publication. It also bears evidence of the form of Indian politics at the time. The pretext for a statement of general political philosophy here is a discussion of the cost of the Chitral expedition of 1895 in far northwest India. By the Indian Councils Act of 1892 the Viceroy's Legislative Council had been given power to discuss the annual budget, and it was under the guise of budgetary criticism that such nationally-known political figures as G. K. Gokhale made more general political criticisms of British rule in India. Gokhale's famous annual budget critiques began in 1901; this earlier example shows how the Act of 1892 had set the tone of political discussion in India.

Hindu: Everything you say is crooked. Your way of playing the game is full of cheating.

Englishman: Now don't get off the track. Tell the truth.

Hindu: All right. Do you remember that your expert said the Chitral Expedition would cost one and a half million rupees? And now the expenses have mounted to fifteen millions. Now, who is being dishonest?

Englishman: Well, suppose that in a battle with the enemy you have to use more guns and fire more often than you estimated, is that the fault of the estimated figure? How can one govern in this way?

Hindu: We are not criticising that. But who is responsible for the expenditure of twenty-five million rupees out of the Indian treasury?

Englishman: What right have you to ask that question?

Hindu: It is our right as your subjects to give advice to our respected rulers and make them rule properly.

Englishman: And supposing we do not listen to you?

Hindu: We shall drive away anyone who tarnishes the good name of the Empress.[14]

Englishman: What gives you the right to utter such bold words?

Hindu: We have learned from writers like Mill, who tell us the truth and make us resolute.

Englishman: And what do they say?

Hindu: They say that one can oppose government officers with justification only under two conditions. The first is that there remains no other resort but revolution. The second is that there should be no doubt about the ultimate success of the party one joins.

Englishman: How long is this senseless talk to go on?

Hindu: Until the nation again gives birth to fathers like James Mill and sons like John Stuart Mill.

My cousin Achyut Kolhatkar, who later became famous as an editor, learned his first lessons in journalism from my father and cultivated his peculiar sharp and witty style. As regards social reform, my father was a traditionalist. My cousin Achyut's

---

[14] By bad government.

father, on the other hand, was among the first generation of social reformers in Maharashtra. When he married a widow, my father even published a strong attack on him.

Satara was the place where every new political movement was first discussed. And my father was a prominent participant in such discussions. The Rajas of Aundh, Bhor, Phaltan, and Satara[15] used to come to our house. I remember the Maharaja of Satara's horse-carriage standing out in front. Once or twice I was taken for a ride in it and was given some biscuits and peppermint balls.

About my mother I can only say that she was the typical ideal mother described by everybody. She was loving and large-hearted and of a religious mentality. She came from a family named Gokhale in a village near Satara. Her father had three daughters and one son. They were a poor family, and my mother, who was the eldest child, was fair and very good looking. A marriage broker happened to see her and suggested to her father that he could marry her to a rich old man. But her father refused, and she was married to my father.

My sister Manu was the oldest among my brothers and sisters. She was very handsome and used to sing songs which she herself had composed, for she had a very sweet voice. She was married to a young man in Miraj who was a lawyer and an athlete as well. My elder brother Mahadeo left school after the seventh grade and was working in the press and on the editorial side of my father's paper under Father's direction. He was lean, tall, and good looking. He had a good voice and used to take part in the *melas* at the time of the Ganapati festival.[16]

---

[15] Titled gentlemen, all either rich landholders or at best rulers (with strictly limited powers) of petty principalities.

[16] In the public festival, instituted by Tilak, honoring Ganapati, the elephant-headed god, an image of the god is ceremonially set up in homes and public places for ten days, during which various programs of instructional lectures and entertainment are given. At the end of the ten days of festivities the image is taken out in procession and immersed in water. The fears expressed later about ritual pollution (of Brahmans) arose from the fact that all castes, high and low, could participate.

It was he who first took me to see a play, which happened to be a musical comedy. I was too young to enjoy the acting and music, but when the demon entered the stage and carried off the princess, I was so frightened that I fainted and the next thing I remember was opening my eyes and seeing the actors crowding round me in a backstage room in all their costumes! My two other elder brothers were schoolboys. That was our family.

Our house in Satara was near a large well called Bajirao Well. Only a couple of Brahmans practising as priests were neighbours; all the others were Gosavis or Marathas in the service of the Maharaja of Satara. Thus I became an egalitarian from a very early age and had Gurav, Sutar, and Maratha[17] boys and girls as my playmates and companions.

In the same month that I completed my sixth year, my dearly loved father died (March, 1897). What can I remember about him in this period? Whatever impressions I have of him are vivid and have not been blurred by time. Since my father was a leading citizen with many relatives in town, one would normally have expected two or three hundred persons to accompany his funeral procession. But the epidemic of plague which was raging in Satara at that time had so terrified everybody that only three or four people took his dead body in a bullock cart to Mahuli and cremated it there.[18] As a matter of fact, my father had died of a heart ailment and not of plague, but everybody feared this dreaded new messenger of death. These first six years of my life, just when I was getting to know the world, were spent

---

[17] Guravs are the caste of attendants in the temples of Shiva; Sutars are carpenters, and Marathas are the major agricultural caste of Maharashtra.

[18] In Maharashtra, the dead are carried on a stretcher-like contrivance of bamboo and rope, and it is the duty of friends, neighbours, and relatives to carry the body or "give the shoulder" for at least a short distance in the procession to the cremation ground. Taking the body in a bullock cart is considered derogatory.

under the loving care of my father. He it was who gave me my first lesson in writing.

My mother used to sing a song about some mythological event which had a fine description of elephants and horses in it. I used to like the song very much and would press Mother to sing it while she was arranging her hair in the morning. When she had plaited the hair into a kind of pigtail, it looked very much like the trunk of an elephant, and I used to play about with it before it was tucked up into a circle. When my father died, the braid was gone and so also the trunk of my elephant. My mother sat in a darkened room because of her grief at the death of her husband, and I cried because I had no elephant trunk to play with. I remember even today the loving touch of my mother.

After the death of my father I went to Poona with my eldest uncle. My cousin, who was called "Uncle" Achyut, was studying at that time in the Deccan College. Why this cousin of mine was called uncle, I have been unable to discover to this day. Achyut's mother had died when he was less than two years old. My uncle Balwantrao, eldest of the six brothers, had until then no child, and being the eldest he was the mainstay of the whole joint family. Thus the care and upbringing of the baby Achyut naturally devolved on him and his wife.

Our family at that time could not definitely be called either a joint family or a separated family. The only ancestral property was a piece of land measuring only a few acres. As Balwantrao was the eldest, he used to look after it. Naturally my other uncles and my father had to establish their own family units by their own labours. But even then, at the time of marriages and other festive occasions or in times of difficulties, they all acted as if they belonged to a joint family. The separate family units had not quite drifted apart from each other. A sign of this feeling of being a joint family was that Achyut included the name of his foster father in his formal name and called himself Achyut

Balwant Kolhatkar instead of Achyut Waman Kolhatkar (Waman being the name of his real father).[19]

During my stay in Poona I missed my mother and my Satara playmates. My uncle told people, "Our little Chintaman dreams about his boy and girl playmates," and teased me.

We used to get *Karmanuk*,[20] *Kal*,[21] and *Kesari*.[22] My exercises in reading Marathi made use of these papers as textbooks.

One morning in Poona the news that the tyrannical British official Rand [23] had been murdered at midnight was whispered from person to person. Even while the words were being whispered, everybody was nervously looking about for fear that Rand's ghost would come to persecute the speaker. Although everybody was happy that the hated tyrant had breathed his last, the expressions on people's faces were such as to show extreme grief. But even then, people like Balwantrao put on their going-out clothes and took a turn by the office of the *Kesari*.

I was in Poona for five or six months. During this period Achyut went through a dangerous illness. He had typhoid fever for forty-two days and was cured by Indian medicines. As soon as Achyut was declared convalescent, Balwantrao decided to take him to Kaloshi for a change of climate.

About twelve or thirteen miles from Satara, at the foot of the Mahabaleshwar plateau, lies the headquarters town of that district. About a mile and a half away on the banks of a river is situated the village of Kaloshi. My uncle Balwantrao had purchased fifty or sixty acres of land there where he had built a house,

---

[19] The same Wamanr who appears later in this selection.

[20] A weekly devoted mainly to stories, novels, poems, and humorous articles.

[21] A nationalist weekly representing orthodox Hindu opinion.

[22] Tilak's paper, representing the same viewpoint as *Kal,* but slightly more progressive in its attitude toward reformers and Muslims.

[23] Walter Charles Rand was the official appointed by the British to take strong measures against the plague which struck India in 1896–1897. This included the use of troops in fumigating private homes, considered a gross invasion of privacy by Hindus; and his autocratic methods and tactlessness in so doing earned him a reputation for tyranny. It was in connection with his murder that Tilak was first tried for inciting to sedition.

dug a well, and made a considerable estate. He also lent money to farmers of several villages round about. Most Brahmans who had land in these parts or were village officials of Government lived in the chief town. Balwantrao's house in Kaloshi was the only Brahman house in a village for several miles about.

It was in 1894 that Lokamanya Tilak started the Ganapati festival, and the plague epidemic began its frequent visits to Maharashtra in 1896–1897. Some people thought it was a kind of protest of the orthodox god against inevitable pollution at the hands of all kinds of people in a public festival. Also, the mouse, the traditional carrier of Ganapati, was the carrier of the dread disease and this lent some support to this superstitious belief. The banner of the victorious god of death was now fluttering proudly on the back of the mouse. As the poet Gadkari once said, in those times one had to be more afraid of a dead rat than of lions and tigers.

As the plague epidemic had started in Satara also, my mother and my brother's wife came to Kaloshi. My two elder brothers remained in Satara to look after the press. The third brother had already gone away for his education.

Our house in Kaloshi was outside the village. Coming from Satara, one crossed the river, then forded a rather wide stream, and finally reached our house. It had a big well lined with stone, a round stone platform at the base of the fig tree sacred to Datta, the three-headed god, and an orchard and a flower garden round the house. Here I again made friends with my contemporaries, necessarily of course of non-Brahman castes, and thus took up the kind of life I was more used to in Satara. On our farm there were the usual cows, buffaloes, and bullocks, but also a horse. I enjoyed these new surroundings and the new activities, roaming around on the bunds round the fields, playing in the water coming from the *mot,* riding the horse, and being made much of by the farm hands as the son of the master's dead brother.

Suddenly the pleasure vanished. The atmosphere became

dark. News came from Satara that my eldest brother Appa was down with fever. People went to bring him to the farmhouse, even though it was bitterly cold. A small hut was constructed out of millet-stalks a short way from the house, to keep him should it prove to be a case of plague. The plague had put such fright into people's hearts that with its arrival, they abandoned their houses and became wanderers; towns were deserted. As the malady attacked anybody who ventured near a patient, nursing him was unthinkable. All our thoughts were about Satara.

Next day, we saw somebody approaching by the path near the stream. It was my brother, so weak that he had to be supported on his horse by two or three farm hands. He was wearing a silk coat and a disordered rose coloured turban. He lifted his head with great effort and threw a glance at our house. When I saw his face, I called out "Appa!" and ran towards him. But somebody caught hold of me and took me away to a house in the village where I stayed the whole day. The womenfolk there tried to calm me, but I longed all the time for Appa. I do not remember when night came and where I slept.

When I awoke, I found my mother near me. She pressed me to her breast and burst into tears. My sister-in-law was also sitting nearby and sobbing. After a little while I said, "Mother, our Appa . . ." and she replied through her sobs, "Oh, Chanya,[24] your Appa is gone." I thought of Father whom I would never see again and of this brother who was also gone out of my life. My cousin Achyut tried his best to calm me, but all that he said did not change the fact that I could never again see my brother.

As I had seen my brother arriving on horseback I was curious to know what had happened to him afterwards. I saw that the millet-stalk hut built for him had burned down and I was puzzled about the whole affair. Ultimately my curiosity was satisfied by a farm hand when I pressed him very much and would not let off.

"Appasaheb could not even get down from the horse, he

---

[24] The author's pet name.

was so weak," he said. "He was lifted down by my father and your uncle. Achyutsaheb was also sent away to the temple of the village goddess. Your mother and sister-in-law were nursing Appa, but he was unconscious right from the time he arrived. By evening he died. Everybody began to cry, but your uncle asked everybody to be quiet. Then he, my father and two others cremated the body yonder on the bank of the stream. The hut with all the clothes and bedding was also burnt down."

At this recital I again began to cry. But the farm hand said, "Oh, please, Chintaman, do stop. Haven't you promised that you won't cry? If your uncle sees that you are crying, he will scold me," and then, as if to keep my promise, I controlled myself and stopped crying.

To lose a dear husband and a grown-up son in the course of eight months was a terrible blow to my mother; and further, there was the fourteen or fifteen year old widowed daughter-in-law. But one more blow was to come. On the sixth day after my brother's death a letter from my mother's family home brought tidings that my mother's only brother had also died of the same dread disease. Every house had the same experience in those days, and everyone asked God what had angered Him so and why this terrible punishment was being meted out to us.

Just as even a raging forest fire is finally quelled, the epidemic subsided and conditions in Satara began to return to normal. Families, who had abandoned their houses and gone out to live in temporary huts all over the countryside, gradually returned. My second brother had boldly remained in Satara throughout. The deaths of father, brother, and uncle appeared to have created in him an attitude of not caring for consequences.

The changed course of a river, the stump of a tree broken off in a storm, are things included in history. Man also drinks up the cup of sorrow and plunges once more into the stream of life with ever-rising hope. God has created this tendency to look to the future in man, and man turns his back on the past and starts on his path ahead.

At this time, Indian games were becoming popular among young men. Two sons of the Maharaja of Satara (well, it is no use calling them princes when the Maharaja—literally the great king—had himself no kingdom!) were expert players of one game, *atya-patya,* and had organised a team. They used to invite teams from other towns and organise matches and tournaments. That year, the team from Miraj was reputed to be very good, so a match was arranged for it with the Satara team. The Miraj team was captained by my sister's husband.

The match at Satara was very keenly contested, but finally the Miraj team won. Meeting her son-in-law and hearing his praises gave my mother a short respite from her shattered life. But even that was to prove very brief; only an interval of three months separated the death of Appa from the tragedy that followed.

My brother-in-law was a well-educated and successful man, but his domestic life was entirely governed by his mother. In fact, he never got free from his mother's apron-strings. His love for his mother went so far that even when he saw the extraordinary ill-treatment of his wife at her hands, he did not utter a word of protest. Apparently the fact that my sister came from a respectable family and had received some education, unlike most girls of those times, were crimes in the eyes of her mother-in-law.

Her ill-treatment included actual physical violence; she was beaten and also starved. She was made to sleep in the stable, had to do hand-polishing of rice used in the house and got only the broken rice together with some very sour buttermilk which she hated, and was given only the coarsest of *saris* and sackcloth for bedding. She was continuously abused with the most offensive of epithets. On special occasions the poor girl's father and mother were also roundly denounced with selected epithets.

But my sister went through all these ordeals with the determination of a true Hindu woman. Then the mother-in-law allowed her, after she had her first flux, to go to her husband as a kind of favour. This resulted in the birth of a daughter.[25] Then the tragedy reached its climax. My brother-in-law developed diabetes and was confined to bed, and the newly born child and her mother were accused of being an evil omen.

During all his illness my sister could hardly see her husband, let alone nurse him. The doctors tried their best but feared the worst. One night my sister caught hold of one of the doctors and pressed him with all the earnestness at her command to tell her the worst. The doctor was moved, because the story of the terrible ill-treatment of the helpless young woman was known to young and old in Miraj. He merely heaved a sigh and grunted.

My sister at once realised the true state of affairs. Then she appeared to have come to some kind of decision. She called in, one by one, all the married women she knew whose husbands were living, gave them red *kunku* and yellow turmeric powder,[26] and presented them with some small objects from her mother's house, taking precautions not to let anyone know what she was doing. When no one was about, she jumped into the well in the courtyard and ended her life.

When the people who had gathered together because of my brother-in-law's critical condition heard something fall into the well, they hurried to the courtyard. One or two jumped in after some discussion, but by the time she was pulled out she was dead. Just at that moment, somebody cried out that her husband had breathed his last. Whether from the sick bed or from the bottom of the well, the two souls had the same destination and went along their path together.

The news of the double tragedy spread like wildfire in the town and everybody rushed to the house. Everybody said,

---

[25] Daughters were much less desirable than sons, as only sons could carry on the family name. A bride's precarious position was not secure until she produced a son.

[26] Applying red *kunku* to the foreheads of married women whose husbands were living and a spot of yellow turmeric powder beneath it was the traditional ceremonial honouring such women, who were considered auspicious. To die before one's husband was the cherished wish of every woman.

"blessed woman," when they saw the dead girl's body. The police carried out a routine examination and handed back the body for cremation. But now, just as certain playwrights, even after they have reached the climax in the unfolding of the drama, continue to harp on the same theme and disgust the discerning spectator, the mother-in-law stepped in with an anticlimax.

As some married women from the neighbourhood were preparing the body in a manner suitable for a woman who had died before her husband,[27] the mother-in-law cried out, "Wait, do not take the widow[28] like that. She has become a bare-headed one[29] after her husband's death!" These words horrified those assembled. They silenced her by their denouncing words and scornful laughter, put the ceremonial red *kunku* powder on the forehead of the dead girl, placed the traditional coconut and grain in the end of her *sari,* strewed flowers on her head and body, and carried out all the prescribed rites for a woman who dies before her husband.

It was afternoon before the legal formalities and the religious rites were over. Then a long procession of mourners, young and old, started towards the cremation ground. The dead woman as an eternal *soubhagyavati*[30] preceded her husband's body in the funeral procession in the traditional manner. Many people, particularly the late sportsman's colleagues, threw little flowers of wrought silver or gold or fresh flowers over the bodies. Even though the cremation ground in Miraj is three miles from the town, a large number of citizens followed the procession and with heavy hearts set fire to the funeral pyre.

---

[27] The bodies of such women, in Maharashtra, are clad in a green *sari* with green bangles on their wrists and red *kunku* marks on their foreheads.

[28] The Marathi word she uses has the meaning of both widow and prostitute and is not used for a widow unless the speaker intends to show the utmost contempt and to defame her; incidentally a revealing commentary on one aspect of the social problem presented by prohibition of widow remarriage.

[29] That is, she ought to be shaved like a widow. This custom was prevalent only in the Brahman castes and in one or two other higher castes.

[30] This untranslatable word traditionally means a woman whose husband is living, hence a woman of good fortune.

Some people tell a wonder story about this funeral. After the pyres were lighted, a cow came up to them again and again, even though people tried to drive it away. Finally someone suggested that it should be allowed to do what it apparently wanted to do. So people moved to one side. Then the cow performed the sacred round of the pyre in the traditional right-hand circle. We can, of course, say that this was a story started and spread by those who were touched by the tragedy, but the newspapers gave it considerable publicity at the time.

When Achyut heard of this sad affair, he wrote a letter from Poona to my mother. It said,

I received your letter, which saddened and shocked me. I admire the courage shown by Tai. (Tai was my sister's pet name.) When I think of her behaviour, I say to myself, "What meritorious action!" I think she acted in a way which is very creditable to our family. As the poet Moropant has said, "What great good fortune that a woman should die before her husband." My revered aunt should try to think of her daughter as an ornament to our family and try to console herself. The series of calamities she has had to face is greater even than those which befell the women in our epics. But God, the friend at the end of one's days, will not leave her . . .

That was the end of our Tai. Even today, after so many years, my heart becomes full when I write this terrible story of her life.

My mother's condition was like that of a sinless, dumb cow. Even her tears dried up. She could hardly say anything. To whom could she talk—and about whom? And how could she express what she felt? She seemed to have lost her bearings completely. My father's cousin Wamanrao, who was at that time judge of the Small Causes Court at Jabalpur, sent a pressing letter to Balwantrao, urging him to send my mother there. Balwantrao tried his best to persuade my mother to go.

"Do listen to me, Sister-in-law," he said. "It will be a change of surroundings for you. Waman will do everything for you. At least for the sake of this youngest son of yours (meaning me) you should go to Jabalpur. However deeply you may mourn the loss you have suffered, the dead are never going to return."

Mother was sighing with anguish. What sin have I committed, she thought, that I should lose within fifteen months husband, son, brother, and daughter? The white forehead of the widowed daughter-in-law made her ever restless. Balwantrao continued, "If you are anxious about Uma (my brother's widow) you can take her with you to Jabalpur. If, however, you are a little doubtful about that course (because Wamanrao was a well-known social reformer and people might say that he would persuade the young widow to marry again or to go to a school against the traditional way of Brahman widows), her father has written to me that she can go to Wai and live at his place." My mother was finding it difficult to live in her house. Every corner and every object reminded her of the dear ones who had gone. Finally she consented to the suggestion and made ready to go to Jabalpur. My elder brother was to remain in Satara to look after the press and to go to school.

From Satara we went to Wai to leave my sister-in-law. We stayed with the Vaidya family, who, three generations before, had given employment to my great-grandfather as a house priest. Since then, however, the Kolhatkar name had made such progress in life that there was no longer any feeling of the employer family and the family of the house-priest between the Vaidyas and the Kolhatkars, merely friendship. We wanted to start as soon as possible for Jabalpur, but Mr. Gadgil of Baroda pressed us to stay on for some time. Because of the kinship and the old friendships at Baroda, my mother could not say no.

Mr. Gadgil had once been the chief judge of Baroda state. Now the queen mother of Baroda was to visit Wai, which is a sacred place of pilgrimage, and Mr. Gadgil was in charge of all the arrangements. The whole town was greatly excited at the prospect of the visit of such a high personage. Priests of various descriptions, religious preachers, and mendicants were attempting to get a share of the money the great lady was bound to distribute by outdoing each other in friendship for Mr. Gadgil and visiting his house. When she came, she spent a great deal of money in organising special rituals, worshipping the images in different temples, organising religious discourses, and arranging dinner parties for Brahmans.

Then one day she was to come to Mr. Gadgil's house for lunch, and everybody set to making preparations. The great lady arrived in a carriage drawn by two horses. From the door to the place on the second floor where she was to sit, women stood on both sides with sheets of white cloth to serve as veiling.[31] The queen mother sat there for a short while, spoke a few words to Mr. Gadgil, and then went in to dinner. She did not eat any of the numerous dishes which had been prepared, but partook only of her favourite dish, a piece of plain millet bread and some butter. Everybody was highly satisfied with all this and considered himself fortunate to have witnessed this great occasion.

I was not at all happy at this delay in our journey, but of course nobody bothered about my feelings. Right from Satara, I had been excited about our trip to Jabalpur. Of course, in the great excitement of the queen's visit, I forgot my vexation. My mother had, in the meanwhile, ascertained the details of our further journey. I could hardly contain my joy. Satara and Wai were of course neighbouring towns and I was no stranger even to Poona. But Jabalpur! The train journey itself would take three or four days and nights, somebody told me! I began to look down on my poor friends in Wai. After all, they were going to stay in Wai, while I was going to faraway Jabalpur. If anybody had asked me why I was so excited, I would have said that it was the train journey of three or four days and nights. I, who have travelled throughout my whole life and have now tired of travelling, am still conscious of the happy excitement of that first

---

[31] Women of Maharashtrian princely families did not show themselves in public, although *purdah* was not generally observed among higher caste women in this region, as it was in North India.

long journey. That is why even experienced and elderly playwrights praise the childhood years and regret that the time is gone, never to return.

Finally the day of our journey arrived and we got into a *tonga* to go to the station. On the trip we had to change trains three times, each change entailing a considerable delay. My mother would not take food unless she had first worshipped a god's image made of earth. For this she carried with her some black earth which was easily formed into an image. But it was difficult to get the particular kind of leaves which were necessary. Mother thought only of the series of disasters that had struck her. She was conscious of her helplessness and used to impress upon my mind how to behave in the house of our benefactor. At last we reached Jabalpur. One or two gentlemen with two uniformed servants had come to receive us.

When we got down, one of the gentlemen came forward and asked my mother if we were the guests of Kolhatkar *saheb*. On being assured that this was so, he asked the servants to take out our luggage. I can hardly describe my feelings of elation at seeing our luggage being taken out of the train by *pattewalas,* as they were called. At Satara, the municipal *pattewalas* used to bring papers to our house in connection with my father's work in the municipality, but they were not so imposing as these. These Jabalpur *pattewalas* were tall and well-built and had full moustaches and beards and looked very awe-inspiring; they spoke the language of North India. At first I was a little frightened, but when I saw them bringing out our baggage, I felt more confident. I had seen many big railroad stations on the way, but the imposing structure of the Jabalpur station impressed me most. That it was bigger even than the Poona station made a lasting impression on my mind.

Outside the station, we got into a *tonga* with a big horse. One of the gentlemen who had come to receive us also got in. Then the *pattewalas* loaded our luggage and we started off. I was observing everything most carefully. The houses were different, the people's dress was different. The few words which I caught of the conversation of the people on the streets were certaintly not Marathi. Nervously I huddled by my mother, wondering whether the people in our new home would be different from those in Satara and whether they would speak and understand Marathi. Then the *tonga* went round a large park and stopped in front of a bungalow.

On the steps of the bungalow, a middle-aged, dark complexioned woman with two children respectfully bowed to my mother. Then Mother made me bend down and greet her. She was my aunt! She said in Marathi, "Oh! Your name is Chintaman, isn't it? This is your sister Shanta, and this is your brother Ananda." Then I felt reassured that the people in this house were like us and spoke our language.

But it was difficult for me to become used to the life at Jabalpur. In the first place, the bungalow had no resemblance to our house in Satara, with its enclosed front yard, open veranda-like front room, middle room, kitchen, back garden, etc. It could also not be compared with the house at the Kaloshi farm. The bungalow was very large, with a number of large halls and several small rooms. They were all cluttered up with chairs, tables, beds, and cupboards, with photographs and many knick-knacks everywhere. The garden round the bungalow was full of fruit and flower trees; beyond that was a guava garden. That was the only place where we could play. The kitchen and dining room were situated in a separate structure a little distance from the bungalow.

Rao Bahadur Wamanrao Kolhatkar, whom everybody called Nana, was tall and very fair in complexion. His face showed the expression one expects of a high official conscious of his dignity and power. His manner of speech and his every movement were such as to impress other people. He had three daughters, one after the other, and two sons. Shanta, who was slightly older, and Ananda, who was slightly younger than I, soon became my particular friends. Two children of the *tonga*-driver also joined us in our play. All Nana's children were of school age, and I also began to attend school at Jabalpur. Although the people there spoke Hindi, our school was conducted in Marathi. We all went to school and returned home in the *tonga*. A teacher also used to come to the house to supervise and supplement our studies. It took me some time to get used to all this high standard of living and the attention paid to studies. Up to that time my schooling had never been consistent and regular. If Nana ever noticed that I was not treated like his own children, he became angry and said, "Do you think that he is an orphan who has come to our house as a destitute child?"

My mother and Nana were nearly of the same age. At Wai they had played together as children. On account of my mother's timid and sensitive nature and the calamities that had been her lot, Nana tried his utmost to make her forget her sorrow. While she was plucking flowers in the garden every morning for the worship of God, Nana would explain to her a verse from the *Gita*. Nana was a radical social reformer who practiced his views. But he also insisted that my mother should have all the facilities for her traditional behaviour including the worship of gods in the house, and everybody had to see that she should have no ground for complaint. Nana, an advocate of women's education, tried to persuade my mother to send her young widowed daughter-in-law to the school started by Karve, but he did not succeed in this.

One day, the Marathi-speaking families in Jabalpur and Nana's colleagues heard with surprise that there was to be a *hari-kirtan* at Nana's house. Many people had assumed that this high official and leader of the social reform movement would be an atheist. But as a matter of fact, Nana had studied a number of religious treatises and he often recited many devotional poems with great pleasure. It was a strict rule in the house that before meals and at bedtime prayers should be said.

The person who was to give the *hari-kirtan* was the father of my widowed sister-in-law. He was known to be a somewhat eccentric person about whose unusual behaviour many stories were told. One of these was that in the wedding ceremonies for his daughter, he had dug long pits on both sides of the streets, made wood fires in them, and heated large pots of water on them for the ceremonial bathing of the bridegroom and the members of his family. Now he had taken a vow to perform 100,000 *hari-kirtans* and then to visit Banaras, the sacred place of pilgrimage. It was thus that he had reached Jabalpur after visiting many other towns.

His usual programme was to visit the notables in the town in the forenoon, persuade one of them to arrange a *hari-kirtan,* arrive punctually at the appointed time with his companions and all the necessary appurtenances, holding the discourse in the evening. He would accept any present that his host might give but did not insist on payment. In Jabalpur, Nana's house was considered a kind of haven by all Maharashtrians, learned men, religious preachers, or artists. In this case there were the additional factors of the priest's belonging to the same town and being a relative by marriage. Naturally he was welcomed with great friendliness and treated with consideration.

After some time, Nana was transferred to Nagpur and we all left Jabalpur with him. I was just beginning to feel at home in the new surroundings when the shocking news of the death of my brother who had remained in Satara reached us. Mother's wounded heart, which had just begun to heal a little, again began to bleed at this new disaster. Nana tried his best to console her, but she was drowned in a sea of sorrow. She decided to go back to Satara. Sometimes a change of surroundings makes one forget one's sorrow. But when things become unbearable, one wants to jump into the centre of the whirlpool. Mother insisted that she and I return to Satara. Nana wanted to keep me for my schooling, but Mother was too nervous to let me remain away from here. My sole surviving elder brother, who had gone to Akola to stay with a cousin for his schooling, was also called back.

And so we returned to Satara, a great change from the

comparatively luxurious life in Nagpur. Our house appeared poor
and simple to me. The school at Satara would not recognize the
fact that I had been in the third grade in the Central Provinces,
and I had to join the second grade again. The one subject in
which I was very poor was the *Modi* script. I just could not
manage to write it properly and had to suffer frequent punishment at the hands of my teacher. Arithmetic also was my bug-
bear, but I tried to create an impression on my fellow pupils by
speaking Hindi, which even the teacher did not know.

Just as the final examination and the festivals like *Dasora*
and *Diwali* came round every year, the plague epidemic also
became a regular visitor, only it had no definite time for its visits.
Sometimes it was in the middle of the rainy season; in other years
it even came during the hot months. Whenever it came, we
moved to Kaloshi to live on my uncle's farm and so were spared
the inconvenience of living in temporary hutments on the open
grassland outside the town. But it did mean that my schooling
was interrupted almost every year, and I never overcame this
handicap during the whole of my life.

Balwantrao, my uncle, tried his best to create in me a love for
learning. Fearing that if this fatherless boy was not properly educated, people would blame him, he often used harsh measures to
make me study. But I thought that he was ill-treating me because
I had no father to protect me.

One day I thought of a way out. I had heard that the sap
of the *sher* tree[32] when put in the eyes made a person blind, so
one day I used this method to free myself from this constant
bother of study. As my eyes began to smart, I began to howl
piteously. Nobody knew what the cause could be, and all kinds
of remedies from milk-drops to honey were tried, but to no
effect. All this while I was crying and rubbing my eyes and
very soon they were swollen and red. I began to think that I
had gone permanently blind and that I need not now do any
reading, writing, or arithmetic. I was made to lie down in a

---

[32] A succulent which grows in this region.

darkened room in the centre of the house. But after a little while, when I opened my eyes just a crack, I was surprised to find that I could see perfectly. I closed my eyes again and re-opened them a little, and still I could see! My hope that I would become blind and thereby teach my mother, uncle, and other elders not to bother me with study, was dashed to the ground.

For about a week, my eyes were treated with butter and pieces of cloth soaked in milk, and then to my chagrin Balwantrao started to insist that I take up my studies again. I repeated my trick with the sap of the *sher* tree, and when this cycle happened two or three times Balwantrao was apparently convinced that my eyes were too weak to undertake studies and let me alone.

Balwantrao usually lived at Kaloshi on his farm but used to come to Satara very often. From his talks and from newspapers, which I was very fond of reading, I was well-informed about world events like the Afghan war and the Boer war in Africa. Some Boer prisoners of war were kept at Satara in an internment camp, and we often went to look at them, because we thought that they were brave to fight against their oppressors. They used to spend their time making toys out of cane and bamboo while we stood for hours watching them. They also organised a cricket team and played matches against the local teams.

About this time, my cousin Achyut was married to the daughter of a very rich man and I had occasion to witness the great pomp and the various traditional ceremonies with which the wedding was performed. The bride and groom threw mouthfuls of water on each other at the time of the ceremonial bath, fed handfuls of food to each other at the time of the wedding feast, and bit off pieces of rolls of betel leaf held in each other's mouth.

This cousin of mine was a somewhat simple soul—at least people thought so. He was so fond of study that he would even forget to drink the cup of milk placed in front of him. He never noticed whether the food he was eating had enough salt and pepper. If he went for a walk, he never remembered to return home at the appointed time. If he went to do physical exercises, he would spend hours at a time doing various jerks and movements. Balwantrao, whose adopted son he was, was very fond of him, and Achyut also loved him dearly.

One fine morning about five or six months after his marriage, Balwantrao got a wire that Achyut had disappeared and could not be found. He was at that time studying for the law degree in Bombay. He was of a religious disposition and had come into contact with political leaders like Lokamanya Tilak. Some thought he had become an ascetic like Vivekanand; others thought he had joined an underground revolutionary group. Lord Curzon's regime was becoming very unpopular at the time, and a great *darbar* was going to be held at Delhi, at which the Prince of Wales would be present.[33] So people feared that Achyut had joined a plot to cause some disturbance there.

Balwantrao went to Bombay and organised a search while everybody made vows to various gods and promised one thing or another if the young man was found. Finally he was located in the Theosophical Centre at Banaras established by Mrs. Annie Besant.

By this time, I had already acquired a taste for Marathi reading, particularly novels, but I now began to read plays also. I began to copy out the long speeches in the prose plays and the songs in musical plays and to learn them by heart. I often went out onto the great grassland plateau and recited these speeches and songs in a loud voice without troubling anybody with the noise. But I rarely got an opportunity to see a play in Satara, because that was not considered respectable in those days.

Somehow I managed to get through the elementary school and entered the New English School. This institution had been

---

[33] January 1, 1903—the second Delhi *darbar,* less famous than its predecessor of 1877 or its successor of 1911.

started a few years previously by the members of the Deccan Education Society of Poona. The headmaster, Mr. Devadhar, was a great idealist and was exerting every ounce of his strength to make the school a success. For me, the only change was that instead of the cotton or jute carpets which we used in the elementary school to sit on we now sat on benches in the English school. Different teachers now taught us different subjects. My hopes that corporal punishment was confined to the elementary school were soon dispersed when I found that the teachers in the English school made free use of their hands and canes. My expectations and those of many others like me that the English school was a place of enjoyment were proved to be utterly false.

At about this time, a famous dramatic troupe of the day came to Satara. One of their members was a cousin of mine who was serving as a house priest with the troupe. When the actor who played the principal female roles wanted a room away from the big house where the troupe was staying, my cousin recommended him to my mother, and so the actor came and lived in a room in our house. He was a most exemplary tenant, quiet, well-behaved, and orderly. I got to know him quite well and through him I received free tickets to a number of their plays. Some of the other actors in this troupe were also well known for their peculiarities and eccentricities. The owner of the troupe was fond of good clothes and good living. When he went out for a walk, he took a dozen dogs and two or three attendants to look after them. The troupe was earning good money, and the actors were well looked after. The boys of the troupe had a teacher who travelled with them to look after their studies. There were, in all, nearly seventy-five or eighty persons travelling, eating, and living together. One teacher in our school who was very fond of plays naturally saw me at the performances. He invariably asked me the next day in class what I thought of the performance, and we occasionally had short discussions about the merits and demerits of different actors, the stage scenery, or the costumes.

Soon after this, my cousin Achyut, now returned from Banaras, gave up his law studies and came to Satara as a teacher in my school. He used to teach Sanskrit and history and was very conscientious in his work. Though he was a social reformer, he was also an ardent student of ancient books. He used to go through the streets of Satara accompanied by his wife, which shocked the traditionalists in this orthodox town. He even gave a religious discourse in a neighbouring temple but introduced many innovations like the Urdu song, "The Lord Allah is the protector of the whole world," which he used as his main theme. Naturally the use of the name of the Muslim God Allah in a Hindu temple shocked many people. But he delighted in thus shocking people's sensitivities and soon took up another song, "The God Shiva put the moon around his neck"—and so the audience was happy again.

One day a farm hand came from Kaloshi to say that Balwant-rao was very ill. Achyut and I immediately set out for Kaloshi only to learn that my uncle had expired while being brought to Satara. Achyut had dearly loved his adopted father, and he deeply mourned his death. He shaved his moustaches in the traditional manner while performing the funeral rites and never again let them grow.

A small but significant incident that took place at this time may show the reader how Achyut was always thinking of ways to create some diversion. One day an anonymous article appeared in a local weekly, strongly criticising the teachers in the New English School. Nobody was spared. A sentence about Achyut read, "A teacher, who has shaved off his moustache and who goes on the streets accompanied by his wife, is trying to create the impression that he has just arrived from England." A long time afterwards it was discovered that Achyut himself was the author of that article.

I remember vividly an incident that took place about this time. Some of my fellow students had purchased some pen-holders with hollow glass handles filled with coloured water.

When I asked my mother and elder brother for money to buy some, I got a flat refusal. Then I submitted a false account of the money Mother had given me for some shopping and bought two of the coveted pen-holders for one and a half annas. But soon my mother became suspicious about the prices in the shopping account I had submitted and began to question me. But I would not confess. Then she stopped speaking to me, became very aloof in her behaviour towards me, and reported the matter to Achyut. He called me to his room and questioned me in a persuasive manner without any threats, and finally I confessed to my misbehaviour. He gave me an earnest sermon on the value of honesty and truth and let the matter drop.

Two of my fellow students, Mehendale and Hinge, wanted residential accommodation in Satara, so I persuaded my mother to let them room at our house. Mother probably thought that in their company I would pay more attention to my studies. On the contrary, my fondness for drama grew in their company, because they were both great lovers of the theatre. We now began to make plans to form an amateur group and stage a play. After much discussion we selected *Tukaram* and then began to decide who should take which part. My own desire to play the leading role or at least that of King Shivaji was not fulfilled, and I got a minor role. The rehearsals were held at our house; and besides my friends Mehendale and Hinge, a young man named Bhusari who was related to the rich Mutalik family was associated with our group. After about three and a half months we were ready to perform the play. I did most of the directing, as I was the one who had seen the largest number of plays and had also learned by heart a number of soliloquies from several plays.

Although the daily rental of a theatre in Satara was under ten rupees, none of us had even that modest sum. So we performed our play in the second floor hall of a nearby house with a curtain of red cloth dividing the "stage" and the audience. Many people attended the show, mostly relatives and friends of the actors. Some of them even had to stand outside and take a

peep through the windows. A few even stood in the street outside. The total number, including children, must have been
about fifty. Of course our costumes, like everything else, were
mostly borrowed or old articles of dress, and the paint that we
used was crude in the extreme. But the thrill that this first performance gave me has never lost its intensity.

Although I was never directly involved in politics or in the
revolutionary activities going on at that time, I was impressed
with what was happening then in the country. The whole atmosphere was such that no young man could remain aloof. I was
very fond of reading Marathi newspapers and had also listened
to discussions between Balwantrao and Achyut. Such events as
the murder of Mr. Rand, the sentencing of the Chaphekar
brothers to be hanged for the crime, the partition of Bengal, the
occasional shooting by a British soldier of a villager mistaken
for an animal during a hunt, the session of the Indian National
Congress at Surat, the destruction of crops by locusts, and the
applications of farmers for a loan from Government which Balwantrao had persuaded the farmers to sign at one time did not
fail to excite us; and in school we were particularly stirred by the
death penalty awarded to a sixteen-year-old revolutionary.

All this resulted in the establishment of a secret society of
volunteers who had taken an oath for the freedom of the
Motherland. I was one of these and my friends Mehendale and
Hinge also joined the organization. We used to sit together and
plot a revolt. Although my mother's sight was not as good as it
had been, she was observing me carefully and must have realized
that I was involved in something underhanded. When she
questioned me, I of course made evasive replies, but she succeeded in prying the story from Hinge and Mehendale. Then
she persuaded Mehendale to write a letter for her to Achyut in
Nagpur saying that I was not attending properly to my studies
and asking him to send for me.

This put an end to my "political" activities, and I went to
Nagpur. There I at first lived with Nana, with whom we had

stayed at Jabalpur and who was a little surprised to see me but urged me to attend to my studies and not to make my mother's last days unhappy. Achyut, although he had passed the law examination of the Central Provinces because Nana wanted him to go into state service there, had joined instead the editorial staff of a Marathi weekly called *Desh-sevak*. This paper was generally thought to represent the Moderate group in politics, but Achyut began to write strongly worded articles, highly critical of the British government, like those in the papers representing the Extremist group.

My attempts to join a school in Nagpur were unsuccessful. In one high school there was no vacancy and in another they refused to admit me because I was related to Achyut, who by now was becoming well-known as an Extremist in politics. I therefore had considerable free time and began to take on miscellaneous jobs in the press where the *Desh-sevak* was printed. I also got in touch with an amateur dramatic club and was to play the role of the heroine in the Marathi version of *Taming of the Shrew,* but all that was stopped by the orders issued by Government for Achyut's internment on account of his Extremist views in politics.

As Government had adopted the policy of confiscating the properties of political suspects, Achyut, in consultation with a clever attorney, had made some sort of arrangement about the farm at Kaloshi, which he had inherited as the adopted son of Balwantrao. Now, when he was arrested, he asked me to go to Kaloshi and look after the farm, partly because he realised that I was no good at my studies. Achyut's attorney was apparently in sole charge of the farm at Kaloshi, and my mother and I had to ask him for money when we required any. He was not very enthusiastic about my going to Kaloshi, and I returned to Satara for some time but no longer attended the high school.

Soon, however, the attorney wrote to me to proceed to Kaloshi and take over the management of the farm, also sending me some money. My mother did not want me to go, particularly because there was no one there who could cook for me.[34] But I assured her that I would cook my own food and began my life at Kaloshi. I used to come to Satara once every few months, and each time Mother gave me a supply of food that would last for some time. Very soon I became so used to the life on the farm that even my speech began to resemble that of the villagers. People at Satara, on hearing me, sometimes reminded me that I was not in Kaloshi, but Satara.

At Kaloshi I became friendly with the young farm hands. At night I would read aloud the epics or stories from Indian mythology and many people came regularly to listen. I also taught five or six of the farmhands to read and write. I cooked for myself for the first month or so and then got tired of it. Then the wife of our tenant Sawant suggested that if she prepared the dough for my flat bread in milk instead of water I could eat it.[35] But even that pretence was soon given up, and I soon took all my meals with the Sawant family.

I also took part in the meetings of the village council; in fact the old members made me the chairman. I soon acquired great skill in carrying out all the different types of work in the field.

At about this time, the students in my old high school at Satara were planning to stage *Zunzarrao* at the time of their annual gathering; but they could find nobody suitable for the leading part. One of my old teachers who knew my fondness for drama suggested my name. I gave my consent with some hesitation as the date of the play was only three weeks off. But I did my job well and earned praise from everybody, including the Headmaster.

---

[34] That is, there was no Brahman available. Since Kolhatkar was a Brahman, he should not have accepted food cooked by those of a lower caste, but ritual was sacrificed to expediency, with no apparent psychological or other ill effects.

[35] Milk, as a product of the cow, is not considered ritually polluted even if handled by members of low castes.

Ordinarily we sent the produce of the farm to the weekly Monday market at the District headquarters town. There I used to meet and chat with a number of petty government officials. Once I decided to take a crop of peanuts to Mahad, which is near the west coast and where, because it was a bigger town, I expected to get a better price. This proved to be a costly venture. The owner of the agency firm through whom I arranged the sale suggested that I should buy chilies, which were expected to sell at a higher rate later. So I sold the peanuts and purchased chilies out of the proceeds. Unfortunately, the market for chilies fell rapidly, and I sustained a total loss of about Rs. 300. I had to ask the attorney in charge of the farm for some money to pay the agency firm.

One day during the next rainy season, while I was engaged in various activities in the fields, I was informed that an inspector of police had arrived at the village and was calling me for an interview. I became a little nervous, especially because only the previous Monday I had received a letter from Achyut from prison. The police officer, whom I knew, did not even care to return my greeting and announced that he wanted to search my house. Without thinking of my legal right to see a properly drawn-up search warrant, I allowed the search to proceed. Naturally they found nothing objectionable. Then the officer demanded to know where I kept the weapons. At this I began to laugh and pointed to the agricultural implements which were kept in a corner of the cattleshed. But the officer said angrily, "Don't be funny. Where are the sword and the musket?"

"But Officer," I replied, "I don't have any gun. If I had, I could have killed the wild boar which came around here the other day."

Then the officer demanded to see my papers, books, and letters. I told a young farm hand to show him where my books and accounts were kept and while they were engaged in looking through them handed over Achyut's letter from the prison which was in the pocket of my coat to a boy with instructions to destroy it. The only thing that the police found was a copy of a play named *Rashtrodhar* which had been proscribed by Government.

Although the officers had orders to arrest me and take me to Satara the same day, in view of the late hour and the difficulty of crossing the river at night, they agreed to let me remain at Kaloshi until the next morning. On the way to Satara, many farmers came to say goodbye to me. Each one had brought a small vessel full of milk. One said, "My old mother asked me to insist that you drink this milk," and others said, "My aunt (or my sister or my wife) has sent this milk, and you must drink it." Every one of my acquaintances bid me farewell with a very heavy heart.

After I reached Satara, I was lodged in a temporary jail where the police carried on their investigations. My home at Satara had been searched at the same time as the search at Kaloshi, but there also the police had been unable to find any incriminating evidence. Now occurred the scene described at the beginning of this story. Then they decided, in consultation with the prosecuting attorney, that I should be used as a state witness who had been granted pardon. I was coached to state certain things which would involve other persons charged with conspiracy, among them Mehendale and Hinge. The "evidence" that I was supposed to give in court was rehearsed in the presence of the Collector. But all this made me very restless, and I knew that my evidence could condemn the accused to life imprisonment.

I then consulted a famous criminal lawyer in Satara and told him everything. He advised me to say before the Collector whatever the police wanted me to say. Later at the sessions trial, he would tell me what to do. But I was very nervous about making statements before the Collector about many things not known to me at all.

Finally in the sessions trial I contradicted my original false testimony and testified that I had no knowledge of any conspiracy. The police, the state prosecutor, and the judge were very upset, but they could do nothing. The accused were acquitted, and I at once returned to Kaloshi.

Soon afterwards Achyut was released from prison. When he came to Kaloshi the welcome he received from the farmers of the neighbouring villages was really extraordinary. These illiterate and poor farmers understood that Achyut had suffered imprisonment for his country and did everything they could to show their admiration and gratitude.

Achyut, the attorney who was virtually the manager of the farm, and I now examined the receipts and expenditure in the farm account books. When they reached the item regarding the sale of peanuts, purchase and sale of the chilies, and the ultimate loss of Rs. 300, the attorney said very harsh words to me and insisted that I should make good the loss. My expectation that Achyut would take my side did not prove to be true, for he merely made some noncommittal remark. This so infuriated me that I signed a promissory note for Rs. 300 and left for Satara after informing them that I did not wish to remain at Kaloshi any longer, although it was late at night. I reached Satara after walking the thirteen or fourteen miles at about five in the morning. My mother received me lovingly, but when I told her what had happened, she began to shed tears, in which I joined in spite of myself.

When my elder brother learned that I had returned from Kaloshi, he too was very angry. Already he was displeased that I had left school and taken to farming, that I had associated with revolutionaries, and that I was interested in acting. This was the last straw.

Now the question before me was what to do to earn my livelihood. I turned down such careers as becoming a clerk or a compounder of medicines under a doctor and decided to try acting with some dramatic company. I wrote to the manager of

a well-known company, the *Shahu Nagarvasi* Company, and to
my great surprise I received a reply that I should immediately
report for work. At this most unexpected good fortune I felt I
had found the true field of my life's work and thanked my stars
for this great favour.

IV. N. T. KATAGADE,
Gandhian Constructive Worker

INTRODUCTION

N. T. Katagade (b. 1895), nicknamed "Pundalik," author of the selections which appear below, represents a group of Indians who were powerfully influenced by the political movements of the first two or three decades of the twentieth century. This selection and the preceding one by Kolhatkar indicate the very considerable influence exerted over the young people of Maharashtra by Bal Gangadhar Tilak, leader of the so-called Extremist school of politics, and especially the influence of his weekly newspaper *Kesari,* which fearlessly criticised government policies and actions and carried on a persistent campaign for Indian independence. In the matter of political versus social reform, it was the view of the Extremist school that political independence must precede social reform. Violent methods were more or less openly accepted, at least by Tilak, on the theory that the end—independence—justified the means. Pundalik's account bears testimony to the appeal these sentiments held for impatient and idealistic young men.

The inadequacy of force alone as a theory of action, however, was constantly maintained by Tilak's opponents in the Indian National Congress. The Moderates or Liberals urged the use of only constitutional and legislative methods in an attempt to persuade rather than force the British to grant independence. Meanwhile the nature, scope, and role of social reform in politics continued to be an important issue. How Mahatma Gandhi, after the passing of both Gokhale and Tilak from the political scene, united demands for an acceptable method of political action with those for social reform and restricted his movement to nonviolent, if not strictly constitutional, means will be familiar to most readers. How his iron discipline guided the young Pundalik, who might otherwise have drifted into a violent revolutionary conspiracy, into a life dedicated to social reform, is told below.

Although it may not be immediately apparent, Gandhi himself acknowledged that his method of social reform was the direct outgrowth and logical extension of nineteenth-century Maharashtrian social reform movements and especially of the work of G. K. Gokhale in this field. Where Maharashtrian reformers like Maharshi Karve preferred to attack the problem at a comparatively sophisticated level through the medium of institutionalized higher education, relying upon changes in values thus introduced to percolate down through society, Mahatma Gandhi attempted a total reconstruction of village society at the most rudimentary level. Theoretically his efforts were meant to apply to all of India; practically, certain selected areas were made "laboratories" for his theories. Thus the first *satyagraha* (nonviolent campaign of resistance) which occurred in India, directed against the British indigo planters of Champaran, Bihar, in 1917, was far more than a public political demonstration, as we see from Pundalik's account of it here.

Of particular interest is the manner in which Pundalik drifted into Gandhian constructive work. Various circumstances closed the doors of higher education to him, and, without the training necessary to support himself at a craft, he became a hanger-on in the train of a regional politician. It was his very availability which made him more eager to join Mahatma Gandhi's frankly experimental enterprise than he might have been as a young man with a greater investment in higher education or a career achieved through regular educational channels. Here, then, we see another response to the narrowness of the established channels of occupational achievement and social change. Where the young men of Poona had banded together to provide an alternative to purely Western-sponsored and -operated institutions of higher education, the constructive workers turned to the implementation of Gandhi's program of basic education in hygiene, crafts, and literacy for the masses at the village level.

Pundalik has continued to be active in the movement; he now directs a constructive workers' training camp in Southwestern India near Belgaum (Mysore State). After Independence in 1947, constructive work and politics went their separate ways, fusing again only in 1955 in the Bhudan movement of Acharya Vinoba Bhave. Although constructive work is carried on unobtrusively and with far less publicity than the government-sponsored Community Development Program, the ideals which inspired it continue to command allegiance in modern India.

The following selections are taken from *Pundalik,* published in 1950 by the Miraj (Maharashtra) Sneha Samvardhak Sangh (Miraj Association for Friendship). It is an unfinished work, taking Pundalik only into his early years in the constructive work movement. He has never published a sequel.

E. M.

PUNDALIK

N. T. Katagade

LOVE OF MY PARENTS

My earliest memories take me back to my sixth or seventh year. A beautiful stone image of Maruti, the monkey-god, stood in the courtyard of our house and opposite it an image dedicated to a local saint. On the raised platform between the two images my brother and I used to sleep.

Upon awakening in the early morning I would open my eyes only a little and then put my hand over them, for I wanted the god Maruti to be the first thing I saw, so that the whole day would bring only good and pleasant things. But my brother, sister, mother, and sometimes my father got up earlier than I for their early-morning prayers; as soon as I opened my eyes I would see not the god but one of them. The day would then begin with irritation and quarrelling. However, if I had a holiday from school, or if I learned that some special delicacy was being prepared in the house, then I was readily convinced that it would be a happy day. My dark mood would disappear. Now I recall how affectionately the members of my family took part in such episodes, and I cannot help thinking of them.

"Made-in-India": My Involvement in Swadeshi[1]
Activities

In Miraj, the town where we lived, a singing troupe was organized to promote certain patriotic activities. Together with a
number of other thirteen- and fourteen-year-old boys I volun-
teered to join the troupe. I had quite a good voice and was in
great demand for every performance. Under the influence of the
songs we sang I took a vow not to eat foreign sugar. For such
a patriotic act my friends and I were highly praised, although
later we realised that people were really making fun of us. Whenever we took part in a banquet where many people were present,
I would be pressed to sing a song. As a matter of fact, I was
usually waiting to be asked. One very popular verse I had no hesitation in repeating several times during the course of my performance was:

Oh, how can you smack your lips with relish
When what you eat
Is a foreign-made sweet?

It was known to all—my family, my school friends, our
neighbours, and my father's friends—that Pundalik did not eat
foreign sugar. So, if occasionally I received a *pedha* or some other
sweet, my friends and companions would gather round me and
say, "You do not eat sugar. What are you going to do with this
sweet? Why don't you take a pinch of the sacred ash from the
temple and put that into your mouth?" But I would reply, "Even
if I don't eat sugar, I have brothers and sisters. They haven't
taken any such vow." When I reached home, and my brothers
and sisters naturally asked me for the sweet from the temple, my

[1] Literally, "belonging to one's own country" or "homemade." Here it
refers to a boycott of foreign goods in preference for Indian produced goods
which became a tactic of the freedom movement and was at its height between
1905 and 1910. Pundalik's recollections seem to commence at about 1905.

ready reply was "I have so many friends who know about my
vow, so how do you think they would let me keep the *pedha*?"
It goes without saying that on my way home the sweet had long
since been quietly consumed under cover of dusk.

But once this trick of mine was exposed. My father was a
dealer in gold and silver. There had been a big auction of old
ornaments in the local Raja's house, and my father had made
quite a profit. As was customary upon such good fortune, he
celebrated by distributing *pedhas* to his friends. I was entrusted
with the task of taking a packet of *pedhas* to Attorney Navare,
from whom I was taking English lessons. On my way I managed
to open the package in my pocket and eat one *pedha,* thinking
that a reduction in quantity by one would not be detected. But
soon, one by one, all the sweets were consumed and, when I
reached Shri Navare's house, only the wrapper remained. I simply took my English lesson and returned home in the evening
as usual. Four or five days passed, and I was beginning to feel
that my theft had gone undetected.

One day my father, as was his habit, visited his friend Shri
Navare. I had already arrived for my lesson. As soon as Attorney
Navare saw my father, he demanded *pedhas.*

I was sweating with fear. The theft was bad enough, but
how shameful it would be if the breaking of my vow became
known! My father replied to Shri Navare, "I already sent *pedhas*
to you by Pundalik. I gave them to this great patriot because he
has given up eating foreign sugar. I though they would be *sure*
to reach you. Is he here?"

There was nothing to do but show myself. I can still remember the conversation that took place. Attorney Navare said to
me, "Pundalik, please do not give us any such lie as 'I gave the
pedhas to friends,' or 'I brought them here and put them somewhere and then forgot all about it, and they just disappeared
from the place where I put them,' or 'I forgot them somewhere,'
or 'Somebody took them from me.' Just tell the truth and be done
with it."

I liked this advice and told the truth. As soon as I had finished the confession, my father caught hold of me and took me home, beating me with his walking stick and telling everybody the entire episode all along the way. My brothers and sisters laughed at me, but my mother was deeply grieved. On that day I seriously decided to give up foreign sugar. I stuck to my resolve for all of six years. Later, seeing that even great patriots did not keep such vows rigorously, I hardly know how or when, my vow also evaporated.

A Dancing Tuft of Hair Brings Merriment and a Whipping

When we were young, we boys had tufts of hair at the back of our heads.[2] Although we were not very fond of these tufts, my father was most particular to see that their size was never reduced, not even the slightest. Every day, early in the morning, my father would teach us the proper way to recite a devotional hymn. In this recitation one is supposed to move his head up and down to emphasize certain syllables. One day, while my elder brother Gopal and I were reciting this hymn, the lamp threw our shadows on the wall. The moving shadows of the knotted hair-tufts bobbing up and down seemed hilariously funny to us. In order not to irritate Father we tried mightily to restrain ourselves but finally exploded into a loud peal, awakening our mother, who was sleeping nearby.

My father did not understand. Once before, while teaching this prayer to us, he had dozed off and now he assumed that we were laughing at him. He shouted at us, "If you laugh when learning your prayers, I will give you such a sound beating that not a square inch on your body will remain intact. Now pay proper attention." We immediately recognized his serious tone.

---

[2] This was the custom among Brahmans. The base of the tuft was supposed to be as big as the hoof of a cow, and the remaining hair was shaved off the head.

We had had past experience of his violent anger and kept quiet. The recitation started again. We decided to say the hymn without moving our heads, but Father demanded, "Well, do you find it so difficult to move your heads? Are you ashamed of moving them up and down?" So saying, he took up a cane.

My mother, who was still lying in bed, said to us, "Why don't you move your heads? Why must you court a beating so early in the morning?"

Fearing Father's wrath, we began to move our heads in the prescribed fashion but again the dancing shadows of the hair-tufts bobbed before us. Father gave a final warning and turned his back to us to lead the recital with the intention of overlooking mere smiles so long as we made no noise. But again, at the sight of the bobbing shadows of the hair-tufts we could not contain ourselves and burst into loud peals of laughter. My father's patience was exhausted and he began to cane us, distributing the strokes impartially just as the driver of a bullock cart whips first one bullock and then the other. Although tears were streaming in torrents from our eyes, we still could not stop laughing. It was only after Mother intervened and got a few strokes too that Father regained his temper. The beating had raised welts on our bodies, the sight of which upset Father so much that he rushed into the back yard, drew up a big copper vessel full of water from the well, and poured it over his head without even removing his shirt. Then he came into the house, prostrated himself before the god in our family shrine, and took a vow that he would never again teach us anything. He kept this vow until his death and never again taught us anything. Any instructions he wanted to give us he would relay through Mother.

This whole episode naturally caused much discussion. Our younger brothers and sisters wanted to know just what had happened. Finally Mother undertook to explain our behaviour to Father, but he still stuck firmly to his resolve.

There Is No Recourse against Punishment by Elders

This was not the end of the hair-tufts, however. Father did not like us to go about without properly knotting our hair-tufts. In our lane lived a large number of my father's contemporaries, one of whom, an old man named Sangrolkar, used to call me over if my hair-tuft was not properly knotted. He would catch hold of my ear, make me sit down and get up five times, and then order me to knot my hair properly. On one such occasion I rebelled and refused either to take the punishment or to knot my hair. But "Uncle" Sangrolkar gave me a sound thrashing and then punished me as usual. Smarting under this indignity, I went crying to my father and told him the whole story. But my father took Shri Sangrolkar's side, saying that all old people had the right to punish youngsters. I asked, "Does he belong to our family?"

"Even if he does not belong to the family, he lives in the same lane," said my father. "You must not answer back to an old man. You must obey him. That is right for young people."

I: "Well, let that be. But why must I tie a knot to my tuft of hair? I can wear my hair any way I like."

Mother was standing nearby listening to this conversation.

Father: "Well, others are not harmed if you do not knot your hair. But if you take so much as one step without the knot, you commit a sin equal to the killing of a cow. If you wish to avoid that, you must knot your tuft of hair."

I (looking at Mother but addressing my remark to my father): "But what proof is there that what you say is right? Suppose I say, if you take one step after knotting your tuft, two dead cows come to life, would one be expected to believe that too?"

Father exclaimed, "Pundya,[3] you have gotten into the habit of having these arguments with your elders!" Whereupon he too

---

[3] A pet name for Pundalik.

gave me a whipping. At almost the same time, "Uncle" Sangrolkar entered the house chewing *pan* and heard what had happened from my father. I was lying on my mother's bed in the
inner room sobbing. I was called outside, but Mother was on my
side this time and warned my father not to harass me further,
pointing out that even children had ideas of honour and dignity.
Father assured her that I would not be ill-treated and asked her
to send me out.

I went out against my will. I did not look at "Uncle" Sangrolkar. My mother stood in the doorway of the inner room. My
father and "Uncle" Sangrolkar were exchanging smiles. For some
time nobody spoke. Finally "Uncle" Sangrolkar asked my father,
"Well, what have you taught Pundya today?" Father said, "You
ask him, and that may serve as a kind of test." I was on the
point of bursting into tears, but I feared my father would flare
up again if I did not answer. So I said, "Obey all elders, never
enter into an argument with them. All elders in the lane have
to be honoured in this way."

Father: "Quite right. Well said. Now the test."

"Uncle" Sangrolkar: "Stand on your hands with your feet
up, touching the wall."

Although close to tears, in order to obey an elder I stood on
my hands.

"Uncle" Sangrolkar: "Now let us see you cry."

Of course I obeyed this order very readily, as I was already on
the verge of crying.

But then "Uncle" asked me to try to laugh. I did my best to
obey even while tears were rolling down my cheeks. Both my
father and "Uncle" Sangrolkar rocked with laughter at my
plight.

My mother, however, did not care for this at all. She suddenly came out and took me inside, saying, "Is it proper for
grown men to tease a boy like this? I don't like it, and I don't
care whether certain people come to the house or not." At the
tone of her voice they stopped laughing at once. And so I was

rescued. "Uncle" Sangrolkar did not come to our house for about eight days after that.

Thereafter, if by chance I saw "Uncle" Sangrolkar when my hair was unknotted, I voluntarily twisted my own ears, sat down and got up five times, and knotted my hair in his presence before going on my way.

THE MHASOBA OF AKKALKOT[4]

When I was in the second grade in the Marathi school we had a teacher named Shri Kane. He had a reputation for being a very good teacher and it was said that no student in his class ever failed, as they all worked very hard. Though I had never seen Shri Kane give corporal punishment to any of his pupils, I soon learned the secret of his success. We all did our homework until late at night and again very early in the morning. Even our parents were surprised at this. It was not necessary for anybody to call me in the morning. I got up by myself, and the family admired me for it. But the underlying secret was quite unknown to outsiders. Before the end of each school day, Shri Kane used to deliver a short speech. It was always the same. "You must do all the homework I have given. Don't neglect it. I swear by the throat of your parents.[5] I swear by your teacher, by Ganapati and by the Mhasoba of Akkalkot. If anyone breaks an oath by his parents, he dies of starvation; if one breaks an oath by Ganapati, he is forever lost to all learning; and if one breaks an oath by the Mhasoba of Akkalkot, the god will enter the bellies of students, open their bowels, and whatever they have eaten will come out. So, if you wish to escape all this, you should study hard." I at least was so terrified by this speech that every day

---

[4] The Mhasoba, a non-Aryan godling worshipped by Hindus in this area, is regarded as belonging to a lower order than such universally known gods of the Hindu pantheon as Shiva and Vishnu. The town of Akkalkot is one of Mhasoba's residences.

[5] This is the usual form of oath. It is believed that if such a request is not complied with, the person whose throat was sworn upon may die.

when I went to school I expected to see some one of us with his stomach slashed open and his bowels hanging out.

I Join the Ambabai Gymnasium; Wrestling Match between Brother and Sister

A few enthusiastic students had established a gymnastic club near a temple of the goddess Ambabai. Instead of "the gymnasium near the Ambabai temple," it soon became known as "the Ambabai Gymnasium." At that time about fifteen or twenty students used to visit it regularly for physical exercise. Once when I had been defeated in a scuffle with a fellow student at school, I mentioned this to my elder sister. She advised me to learn wrestling and began herself to give me lessons. We must have been ten and twelve, respectively, at the time. The people in charge of the Ambabai Gymnasium were of course ready to admit me there, but they were not prepared to admit my sister, as women were strictly excluded. The padlock that they used for the outer door of the gymnasium could be slipped off through the hasp, and since nobody was there in the morning before ten or eleven o'clock, my sister and I used to go there at this time to practise wrestling. Some of the senior students who were among the leaders of the club caught us a few times and gave us a severe warning, but we paid no attention and continued our exercise. Then they began to use another lock, but the old-fashioned, half-broken door could be lifted from below and pushed back, and we used to slip in that way and carry on our practice. I could not understand why they should object to girls. Finally they kept a watch on us and began to beat us. We, in retaliation, would pull out flowering plants in the garden. When finally the matter reached my father's ears, he began to accompany me to the Gymnasium and teach me wrestling. Both of us became members of that institution.

I soon made a good impression on the managers of the Ambabai Gymnasium. I cannot possibly repay the debt that I owe to the institution which left such a good impression on my character in my boyhood. The organizers wanted to raise a generation of healthy young men free from bad habits, who would use their mental and physical powers in the cause of Extremist politics in the country.[6]

A STONE AIMED AT THE PRAYER UTENSILS

A lady friend of my mother's who lived near our house often came to visit us, and all of us brothers and sisters frequently returned her visits. Our families had a long history of friendship and neighbourliness. Once the lady's husband was down with a long bout of fever. Everyone in their house had become nervous and anxious, as the head of the family was ill. So she decided to offer prayers to the goddess Ambabai one evening to see if this would change her fortunes. She was walking along the street towards the temple with the prayer utensils in hand when I saw her from the second floor gallery of our house, which overlooked the street. Nearby lay a stone. An irresistible temptation to aim at the circular tray in her hand holding the prayer utensils came over me. The thought was translated into action in no time. The stone hit the poor woman's hand, breaking her glass bangles.[7] Down fell the tray with all the prayer utensils on the ground. As the stone could have come only from our gallery, she came straight into our house. When my mother welcomed her and inquired about her husband's condition, the poor woman began to sob uncontrollably.

Having no idea what her friend had come to report, my mother tried to console her. "Oh, please don't cry," she said. "He

---

[6] That is, Tilak's party. Note its obvious influence upon Pundalik and all his schoolmates. The Extremists' stress on physical fitness and potentially violent activities such as archery appealed particularly to eager, if half-educated, boys like Pundalik and is still a feature of Hindu revivalist parties in India, despite the absurdity of it all at this level. See also remarks in the introduction preceding this selection.

[7] Only unmarried girls and married women whose husbands are alive wear bangles in Maharashtra.

will recover from his illness. Don't we see many sick people recovering from their illness? One can only trust in God." As she said this, she put a *kunku* spot on her friend's forehead. Hearing their conversation from my upstairs room, I realised how mischievous and foolish I had been. Now I heard the lady say, "While I was on my way to the temple of Ambabai with all the prayer utensils, a stone fell on my hand and broke my bangles, and all the preparations for the worship of the goddess fell down in the street! I wonder whether my husband will ever recover. I am feeling so hopeless—desperate!" My mother exclaimed, "Oh, what Mahar[8] threw a stone at you?"

"Oh, Chandra, how can I explain it to you? The stone came from the direction of your own gallery!"

Shocked, my mother replied, "None of my children is at home, or one of them would have been falsely charged with this foul deed. Come with me. You can see for yourself."

Cold with fright, I pulled down a large basket we used for storing dried chilies and hid in it. They did not find me, but after they had gone away I had a violent coughing fit from the chili smell I had plentifully inhaled. This finally betrayed me, and naturally I got a thorough whipping. But even that did not calm my mother's rage. She dragged me to her friend's house and in her presence again beat me. It was that kind lady who rescued me that day from my mother and kept me with her for the rest of the day.

TOP OF THE CLASS

While I was studying in the Marathi fifth grade, my father asked me, "Pundya, what rank have you in the class?" Without thinking I blurted out, "First." Actually I was only fourth or fifth in my class. If I had corrected myself then and there or taken back my statement, the matter would have rested there.

---

[8] An untouchable caste of Maharashtra and a term of strong abuse among higher castes.

But later, after I spent two days thinking over the matter, I decided to stick to my version. If any visitor came to our house or when he met any friend, my father boasted about my cleverness: "Oh, Pundalik is very intelligent. He is first in the class." Naturally I used to hang down my head and remain silent. Others thought that I was very modest but I alone knew what disturbing thoughts were passing through my mind.

One day my father casually mentioned that he would accompany me to the school in order to see the teacher. What could I say to this? I was wet with perspiration. But there was nothing for it but to go to the school with my father. Before we started, however, I went to my mother and told her the whole truth. I explained to her how a false statement had suddenly slipped out and how I hadn't the courage to change it. She appeared to be convinced.

I went to school with my father. As soon as he entered the class, all the boys stood up. My father asked the teacher, "How is my son Pundalik's progress in the class? Does he study at all?"

"He is not bad, but he would be much better if he would work harder."

Father: "Do they arrange the students in order of merit in this school? What is his rank?"

Teacher: "Oh, why not ask him? I don't remember at the moment."

I had no answer to this, except to burst into tears. My father explained that a couple of days before I had told him that I had the first rank in the class. A few boys shouted that I had never had the first rank. My father felt that he had been dishonoured and asked me, "Well, Pundalik, what punishment do you deserve for this?" I gave myself a moderately hard slap on the cheek to express my repentence and remained silent. The teacher appeared to be satisfied with this punishment, but not my father. Taking me to each class in the school he made me declare: "I lied to my father that I was top of the class. This falsehood has been discovered today." He also told all his friends about my misbe-

haviour. If I was present at one of these recitals, he would begin
with, "The other day Pundalik put me in a very false position
. . ." After some days of this, I complained to my mother.
Whether it was she who intervened or whether it soon became an
old story, I do not know, but my father finally left off referring
to it.

Later when I did take first place, I used to ask Father to
come with me to the school to ask about my rank. But he never
did come to my class again.

MOTHER'S DEFEAT—AND ULTIMATE VICTORY

After I finished fourth grade in the elementary school, there
was an extended discussion between my father and mother about
whether I should be allowed to go to the English school. It
seemed that some exceedingly important matter was to be decided. While we children listened attentively to the conversation
of our parents, my elder brother Gopal would sit in a corner with
a sorrowful expression holding a book in front of his face, because he was the cause of all this difficulty.

While Gopal was in the fifth grade in the English school, he
became addicted to smoking *bidis* for which he used to steal
money or occasionally get money from Mother.

After I finished fourth grade my father had gone to the
English school to see the Headmaster and discuss with him the
question of whether to put me in the English school too. Naturally, when a father visited the school, his son was always sent
for and inquiries made about his studies, so the Headmaster
asked one of the students to fetch Gopal. The fifth grade class
was near the office and the students were at recess. My brother
and some of his classmates were engaged in smoking *bidis* and
blowing out smoke clouds through their mouths and noses when
the messenger from the Headmaster came; and my brother was
still inhaling the smoke when two of his friends caught hold
of him and pushed him into the office. How long could the poor

fellow stand before the Headmaster and his father without exhaling the smoke? Finally smoke began to come out of his nose. This so infuriated my father that he seized Gopal by the arm and gave him a hard slap on the cheek. Naturally the remaining smoke in his mouth was blown out into my father's face. As a result, the subject of my joining the English school was never opened.

My father took Gopal home and shut him up in a room, convinced that it was the English school that had spoiled my brother. Gopal was never again allowed to go to school, nor was either of my two sisters sent to the English school.

My father did not want me to join the English school, but my mother thought that at least one person in the house should know English in the times in which we were living. My brother had realised that he was the cause of the other brothers and sisters being deprived of English education and hoped that if ultimately I was allowed to join the English school, the judgment against him would also be modified. I do not remember the details of the arguments used by my parents, but they appeared to be very cross with each other.

Finally one day a set of books for the Marathi fifth grade, not the English first grade, was bought for me and my father's opinion prevailed. Mother had to yield. But arrangements were made for me to learn English at home.

Since my maternal uncle also wanted me to join the English school, I was allowed to join it one year later, after I had finished the Marathi fifth grade. My father, however, could not be persuaded and refused to bear the cost of my education. So my maternal uncle paid the money and arranged to send me to a friend of his, Attorney Navare, for private tutoring. Four others and I went to his house every afternoon during my year in the Marathi fifth grade. As I was more attentive to my English studies than to Marathi, I got very poor marks in the Marathi fifth grade that year. Though my English progress was good and I could have joined the English fourth grade, Shri Navare advised me to join the English first grade and that was what I actually did.

In the Miraj High School there is a small separate classroom away from the main building where the English first grade class used to meet. Teachers and students alike referred to it as "the Mharoda." [9] As soon as my name was registered in the first grade of the English school, the Headmaster told the office servant to take me to the Mharoda. Shocked, I declared that I was not prepared to sit in the Mharoda and went straight home. When next day the peculiar name of the classroom was explained to me, I began to attend school regularly. Because of my earlier private tuition in English, I maintained top rank in the class throughout the year and gained much in self-confidence.

WHAT MAKES YOU A PATRIOT?

At the time of the final examination in the English first grade came the news that Lokamanya Tilak had been sentenced to six years' imprisonment. [10] We all decided to do what the students in the matriculation class would do. We were all under the impression that some great Indian had been put behind bars by the foreign government and that our school was doing something to get him released. From that day, we younger boys in the singing troupe began to get training in archery. We also devoted much more attention to physical culture and gymnastic exercises.

Some older people began going around town and collecting a handful of corn from each family which could be used to feed the poor or the money realised from its sale utilised to support the political movement. We younger students accompanied our elders with a cloth bag round our shoulders and collected corn once a week. Some of the older students started a reading room,

---

[9] Colloquial for "Mahar-wada," the residence of the Mahars, which is always situated at a distance from the village.

[10] Tilak's second sedition trial in 1908. Public figures in India are usually known by honorific titles; thus Lokamanya means "approved by the people."

especially for political newspapers, which we occasionally visited. Weekly meetings and discussion groups were held there also. Once at such a meeting, I asked, "How can one become a patriot?" Somebody replied, "You must have a good aim in archery, you must ride well on horseback, and you must be present regularly every week to collect handfuls of corn from each household." I felt very proud to move among these older students.

Whenever I behaved badly at home or quarrelled with my brothers or sisters, I was at once asked, "Is this how a patriot is expected to behave?"

PLAGUE

When I was in the third English grade, an epidemic of plague started in Miraj. I wanted to buy a book of Marathi poems which was a text for my class, but Father said when I went to ask for the money, "There is plague in the town, people are preparing to leave town. It is possible that the schools will close down in four or five days. It would be better to buy the book after the schools open again. What is the point in buying the book now and having it soiled?" I agreed with this, and left for school where I began to give out a "prediction" to my schoolmates that the school would close down in four or five days. One of the teachers, Shri Khare, overheard me informing another student of this.

The next day on my way to school I met a boy returning from school. He told me, "I am going back to my house to bring a notebook I have forgotten. But do you know, there is a dead rat in the entrance to the third grade class in the school, with its head pointing outwards and with a broken tail. It has two bubos of plague, and its head is crushed." At this news I was in no hurry to go to school and loitered about until I met three or four other students from my class. To them I said, "Shall I predict a future event? You know, I have not yet been to the school, but I can tell you that we will find a dead rat in the doorway of the third grade classroom. It has its head pointing outwards and its head is crushed. Now the school will close in a day or two." While I was pompously "predicting" this future occurrence, another teacher who was following us overheard our conversation.

During the first period, no class had a teacher, because they had all assembled in the Headmaster's office and were discussing the plague rat. One teacher suggested that the rat never died in the school but that somebody had put it there. Then another teacher reported my description of the rat to my friends and Shri Khare reported my "prediction" the previous evening that the school would be closed in four or five days.

Soon I was asked to go to the office. Naturally I had no idea why I had been called. The Headmaster called me to him and patting me on the back said, "Pundalik, would you do something for me? Nobody else can do it. It wants a really clever boy like you." Naturally I was very flattered. He continued, "I want you to find out who put the dead rat in the third grade classroom."

"I am sorry," I replied. "I cannot serve as a kind of C.I.D. agent." [11]

"Then do you know anything about it?"

"No," I told him, "I have no knowledge about it."

Then Shri Khare intervened, "Have you given anyone a 'prediction' that the school would be closed in three or four days?"

This made me hesitate. I did not know what to reply to this. If I answered in the affirmative, I was afraid that I would be charged with having put the dead rat where it was found. If I replied in the negative, I feared that I would be confronted with those to whom I had given the prediction. While I was thus thinking about the dilemma, one of the teachers, Shri Sathe, became convinced that I was at the bottom of the whole thing and began to beat me, first with his hands, then with a cane,

---

[11] The Criminal Investigation Department of the Government of India, the secret police, were much interested in the activities of nationalists, as Part II of *Pundalik* shows.

and finally he even gave me some kicks. At last the other teachers rescued me from him, but some declared that I should be driven away from the school altogether. The Headmaster told me, "When God gives you the desire to tell the truth, then come to me again," and I was asked to leave.

I spoke to nobody about what had happened in the office but packed my books and went home. At my wits' end, I told everything to my father. Somehow I had managed to control my emotions until I reached home, but there I burst into a violent fit of sobs. Father was taking his meal. I sat on a chair nearby, and with his hand arrested on the way to his mouth he heard my story. Then he declared, "I would not want to think or say anything against it even if a teacher should kill a student. A teacher is and should be all-powerful!" When I heard this I felt completely lost and in my desperation, the following words escaped my lips: "What is the good of having a father like this? I might as well consider myself an orphan."

At this my father put down the food in his hand, washed his hands, put on his going-out clothes, took his usual walking stick, and, ordering me to accompany him, began rapidly to walk towards the school. He was walking so fast that I had to run in order to keep up with him. By the time we reached there, everybody was talking about the event; and seeing me return to the school along with my father, a crowd of students gathered near the Headmaster's office.

Here I should like to explain in passing the relations between my father and the Chief of Miraj State. The latter was a connoisseur of precious stones and had considerable knowledge of their properties and value. As Father also dealt in jewels, he was often called in by the Chief to judge precious stones. These visits were quite frequent, in fact every alternate day. Particularly after the Chief had purchased a new car, his car very often came to our house to take Father to the palace. When jewel merchants came from Bombay to sell some ornaments to the Chief, my father was always called in as a consultant. Occasionally I ac companied him, and I had begun to get some experience in judging the quality of pearls. Once or twice a couple of imitation pearls were mixed with real pearls and I was asked to pick them out. This I had been able to do successfully. My father had never taken any money for the time he spent with the Chief or for the expert advice he gave, but all this led to a considerable acquaintance between them. Occasionally the Chief had to visit our house, and my father's prestige in Miraj was naturally very high.

By the time my father reached the Headmaster's office his temper had risen to boiling heat. He immediately demanded of the Headmaster, "Why was Pundalik punished here today? What is all this I hear about this plague rat? If it is proved that he put the dead rat in the classroom, I would consider the punishment he has received most inadequate. I shall then drive him out of my house. But if that is not true, then I wish to file a suit against the teacher who beat him. Please call Shri Sathe here."

Shri Sathe was actually in the library. But the Headmaster stated that he had gone home and offered to send a servant to call him. In the meanwhile the two of them began to discuss the whole affair—how I had come to make predictions about the closing of the school in four or five days, how I had come to know where the rat was, how many bubos it had, and so on. The boy who had first told me about the rat was also called and questioned.

While all this inquiry was going on, the horn of the Chief's motor car was heard on the road outside, and my father threatened to stop him and tell him the whole business. The Headmaster earnestly requested him to do nothing of the kind. Just then Shri Sathe came into the office. My father did not speak a word with him, but continued to ask all questions of the Headmaster, who in his turn told Shri Sathe about the information so far elicited.

Shri Sathe then apologised to my father and said, "I am sorry

I made a mistake," to me and, bowing a little, made a *namaskar*[12] to me. I just stood there while all this went on, but my father could not bear to see me standing while my teacher bowed to me. He began to give me blows with his walking stick, saying, "You fool, you stand there looking on while your teacher is doing *namaskar* to you! Are you a human being or a beast? Put your head on his feet at once." So I put my head on his feet, but he lifted me up and embraced me, and both of us began to weep. Until I left the office with my father, Shri Sathe sat near me and caressed my cheek with his hand.

The mystery of the dead rat was never solved, but it was assumed that it had probably fallen from the roof and that was how its head was crushed. The school remained closed for about two and a half months.

FIRST ENCOUNTER WITH PROFESSOR VIJAPURKAR, 1907[13]

Annasaheb Vijapurkar and a group of his students were staying for about three months in a large house belonging to the Chief of Miraj on the banks of the river Krishna. In his spare time he and one or two assistants visited people collecting money for his school. One day he came to our house while my father was pounding betel leaves in a small mortar and I was sitting near him. The day before, he had got from a sale some fifty or seventy-five rupees which I had placed in a cupboard, as that was a duty usually assigned to me. I knew where the key of the cupboard was kept.

---

[12] Joining the palms and bowing the head to indicate respect. This gesture is usually made to an elder by his junior.

[13] Professor Annasaheb Vijapurkar was a well-known Maharashtrian educator and a pioneer in "National Education," a movement designed to counteract the influence of government or government-supported schools which taught a government-approved curriculum whose purpose, it was charged, was to "denationalise" the students. The National Schools, on the other hand, taught such subjects as the history of India from the Indian point of view. They also included in their curriculum vocational subjects to enable students to be economically independent of government jobs. Their aim was to inculcate habits of "plain living and high thinking."

My father welcomed Professor Vijapurkar and his companion, and the two explained their scheme of "national" schools and said that they wanted my father to give a donation of at least a hundred rupees.

"I am afraid that is quite beyond my means and as it happens, I have not much money with me today. Here are five rupees which I will give you," said my father.

But I intervened and said, "But Father, don't you remember you brought home fifty or sixty rupees yesterday? I myself put them in the cupboard and I know where the key is kept. Should I get the money?"

My father's face went pale on hearing me, but he spoke with a smile, "Oh, of course, I had quite forgotten. Pundalik, go and get twenty rupees out of that." When I came back with the money and started to give it to him, he asked me to hand it over to Professor Vijapurkar. When this had been done, the gentleman asked me, "But where is your contribution?" So I picked up the original five rupees that my father had offered and gave them to Professor Vijapurkar, telling him that this was my contribution. Then a regular receipt was written, cups of milk were handed round, and the two departed.

Later, Mother remarked, "Even if a cause is good, do you think one should give so much money?" To which Father replied, "Well, I was about to close the matter just with five rupees. But this precious son of yours spoiled everything. What is the use now?" Naturally I got a severe scolding.

Next day Professor Vijapurkar came with a *tonga* to take my father to see his school, inviting me to accompany them too. But I replied, "I don't want to come with you. Yesterday because I reminded my father about the money in the cupboard, my parents scolded me. My brothers and sisters made fun of me." Then everybody had a laugh, and my father told me to put on my coat and trousers and come along. So I went to see the *Samartha Vidyalaya*.

THE PICNIC PARTY

One day all the members of our family—our parents, eight brothers and sisters, mother's brother, mother's mother, and three male servants—went to our farm near Miraj for a picnic. We had taken a great quantity of food with us. The young millet ears were roasted, all the things we had brought with us were spread out, and we were just beginning to eat when seven or eight friends of my father's and a couple of servants passed along the road nearby. Father invited them all to join us, but Mother was apprehensive, fearing that the *chivda* she had prepared would not be sufficient for so many people. So she quickly dumped a lot of hot paprika powder into the *chivda* and distributed it to everybody! Naturally everybody thought that it was too hot and somebody asked me, "Do you use so much paprika in your food every day?"

Simpleton that I was, I replied, "Oh, no! But when Mother saw a large number of unexpected guests joining us, she put a handful of very hot paprika powder in it. That is why it is so spicy. Before that it was not at all hot."

Everybody was speechless. Father's friends looked at each other, while Father pretended to eat something and never looked up. When Mother came to serve something to the guests, she looked at me in such a peculiar way that I realised that I had done something wrong.

When, after the picnic, everybody started to get into the bullock cart to go home, I said I would prefer to return on foot with the guests. No one was deceived by this, but not a word was said and I returned home on foot.

I was on tenterhooks all the time imagining the punishment I would get. But, to my surprise, nobody said a word to me. I could hardly eat anything, and after the evening meal I asked father whether I could sleep near him. When he said he had no objection, I lay down near him but could not fall asleep. About midnight I got up and went to sleep near my mother. She woke up and advised me, "Children should not talk about things that do not concern them. They should listen when older people are conversing. You must learn to mind your own business." Then she patted me, and I went to sleep.

ATTACK ON TEACHER

We had a very good English teacher named Paranjpe when I was in the fourth grade in the English school. He was rather short and about sixty years of age. One of my classmates, Vasudev, was the fastest runner in the school. One day he gave me a blow on the back and ran away. However hard I tried, I could not catch up with him, and so I decided to trap him when he came into the class after recess. The next period was English and, when we saw Shri Paranjpe emerging from the office and heading towards our class, everyone entered the classroom. I stood behind the door, having arranged with a friend to stand in the doorway and give a signal when Vasudev appeared.

Vasudev was standing just outside the door. Expecting that I would lie in wait for him, he waited to come in with the teacher. When my friend saw Vasudev, he signalled to me. But unfortunately for me, the teacher entered the class first. Expecting Vasudev to appear, I threw my hands round his waist and pulled him down. His turban was twisted, his shoes were thrown into the corner, his stick flew off, and his clothes became covered with dust.

Terrified, I realised what I had done. Shri Paranjpe got up, put on his shoes, jammed his crumpled turban on his head, and walked straight out to the Headmaster's office. The whole class was speechless with horror. All the students gathered around me at once. Soon a servant came to call me to the office. The Headmaster was a very quiet man. He merely said, "Pundalik, what have you done? Put out your hand."

I: "But please, will you listen to me first?"

Headmaster: "You idiot, what is there to listen to? Do you know how grave your offence is?"

I: "But, at least after I have taken the punishment, I request you and Shri Paranjpe to hear me out."

Then the Headmaster gave me three hard strokes on my palm with his cane and made me beg forgiveness of Shri Paranjpe. After this I explained to them what had happened. The Headmaster questioned Vasudev and a few other students and finally told me: "You see, you must always be very careful in your behaviour."

That day, after school, Shri Paranjpe took me to his house and asked his wife to give me some sweets, which I could hardly swallow. Then with a smile he told the whole story to his wife. After that I visited Shri Paranjpe's house very often, and he remained friendly to me till the end.

FATHER'S DEATH

About this time, my father became ill with dropsy. This was supposed to last for nine days.

As I was a "footer" [14] my mother one day asked me to perform the following ritual: Two small oil lamps are lighted in front of a plate which has been coated with lamp black, and a "footer" is asked to stare steadily at the black surface. This is known as *karputali*. The scene which the "footer" sees in the black surface is then to be interpreted as a portent of future events. What I saw was as follows: "A cart full of firewood starting from our house is standing outside the wall of the town. Although there is light outside, inside the house is complete darkness." When my mother heard me describe this, she fell down in a swoon.[15] The shadow of grief spread in the house.

---

[14] A breach birth.

[15] The cart was interpreted as taking firewood for the cremation of a corpse.

The next day a famous American doctor was called. I was sitting near my father's bed while he was there. Dr. Wanless said, "He may die in a day or two." As I could understand a little English, my maternal uncle and Dr. Joshi called me outside and asked what the doctor had said. Naturally I gave a simple translation of the sentence. But Dr. Joshi said, "Oh, your knowledge of English is very poor. Don't you know that 'may' includes 'may not?' What the doctor said in medical English means 'The next few days are rather critical; but after that the patient will feel better.' Now have you understood?" I said yes and went inside. When my mother and grandmother inquired what the American doctor had said, I gave this new version. This had the effect of spreading the impression that my father's life was not in danger.

Next day my father began to lose his memory. All of us brothers and sisters were brought round his bed for about fifteen minutes. Nobody said a word. Suddenly one of the doctors came in and said, "Please do not bring the children here. That disturbs his peace. Let him sleep quietly for awhile." So we were all sent to a neighbour's house. We children had our noon meal there that day. About three or four in the afternoon we heard the sound of loud lamentation from our house, and without asking anybody's permission we all ran back to our house. I went straight to my father's bed and seeing everybody crying I also burst into tears. But I could not stay there long and returned alone to the neighbours. In the evening my uncle took me and my elder brother to the cremation ground in a *tonga* for the cremation of my father's body. This was the first time I had seen a dead body. We took a bath in the river and returned home.

For nine days none of us was allowed to go into Mother's room. On the tenth day, she had to face the ordeal of becoming "sacred" according to the traditions of the Hindu religion. This proved to be such a shock that she went completely out of her mind. At night she had to be locked up. She used to cry out during her fit of insanity, "What is a head? It is only a vegetable marrow put on one's shoulder." I was not old enough to realise why she had gone out of her mind, so I was also locked up with her to keep her company. I used to sleep by her side. She never took the end of the *sari* from her head, fearing that I would be frightened.

Mother lived for three months after my Father's death. During this time a Muslim friend of my father's often came to our house. My mother's brother and my elder brother Gopal took full advantage of my mother's condition and took away her keys. They also took away her ornaments saying that they would keep them in safe custody somewhere else. My elder brother took possession of what cash there was in the house. We began to have two vegetable preparations with each meal.[16] Then we started to eat fruit after meals. We all thought it was a great luxury. When my father was living, tea was prepared very rarely and then secretly. Now it was made every day. Grapes were sometimes purchased too. People who never came for meals before were now frequent guests. The Kojagiri festival was celebrated on a grand scale.[17] We had a neighbour who kept a concubine; a group of crooked men made him organise singing and dancing parties in his house and completely ruined him. Not only that, my brother actually sued him for some debts and got a court order against him for Rs. 400. I was completely engrossed at this time with study and physical training. I must have been about thirteen or fourteen years old and did not bother at all about who came to the house, what was going on or how the family fortunes were being squandered, for I was provided with everything I wanted. In a sense, we had almost forgotten the death of our father.

HOME LIFE CHANGES COMPLETELY

After the death of our father, we all became a little more independent. The tuft of hair at the back of our heads was con-

---

[16] One is usual in Brahman families of this class.

[17] A festival celebrated on the first full moon day after the monsoon rains. Spiced evaporated milk with almonds is drunk in the bright moonlight.

siderably reduced.[18] My brother started to shave only his chin.[19]
If I was late in returning home in the evening, nobody asked for
an explanation. It was enough if I was there before Uncle and
Gopal came back at night. Nobody insisted that I should perform
the evening worship, so I spent the evenings either in the gymnasium or at political meetings, just as I liked. We students
used to hear such exhortations as this: "You must become revolutionaries; you must murder the British officers. Parents in England must become afraid of sending their sons to work as officers
in India," sentiments which we found attractive. The older
students, however, did not allow us to attend private meetings;
so about ten or fifteen of us organised a group of our own and
began stealing mangoes, jambuls, and other fruit from people's
gardens.

One day (it was the eleventh of the lunar month) my friend
Bapu and I went into the Chief of Sangli's orchard to get jambuls.
Each one carried a cloth bag and climbed two trees. Just as we
were about to come down with full bags, we suddenly noticed an
old woman under the tree. At first she mistook me for her son,
who had come to the garden early in the morning to pluck
jambuls, and said, "Gandya, why do you want to climb the trees?"

"Gandya?" I disguised my voice and answered the old
woman. At this strange voice she began shouting for her son,
"Gandya, run at once. These Brahman boys are stealing jambuls
from the tree." Her son was already on his way. Fortunately he
got a thorn in his foot and was delayed a bit. I said to Bapu,
"If we want to escape, this is the time for it. If the old woman
tries to catch us, we can always give her a push and slip away."
There was no time to think of an elaborate plan. We jumped
down from the tree with our bags and began to run as fast as
our legs could carry us, Gandya in hot pursuit, crying out, "Damn

---

[18] It was a sign of orthodoxy to have a long, fat, pigtail-like tuft. Re-
ducing the size of the tuft was a symbolic step towards emancipation.

[19] Instead of shaving both the head and chin according to the old custom.

it all, can Brahmans stoop to thefts even on the eleventh day?" and swearing violently at us. Neither of us was caught.

Some time later, during the mango season, my friend Keshav and I went to swim in a well in an orchard. Keshav was Attorney Navare's nephew. Both of us had taken with us the *dhotis* and other clothes of our respective uncles. We washed all the clothes, smoothed them out, folded them neatly and started for home. On the way, we caught sight of some fine mangoes hanging from the trees. If we plucked a few of them, we could prepare a mango-drink or put them in straw to ripen. Seeing no watchman about, we knotted a piece of thick cloth into a bag, and, while I climbed a tree, Keshav stood under it. I did not count the number of mangoes I plucked and threw down, but it appears that all this had attracted the attention of the farmer-owner. From a distance, he set his dog on us and started following it. I shouted to Keshav, "You can't possibly run with the clothes and the mangoes, so just leave the mangoes and walk slowly away with the clothes. After all, you didn't even pick up the plucked mangoes." So I handed over my clothes to Keshav, put all the mangoes in the bag, and began to run clad only in a loin-cloth. The farmer's watchdog naturally paid no attention to Keshav, who was standing still, but came after me in hot pursuit. Whenever the dog came too near, I took a mango from the bag and threw it at him. The animal pursued me right up to town and I exhausted the whole stock of mangoes in defending myself. Finally I climbed a tree, and the dog sat down under it to watch.

Meanwhile, the farmer caught up with Keshav, who was walking nonchalantly along with the folded and washed clothes in his hand, pretending that he was not concerned at all with the whole episode. The farmer seized hold of him and took away all the clothes. Keshav protested, "I did not climb your tree, I have not touched a single mango, and I haven't a single mango with me. I had nothing to do with this whole affair," but the farmer was quite unmoved by all this defence. At the sight of

Keshav without the clothes I was terribly worried. When he reached the tree, he drove away the dog, and I came down.

By this time, lunch was ready. Both of us told our people at home that we had hung up the clothes to dry at a friend's house. Next day, both of us declared that we had forgotten to bring them back and managed to escape any serious consequences. In the afternoon, we did not attend school and instead held a council of strategy. We discussed all the possible ways to get out of this muddle. Finally a possibility occurred to us. We went to an old friend of my father's and told him the whole story. Narudada[20] was quite friendly with the farmers and personally went to the owner of the mango trees, who told his version of the incident. He saw that the particular tree which I had plundered had almost no fruit on its branches. He also saw the heap of plucked mangoes still lying under the tree. So Narudada agreed to pay Rs. 5 as compensation for the damage and came back with the clothes. We were now faced with the problem of securing the sum of Rs. 5. One of the suggestions we considered was this: Keshav's uncle had a three-year-old daughter whom we sometimes took for a walk. We could take away her two silver anklets and pretend that we did not notice where they slipped off. We had a long discussion about this but finally gave it up. Narudada had already borrowed five rupees from my uncle and had paid off the farmer, but we were not aware of this. Probably everybody in our families had learned of the affair through Narudada, but nobody said a word to us. Once or twice when a proposition like "What is wrong in stealing jambuls or mangoes from other people's trees?" was discussed, we would stand up against it, and the elders must have been enjoying our discomfiture. Every now and then Narudada would send notes to me marked "Strictly Private" saying, "When are you going to return my five rupees?"

After this experience, I have always refused to accompany my friends whenever they wanted to go on an expedition to steal mangoes, jambuls, or peanuts from somebody's fields.

---

[20] Naru—personal name; *dada*—elder brother.

All this happened during about three months after my father died. One night, a pestle and mortar kept on a high shelf were brought down by a cat. The noise of these objects rolling on the ground awakened my mother, who called me and said, "Do you see, he is grinding the betel nut in the mortar, let us go to him." So saying, she took down the end of the sari covering her head. Naturally, I was frightened at the sight of the shaved head. In her agitation she realised this and again covered her head, but it was only after the door was opened and the pestle and mortar on the ground shown to her that she calmed down.

KALI[21] ENTERS THE HOUSE

In that year during the nine-nights festival,[22] our house appeared to have been the target of the wrath of God. On the first day of the festival, my grandmother had a swelling all over her body; she died on the sixth day. The next day my mother began to have severe pains in the stomach, and the following morning when the doctor was called he told us it was a question merely of a few hours. Of course my younger brother and I heard these words but could not quite realise what they meant. We were sent to a neighbour's house for the day. Since it was *Dasara* day, sweet rice had been prepared. Somebody said, "Let the boys eat the sweet dish first," but hardly was it served to us when news came that Mother was dying. Although they tried to keep it from us, we somehow sensed it and could not even eat the first sweet mouthful. At this, the women began to cry, and we got up and rushed back to our house. There we heard lamentations and halted in the doorway. At that moment, Narudada appeared, took us by the hand and led us to Mother's bedside. She was still alive, and seeing us, motioned us nearer. My mother was sobbing and had embraced one of my sisters who was a child-widow.

---

[21] Kali, an evil spirit, is disharmony personified.

[22] The goddess Durga or Devi is worshipped in many parts of India for nine days before the Dasara festival. This is known as Navaratri or nine nights. Dasara in Maharashtra is a martial festival celebrating the victory of the god Rama over the forces of evil.

Soon afterwards her breathing became laboured, and we hardly knew when she actually died. My widowed sister still lay in her embrace. And so we lost our mother.

Within four or five months of Mother's death my sister Gita died of poisoning. Gita had been married to my mother's brother.[23] My eldest sister was first married to this uncle, but she had died at the time of the birth of her first child, so the second sister, Gita, was given to him as his second wife. Gita was a very handsome girl, but my uncle had got into the habit of visiting prostitutes. He actually had a kept woman. After the death of my father, grandmother, and mother, this prostitute, Radhasani, began to come to our house. Then she even began to eat with us, first once and then both times every day. Gita naturally thoroughly disapproved of this.

One day Radhasani asked for the gold necklace Gita was wearing. Gita informed her husband that she would never yield to this demand. My eldest brother, Gopal, had also begun to spend his nights away from home, so that the only persons at home that night were my uncle, Gita, Radhasani, my widowed sister, myself, and my younger brother. My uncle closed the door of the inside room and began to beat Gita to make her hand over the necklace. We children, seeing this atrocity, hid ourselves behind the prayer room in our house. Gita was trying to keep down her wails so that the neighbours might not hear her and think badly of our family; otherwise they might gather together and see this despicable spectacle. She had removed the necklace from her throat and held it firmly in her hand. However much my uncle tried, she did not let it go. Finally Uncle hit her hand with a wooden pounding pestle used in polishing grain, and Radhasani threw her shoe at Gita.[24] At that moment Gita gave up any hope of retaining the necklace. Soon after that Uncle and Radhasani went out of the house. It was about midnight. After

---

[23] Such uncle-niece marriages are quite common in the south of India and in the southern part of Maharashtra, where Miraj is located.

[24] A convention for the most contemptuous possible insult.

the two had gone, all of us brothers and sisters sat together weeping. Even today this scene stands vividly before my mind's eye.

Later, after we had all dozed off, Gita sat on her bed for a long time. She must have fallen asleep toward morning, for she did not get up at the usual time. Uncle returned home at about ten o'clock and tried to rouse her. She flatly refused to get up and look to the cooking and said to him, "Why don't you give me some poison and kill me?" Uncle replied, "All right, I will get some poison." That day, Uncle cooked the food and fed us. My eldest brother Gopal came home very late and as soon as I saw him, I told him about the events of the previous night. He went to Gita, who was still lying on her bed, but she did not speak to him. My uncle served food for her on a plate and took it in to her. After leaving the plate near her, he left the house. Gopal told me to go to Gita and swear by my own life to get her to eat her food. But Gita heard this and said, "Pundalik, please do nothing of the kind. I *am* going to get up in the evening."

About three in the afternoon my uncle came home again, and Gita immediately asked him, "Have you brought it?" Uncle gave her a small white package. Gita arose at once, washed her face, and took some food. By that time my uncle and brother had left again. She took out a very costly *sari* with gold embroidery on it, cut it into several blouse pieces, sent for some coconuts from the market, and went out to the houses of several married women in the neighbourhood, to whom she presented these sacred symbols of good luck.

In our house there was an old maidservant who was in the habit of eating opium whom Gita sent to buy some opium, in case the package her husband had brought did not contain poison; for if after taking it she did not die, people would laugh at her. Hence she was making everything doubly sure. In the evening she prepared an early meal of rice and a thin curry of garbanzo flour and gave us our food. She also gave us all the curds with cream that was in the house. She even mixed the rice with the curry for each one of us with her own hand. She pressed us to eat as much as we could, repeating again and again, "Eat the food I have cooked with my own hands." By seven in the evening we had all finished our meal.

"Now children, go to bed, all of you. I shall now prepare my medicine." With these words she went into the kitchen. There she took out two of her glass bangles, powdered them in the mortar, then mixed in the opium and the powder Uncle had brought. She stirred this mixture in milk and prepared her "medicine." Then she called me and my sister, asked me to sit by her, and caressed me for a little while. "Now I will take my medicine," she said; with that she drank the cup of poison. In a few moments she fell down on her bed and began to cry out loudly. We went to Narudada, roused him and brought him to the house. He called the doctor. My uncle also returned. At about 11:30 that night, Gita died.[25] The doctor probably helped my uncle to escape the hand of the law; possibly he got some money for it. In about an hour and a half the dead body was taken to the cremation ground. At about six o'clock in the morning Uncle came back, took his bicycle, and again went out.

Later that morning a neighbour came in a *tonga* with the doctor and the inspector of police and asked me when Gita's dead body was removed from the house. Without waiting for my reply, they drove on to the cremation ground, but the body had nearly been consumed by the fire.

In this way four members of the family died one after the other, and we children were afraid to go to the house after evening or remain there after dark. Moreover, Uncle and Gopal were both in the habit of returning home very late. I used to spend the evening in the gymnasium, and my widowed sister would only start cooking after I came home because she too

[25] This episode may seem somewhat obscure to the Western reader. Gita was forced to the extreme step of suicide by the double circumstance of being dishonored by her husband, who allowed his paramour to throw her shoe at Gita (see n. 24) at a time when none of Gita's own male relatives was willing or able to protect her. Thus abandoned, she saw no recourse but suicide.

was afraid to go into the inner part of the house alone. She used to stand under the tamarind tree outside our house until one of us returned home. I may mention in passing that because of this habit of hers, my companions in the Gymnasium had begun to call her "Stand." [26] This was of course an offence against a poor girl-widow. When it came to my notice, I brought it to the attention of one of the older men at the Gymnasium, and he stopped this nonsense.

One reason for our fear of the house was a peculiar incident that took place there. One day somebody had put some water pots, one piled on the other, in the inner room and wrapped a red *sari* round the whole contraption in such a way that anybody who looked in from the outside room would think that it was a widowed woman sitting in the corner. That night when my younger brother, my sister and I entered the house, we saw this red-clad figure and ran out of the house in great terror, shouting, "We saw our mother. She is sitting in the middle room." Neither my elder brother nor my uncle had yet come home, but a number of people gathered in front of our house at these strange tidings of a ghost.

One or two of them went in with a lantern and sticks in their hands and peeped into the middle room, returning to report that somebody was in fact sitting there. Soon, many of them had lanterns and sticks in their hands. Some said, "Oh, but there are so many children in the house, and naturally the dead must have been drawn there. It is quite natural!" Our friend Narudada came to the house, went into the veranda with a lantern and a stick and said loudly, "Chandrabai, you are frightening your own children. Whatever unfulfilled wishes you have will be attended to. But why do you terrify your children?" But he too could not get up enough courage to go into the middle room. Then another neighbour went in with a large stone in his hand and without a word threw it towards the silent figure. The pots tumbled down with a crash that sent all the assembled neighbours running

---

[26] In English!

helter-skelter. But now we had learned what the "ghost" was, and we all went in. Supper was late that night, and my elder brother and uncle came home very late too.

Soon after this my elder brother and my uncle got me to consent to the sale of one of our pieces of land. At first there was considerable discussion as to whether I should give my consent to the sale of the ancestral property, which was of course the joint inheritance of all the sons. My advisers in the group of elders at the physical culture institution all strongly advised me not to give my consent. But my brother and uncle took me directly from school to the government office where sale deeds are registered, and I could not bring myself to say no. In the document, my age was given as nineteen.[27] The proceeds of the sale were probably equally divided between the two of them. We also had some agricultural land at Haveri and under the excuse that it was too far off to go there every now and then to recover the rent from the tenants, my uncle mortgaged it with a money-lender for 1,500 rupees. I never learned what became of this money.

Before my father fell ill, he had given a sealed box containing valuable family ornaments to a friend for safekeeping. After the death of our parents and grandmother, the box was brought back, and we found in it a list of the valuables we possessed. A copy of that list was also found in our house. The seal of the box was intact, but inside there were no ornaments, only a few silk *saris* and silk sheets with gold borders worn by men as sacred dress. I still do not think that the friend robbed us. It was probably the work of my brother and my uncle.

LIFE WITH THE PRINCE

When I was in the English fifth grade, the heir apparent of Miraj state was a fellow student of mine. It was in this year that the plague epidemic started in Miraj. The Chief of Miraj sent an

---

[27] Pundalik's relations claimed that he was legally of age [over eighteen] and could thus legally dispose of his portion of joint family property. In fact this was untrue.

inquiry to the Headmaster whether the five top boys in the class would be willing to accompany the prince to a house away from the plague-affected town so that he and they could carry on their education while the school was closed. As I had secured the top rank that month, I was also included in this group. The Headmaster, Shri Gogate, and his family were to accompany the party.

This group started by the evening train from Miraj. Although the train was very crowded, we vacated a whole bench for our Headmaster, and he slept soundly through the whole trip. At every stop we tried by all possible means to prevent any more passengers from entering our compartment. Early in the morning we reached our station. A state horse carriage had come to take us the nine miles to our destination, but we also hired another one-horse cart and during this trip also Shri Gogate slept the whole time. But, surprising as it may seem, immediately after the noon meal, Shri Gogate complained that he had been unable to sleep during the journey on account of the terrible crowd and that therefore he would go and lie down for some time. From that day, we boys referred to him privately as "Mr. No-sleep."

One evening all five of us went out for a walk. None of us knew the local language. As it had begun to rain a little, I opened my umbrella. This apparently either frightened or enraged a buffalo not far from our group and it began to charge me, followed by its master, who was shouting to me to close the umbrella. But as my knowledge of the language was very elementary, I interpreted his words to mean "My buffalo is running away. So please scare it with your umbrella and make it turn around." Using the umbrella as a kind of shield, I tried to turn the animal back, but the result was quite unexpected. The buffalo attacked the umbrella with such force that it was soon a complete wreck. Fortunately we had time to run away and save ourselves.

On the whole we thoroughly enjoyed our stay there. During the *Diwali* festival, we were invited for refreshments by the prince's mother, and she herself served us.

During our stay with the prince, I learned some lessons on

how to behave when associating with the rich and powerful and how they treat the less favoured. I may mention a few points here out of my personal experience:

1) There is always a distinction made between the food served to the members of the Raja's family and that served to his retinue and servants. For these latter, food of a lower quality is prepared. The rich appear to be immune to a realisation of what others may think.

2) Very often, the rich try to economise on essential items and are extravagant when it comes to quite unnecessary expenditures.

3) The rich are so dependent on their servants that often the latter become quite insolent. A rather handsome cook in the Chief's service who used to wear glasses was nicknamed "Barrister" because of them, but if there was a delay even of one day in the receipt of his salary he began to curse in a loud voice and did not mind even if his voice reached the ears of his master.

Two Important Years

The two years of the English sixth and seventh grades were the most important from the point of view of the formation of my character and my attitude to life. Our teacher, Shri Vatve, was a very lovable and simple man. When he was demonstrating a problem in geometry, he would draw a straight line forming part of the diagram over and over again, rubbing the chalk so firmly that a little heap of white chalk powder would form on the ground. One day while he was thus engaged, standing with his back to the class, I saw a cockroach creeping up the back of his coat. Thinking it was a scorpion, I ran to him and killed it with one blow of the geometry book that was lying on the desk. The teacher, sunk in thought, jumped and looked around. He was very glad when I told him what I had done, but, not unnaturally, wanted to have a look at the "scorpion." When he discovered that it was nothing more than a cockroach, the whole class began to laugh and Shri Vatve joined in.

The students of my age used to have frequent discussions about what courses we should select after graduating from high school, what our goals in life should be, how we could be of use to our country, etc. About fifteen of us were very active in these discussions. About the same time a debating society was started in our school. I recall that we attended the third meeting, when an incident took place which I still remember vividly.

The chairman, in his remarks from the chair, used so many English words mixed with his Marathi speech that I was shocked. After one or two others had spoken, I stood up as an unscheduled speaker and said, "The speech which our chairman made today was no doubt very instructive and full of valuable suggestions. We must thank him for it. But it is not so easy to say whether he spoke in Marathi or in English. I cannot tell whether he could not remember the English words and used Marathi words in their place or whether he forgot the Marathi words and used English words instead. It sounded as if either a *saheb* who has just returned from England was trying to speak Marathi or a Marathi speaker was trying to speak the local language in England. Who can say whether the respected chairman was trying to speak Marathi to us or English? I do not think we students will derive any benefit by such speeches. I apologise for having put my thoughts plainly before you and also request the chairman to forgive me out of the largeness of his heart."

These words of mine raised a storm, particularly among the chairman's admirers. There was only one student who stood staunchly by me, although my older associates in the Gymnasium group later approved of my stand. Many students insisted that I should express regret and apologise to the chairman, but I declared that at the end of my speech I had apologised to all and also particularly to the chair and that I was not prepared to go any further. Finally the meeting dispersed in confusion, not before a few blows were given and taken. But I was happy to see that thereafter everybody was a little more careful in not using English words when speaking Marathi.

One consequence of this incident was that the number of students taking part in our group discussion regarding the future increased. We had come to the conclusion that we should serve the country and for that purpose remain unmarried. Also, we were determined to get into contact with some revolutionary group, about which all kinds of adventurous stories, true and false, used to circulate among young people. Of course our ideas at that time were quite childish, and we thought it an act of patriotism to follow a *tonga* in which an Englishman was passing and shout derisive remarks in Marathi, which he could not understand.

THE QUESTION OF MY FUTURE

Although after the death of my parents our economic condition had deteriorated, I had not realised how bad things were. My uncle, however, could well see what was in store for us. Almost everything which could be pawned or sold had disappeared from the house, and being anxious about the future, my uncle once came to the school. He not only made an earnest appeal to me to learn carpentry while I was at the English school but also requested Mestri (as the carpentry teacher was known) to pay special attention to me. From that day that good person used to come to my classroom when the carpentry period was due to begin and call me to his class. Then he would stand in front of me and try to teach me the principles of his trade. The other students of course enjoyed this, as they could then be free to use their time as they liked.

When, however, Mestri found that I was making no progress, he called me to his house and talked seriously to me. He said, "Pundalik, your uncle came to see me the other day. It was he who told me to pay special attention to you and teach you carpentry.

Your circumstances have changed. You are now very poor. So if you do not learn a good trade which will enable you to feed yourself, you are going to be very badly off. I am ready to spend any amount of time with you. A good carpenter can earn good money. You know that I am getting five hundred rupees just as labour charges for making the panels of the temple door." But all his persuasive words were without any effect on my mind, except that I began to realise how poor we had become.

I must explain here that I had previously been conscious of a change in our domestic life. But I had not associated that change with money. I thought that we had fallen from high moral standards in our behaviour, we were not observing the orthodox rules of behaviour in our daily life, we were not offering prayers to the image in our courtyard, we were not scrupulously wearing the sacred cloth at mealtime, and so on. I had been sorry for all this, and as far as I was personally concerned, I continued the observances until I left Miraj. But Mestri first made me realise the financial side of our condition.

On another occasion our poverty was again brought to my notice. A pair of brothers, neighbours of ours, who had been friends of my father, tried to help us after his death. But my elder brother and my uncle had no intention of listening to anybody and things went on from bad to worse. As I was on my way to the final examination in the English sixth grade I met one of these brothers in the street. He took hold of my hand and led me to his house, talking to me seriously all the way. He said, "Pundalik, your father was a friend of ours. That is why I have a friendly feeling for you all. Your family was respected and well-to-do. Even if you had not earned anything, there was enough for a modest life for all of you. But your brother and your uncle have made a beggar of you. You must do something for your livelihood. You will soon have to take the responsibility of your younger brother and your young widowed sister." This greatly shocked me and saying that I had to go to the examination and that I would see him later, I went away. I missed the top rank in the examination and also the scholarship that went with it, but I did get second rank and was promoted to the matriculation class.

GRADUATION CLASS IN HIGH SCHOOL

In the seventh English grade we came into more intimate contact with Shri Gogate, the Headmaster, who taught us English and history. He taught English very well but was not at all good in history. I hardly ever cared to attend his history periods. For about two or three months, he said nothing. Once, when I was leaving his class, he noticed me and asked me why I was leaving. I replied that he did not tell us anything new and that I could easily read everything at home. Naturally he resented this. I do think that my behaviour at that time was wrong, but I also remember that Shri Gogate took a dislike to me and never again treated me well. Even today I think that a student may deserve punishment, but a teacher should never hate him. I soon found that attending classes was sometimes made very disagreeable for me. I actually wanted to make amends for my mistakes but somehow could not achieve this. Instead things went from bad to worse.

In this way about four or five months passed. The term-end examination was held and I passed, but I found that if I made even minor mistakes, Shri Gogate pounced upon them. Things which he would otherwise have passed over were magnified into serious faults on my part.

In the term-end examination the teacher who set the paper in English was very fond of chewing *pan* in class. Any book that he held was sprayed with red marks from his mouth. A few days before the examination, when he was taking our class, I placed my personal copies of the textbooks on his tables and he took them home believing that they were official school copies. He must have used them to draw the question paper, because when he brought them back to class, we found that some pages had small red splash marks. And, as we expected, we did find in the paper a couple of questions we had thought would be asked and had prepared well. When Shri Gogate learned of this rather childish trick, it also increased his irritation with me, and he spoke very sharply to me.

On account of this situation at school and also because Poona had the reputation of being the centre of education and of the nationalist movement in Maharashtra, I conceived the plan of joining a high school at Poona. Accordingly I informed my brother and uncle about it. But they would not consent and said, "We could not possibly afford to keep you in Poona."

I: "What! Have we now become so poor that you are unable to pay for my stay in Poona?"

Uncle: "We were all making a show of being well off. We have been living since your father's death by selling the few valuables we had. But now all that is exhausted. Here is the key to the cupboard. You can go and see for yourself."

So I actually went and looked, but there were only a few clothes there. At last I fully realised what my brother and uncle had done. I consulted some of my older advisers at the Gymnasium and some of the neighbours, and after a long debate it was decided that I should go to the Chief of Miraj and place the whole situation before him.

Next day I awoke at four o'clock in the morning and went to the Chief's residence. He was reputed to be a very early riser who did gymnastic exercises. He came downstairs at about five; and as he knew me slightly, he asked me why I had come so early in the morning. I then told him the whole story of how my brother and uncle had spent all our money and done away with all the valuables. He heard me out and advised me to see him again at eleven o'clock in his city house. I returned home feeling very confused and also slightly guilty. I had not said a word to my younger brother and sister, and my elder brother and my uncle had gone out with some friends for a picnic. Actually I did not feel at all like going on with the matter, but of course I could not avoid seeing the Chief at eleven. I could hardly eat anything and went reluctantly to the Chief at the appointed time. His Minister had already arrived there before me, probably at the suggestion of the Chief. As soon as I arrived, the Chief told me to discuss the matter with the Minister and assured me that whatever was possible would be done.

The Minister took me to his office and asked me who had done away with the valuables which were in the house when my father was alive. I replied that it must have been my brother and my uncle. Then he asked me to make a list of the people in whose houses the valuables, mostly gold and silver ornaments and utensils, were likely to be found. When I hesitated to reply to this, he told me not to be afraid about the consequences and also to remain firm even in the presence of my brother or my uncle. Finally, I mentioned that the valuables might be found in my uncle's shop, or in a separate apartment my brother kept, or in the houses of their concubines, or at the houses of two of their friends whom I named or their concubines. I also added that there might be some places in our house where things could be hidden. Then a clerk brought a petition to which I put my signature, although even to this day I do not know what was written in it.

Immediately police watchmen were stationed in front of all the houses I had mentioned and then a police officer, a clerk, and some policemen began a search. By about eleven o'clock at night all the houses were searched and a list was made of all the things that I recognized as belonging to our family. Just when the house of my uncle's concubine Radhasani was being searched, the picnickers returned. I had not the courage to look my brother and my uncle straight in the eye, but I also did nothing to stop the searches. When it was time to confiscate the ornaments on Radhasani's person, I recognized the ring on her finger as my mother's ring, but somehow I could not bring myself to declare that it was not hers and so it was not taken away. But everything else I declared "my property" was taken charge of by the police. If my brother and uncle had not gone to the picnic, probably they would have persuaded or threatened me and prevented the searches, but by the time they came back the proceedings had gone too far to be stopped. Except for what was required to cook food for the five people in our house, everything, including pots and pans, was taken to the police office and a list made.

Next day the two friends of my brother's and their concubines made an application to the court for the return of the things that really belonged to them. The Minister told me to point out all those articles which I was quite certain belonged to us and let the others be returned.

From that very day my brother and my uncle stopped coming to our house. Now came the problem of how to support myself, my younger brother, and my sister until the property confiscated at my request was divided by the Court. The food grains in the house lasted us for about a month, but after that we had just nothing. So we decided to borrow ten rupees a month from Shri Shiralkar, a neighbour and a friend. But my younger brother suggested that if we could go and eat in Shri Shiralkar's family twice a day until the court carried out the division of our property we would not run into debt. As Shri Shiralkar had a very large joint family of about twenty-five persons, three more mouths to feed would not be a burden to him. I was at first very reluctant to do this but ultimately went and spoke to Shri Shiralkar. Tears came to the eyes of that old friend of my father when I made the request. He gladly asked us to take our food with his family, and both he and his wife treated us like their own children.

But even though the problem of food was temporarily solved, we three were daily becoming aware of our extreme poverty. Also, we got tired after a month or so of going to Shri Shiralkar's house for every meal. In that house too quarrels between the various brothers and cousins were going on regarding the sharing of the ancestral property. One evening, the two eldest brothers actually came to blows, and their respective wives had to intervene and separate them. Frightened, we came home without taking our food. We then decided that it would be preferable to borrow ten rupees every month and cook our own food. This we did for the next ten months. We cooked only rice, flat millet bread, split pea curry and occasionally garbanzo flour gruel. We never bought vegetables and ate only two meals a day—nothing in the morning or between meals. We took half a pound of milk a day among the three of us. I was charged with buying the provisions, and I remember we did not eat any butter or *ghi* during that time. But still I cannot say that we were unhappy. We were devoting all our attention to our studies, our games, and the Gymnasium.

LIFE IN THE MATRICULATION CLASS

I was an ardent reader of the *Kesari,* which used to come to the school address. One day the latest issue of this paper, founded and conducted by Lokamanya Tilak, arrived while a weekly test was in progress, and I made the mistake of setting aside my test paper and beginning to read it. Shri Gogate naturally could not let this pass and gave me a sharp reprimand, so I put the *Kesari* aside and took my answer-book. But Shri Gogate was not satisfied with this. He issued an order that no student should have the *Kesari* sent to the school address. I tried to tell him that I would promise not to read this weekly on the school premises if he would allow me to use the postal address of the school, but without success.

Then two of my schoolmates and I thought over the matter and decided to order two more copies of *Kesari* at the school address. In order to raise money for this, I sold my algebra textbook. Later on, two more issues of the same weekly began to come to students at the school address. Shri Gogate did not say anything, but I think he was extremely irritated by it. Then somebody ordered another copy of *Kesari* in the name of Shri Gogate's son. I did not know anything about this, but Shri Gogate must have thought that I was at the bottom of it.

In the preliminary examination I secured very good grades in all subjects but failed in history.[28] Shri Gogate decided not to allow me to go up for the final examination, although he had allowed one or two other students who had failed in two subjects to go up. Actually I had not done so badly on the history paper and should have passed, but I still believe that Shri Gogate's prejudice about me was the cause of my failure.

Finally I decided to have a serious and detailed talk with Shri Gogate. I wanted to express regret for my lapses and secure his permission to appear for the final examination. I was anxious to continue my studies in college and particularly to go to Poona. Shri Gogate's son was in my class and was a friend of mine and I had hopes that he would also use his influence to help me. That year the calendar of the academic year was being changed and the University was going to hold two final examinations, one in December and the next in March. Only those who had failed in December were to be allowed to take the March examination. I therefore thought that even though I failed in December, I would have another chance in March. But it was essential that I have the Headmaster's permission to take the December examination.

So one day I went to Shri Gogate's house. He was conversing with a visitor in a very jovial mood, and I therefore hoped that he would be sympathetic to me. The visitor, another teacher, asked me why I was there. I replied that I wished to speak with Shri Gogate about permission to appear for the final examination.

Shri Gogate: "Well young man, what have you to say?"

I: "I have got 60 to 65 per cent marks in all the other subjects. I have failed in history only by a very few marks. There is still time for me to work hard and make up the deficiency. Also, there are going to be two examinations this year, but I cannot get a second chance unless I take the first test. So please see that I do not have to waste a year in the same class. Our domestic

---

[28] The final examination for high school seniors (the matriculation class, in Indian English) is conducted by the University. The high school holds a preliminary examination to decide who shall take the final.

circumstances have become very bad, and I am hoping that you will not disappoint me. Please grant me the necessary permission to appear for the final examination."

Shri Gogate: "Katagade, I have been observing your behaviour for the last three years. You behave in school in a very disorderly way. You cut the history class after giving me insolent backtalk. When I asked you to have the *Kesari* sent to your home address, you persuaded two other students to order the weekly at the school address. Who ordered the *Kesari* on my son's name? And when you had the opportunity to live with the prince in the fifth class during the plague epidemic, you led him into bad ways. Taking all this into consideration, I am not going to permit you to take the final examination. Actually, I was on the point of permanently suspending you, but what I have decided is that I shall not issue a good conduct certificate to you." [29]

I: "Sir, all these charges are false. How can a single boy create disorder? Were not others equally responsible? All those who did everything that I did have appeared for the preliminary examination, and many of them have been permitted to go up to the final even though their marks are lower than mine. I admit my error in leaving during the history period and ask your forgiveness. I plead guilty to having ordered two copies of *Kesari* but know nothing about the copy ordered in your son's name. Please give me any other punishment you like, but do not ruin my life. And I do not know how I led the prince astray. If I could have done that with the prince, I would have spoiled all the others too. If the prince is not behaving properly, all five of us should be held responsible and your son was one of the group. And do you think that these false charges should be allowed to ruin my life?"

Shri Khare, the other teacher, who was listening to this exchange, also pleaded on my behalf. Shri Gogate's son also tried to put in a few words in my favour, but all to no purpose. Shri Gogate was not one to listen to anybody. Finally he declared,

---

[29] This in effect meant that no other school could admit him as a student.

"Pundalik, I have made up my mind. I regret that I can do nothing for you. Please leave my house."

I was very dejected and was at a loss to know what to do. Even the intercession of one or two respectable citizens on my behalf had no effect, and I became convinced that I was doomed never to enter a college for further education.

Anxious Six Months

Because I was not allowed to appear for the final examination, my education in the high school came to an end and there was also no hope of my ever attending college. This brought on a severe depression, and I began to avoid all my schoolmates.

My younger brother, sister, and I were still living in the old house. As children, we had been used to very good food, but now we were eating very coarse food—very little milk, no butter or *ghi,* no vegetables. I began to have digestive troubles and suffered very badly for several years afterwards. The suit about the division of the family property dragged on and on, and there appeared no hope of an early settlement. We knew that we could not go on long this way, borrowing money for our daily needs. I refused to think about what would happen if we failed to get a loan. I once suggested to my younger brother that we should go and live with my elder brother, who appeared to be in no want at least of food. But the youngster refused to accept my suggestion.

My elder brother presented in the courts the account books he said he had kept since Father's death showing the money he had borrowed in order to feed and clothe us all. The total of these borrowings came to such a large sum that the whole of the family property would not have sufficed to pay it off.

Sometimes, neighbours or friends invited us to take food with them for a few weeks to help us out, but, when we realised that we were being treated as beggars, we decided not to accept this charity.

After the University final examination was over, I secured the question papers from some of my friends, wrote out the answers and sent them to Shri Gogate with a letter saying that I would have passed the examination if he had not ruined my chances forever. But he failed to reply to my communication.

Departure for Belgaum

About this time, our town saw the rise to prominence of Shri Dattopant Patwardhan, who started the new tradition of "nationalist *kirtans*." Many of my fellow students and I regularly attended his discourses and were greatly impressed by them. Occasionally, either Shri Patwardhan himself or some other local leader made a short speech in the interval between the first and second parts of the discourse. The gist of the *kirtan* was that students were wasting their time in English schools and colleges; they might better apprentice themselves to some great national leader, increase their knowledge and fitness for service to the country by reading and meditation, and try to liberate the Motherland from slavery. Shri Patwardhan also offered to feed and train any students who wished to live with him for this purpose.

My friends and I were greatly influenced, and the others persuaded me to offer myself as a trainee, probably because they saw that my education had come to a stop. Although at first I was very reluctant to do this, I went to see him and discussed the possibility of becoming his disciple. He accepted my proposal and asked me to come to live with him from that very moment. I, however, asked permission to go home and return the next day.

I was now in a predicament. What could I do about my younger brother and sister? How could I leave them to shift for themselves? Then too I wanted to become a revolutionary. What could I achieve by working as an assistant to this man during his discourses? I would have to play some musical instrument as an accompaniment to his singing and that was not a very welcome role to me. I spent the night thinking over such problems and then went to consult an old friend. He suggested that I could use this opportunity to make contact with Shri Gangadharrao Deshpande, a leader in Belgaum, who was reputed to be a revolutionary. He suggested that I should live with Shri Patwardhan for some time, go with him to Belgaum as he was planning, and then try to contact Shri Deshpande there.

Although I was still very hesitant, the possibility of meeting a revolutionary attracted me. I therefore went to live with Shri Patwardhan but went home every night to our house to sleep. When the day came to start for Belgaum, I had to make some arrangements for my brother and sister. I sent my younger brother to go and live with my elder brother, who agreed to receive him, probably hoping to benefit by this arrangement to get the younger brother's share of the family property when the division was made. Later, I found that my younger brother fell into the same bad ways and ruined his life to a great extent, but that is another story. It was decided that my sister should remain in our house, and the neighbours were requested to help her when necessary. After I had made these arrangements, Shri Patwardhan and I left Miraj and arrived at Belgaum.

I soon tired of my life as an assistant to Shri Patwardhan. It was not the kind of life that I cared for, standing behind him during his discourses, collecting money afterward and with no reading or any other intellectual activity. Occasionally some widowed woman would approach Shri Patwardhan requesting to become his disciple, but he always gave a resolute no to all such overtures. I was carrying on a regular correspondence with my friends in Miraj regarding my ideas about my future and my domestic problems.

Finally I broke off my connection with Shri Patwardhan and went to live in a room in Gangadharrao Deshpande's house, still hoping somehow to appear for the University entrance examination, join a college, and finally take the bachelor's degree in law. There Gangadharrao assigned Shri Babasaheb Soman to see that I read English, Sanskrit, and Marathi books. Among the books I read during my association with Shri Deshpande were works on philosophy, religion, and economics by Indian authors, the Hindu epics and the poetry of the Marathi saint poets.[30] Other books I read were a history of Ireland and Mazzini's works.

One day Gangadharrao delivered a lecture on *karma-yoga,* the philosophy of doing one's duty, and I took down notes and prepared an account for publication. This was the first exercise of its kind that I carried out, and everybody praised me for it.

On my frequent trips to Miraj because of the suit over the division of the ancestral property, I had long talks with my friends. We were inclining to the view that the whole attitude of the people had to be changed in order to get them to favour the revolutionary method, and this involved our becoming fit to lead the movement so that people would follow us. Now this fitness must consist of higher education, a degree from a university, and impressive oratory in both English and Marathi. However much reading I did privately and however learned I was, nobody was going to accept me as a leader unless I had the stamp of a university, but Shri Gogate's refusal to let me go up to the University examination blocked all my plans. As I was still very eager to continue my education further, I often used to mention this ambition of mine to Gangadharrao, telling him how much I wished to pass the B.A. examination. I recognised that only Gangadharrao was able to help me achieve my ambition for further education, but he seemed to be firmly convinced that that was not the proper course for a self-respecting Indian. Finally I took my courage in both hands and asked him for financial help. His flat "No" shattered my hopes. He added that he was convinced of the worthlessness of the present system of education and was not prepared to give me any assistance.

---

[30] Pundalik lists *Gita Rahasya* by Tilak; the *Shankarabhasha* or "Discourse of Shankaracharya," the ninth-century monist philosopher; most of the Upanishads, the lectures of Mahadev Govind Ranade, and the epics *Ramayana, Mahabharata,* and *Shrimad Bhagawata.*

In Quest of Education

This brought me to the conclusion that I must leave Belgaum and find some other means to continue my education. But of course I had no money, and I asked Gangadharrao for two rupees to travel to Miraj. He said to take the money out of his pocket-book, but when I looked there were only two five-rupee notes there. So he gave me one of them, and I caught the morning train to Miraj.

There I had long discussions with my friends and older advisers. But no matter how we tried, we could not think of a way to put my plans into action. So I decided to seek my fortune in Kashi (Banaras) where there was a large number of Maharashtrian priests and teachers. I was warned that Kashi was a dangerous place for newcomers and that one had to be very careful about "widows, ascetics, and stray cattle." Many widows used to settle in Kashi, a place of pilgrimage, hoping to entangle new arrivals by all manner of tricks. Then there were the sacred bulls and cows, let loose by supposedly devout people as a tribute to God, which roamed about the streets feeding on grain and corn in the shops and sometimes proving very dangerous to people passing along the narrow lanes. Nobody ever did anything to "God's cattle," who thus grew fat and lazy. Finally, there were thousands of "ascetics," mostly people with no scruples, drug addicts, and thieves, who would not hesitate to rob anyone who could be caught in their snares.

In spite of all these warnings, however, I carried out my plan and went to Kashi. Fortunately, I met there the Headmaster of a high school conducted by Theosophists who was slightly known to our family, as his mother had once lived in our house while undergoing medical treatment in Miraj. This kind lady and her son treated me very well and let me stay with them. But my hopes of joining a high school remained where they were, as the absence of a proper dismissal from my old school proved an insurmountable obstacle. My kind friend, the Headmaster, advised me to learn Sanskrit under a *shastri*[31] and even introduced me at a school where forty or fifty students were taking instruction in different branches of Sanskrit. But after a fortnight's trial I tired of it. Moreover, I could not live indefinitely on the charity of the Headmaster. In the end there was nothing for it but to return to Belgaum. I wished I could take revenge on Shri Gogate, who by his refusal to issue a dismissal certificate had ruined my hopes of further education.

On returning to Miraj, I learned that at Jamkhandi[32] no fees were charged and I could get admitted to the high school without any dismissal certificate. I immediately packed my belongings and went there; but to my utter despair, only a few weeks previously the Chief had issued an order restricting admission to the high school only to natives of his state, because far too many outsiders were taking advantage of his generosity and the state could not afford it. And so I had to return. But at the railway station I learned that the train to Miraj was late, but that the train for Belgaum was due shortly. So I bought a ticket for Belgaum, and after two months of wandering about a large part of India arrived at Gangadharrao Deshpande's house. It was rather late at night but Gangadharrao himself opened the door to me. In his goodness he never rebuked me or laughed at my discomfiture, and I took up the old routine as if nothing had happened.

In May, 1916, after my return, the Bombay Provincial Congress was held in Belgaum. Gangadharrao was the chief organiser, and both Mahatma Gandhi and Lokamanya Tilak attended. I worked as a volunteer on the residential arrangements for the hundreds of guests who had come from outside, the food arrangements, the conference tent, and many other details and was very happy not only to be of use, but also to have the oppor-

---

[31] The usual term for a teacher of Sanskrit literature or one learned in Sanskrit; sometimes also suffixed to names.

[32] Another small princely state now in Mysore.

tunity to see and meet all these important leaders. Mahatma
Gandhi had not at that time adopted his well-known *dhoti* cos-
tume but wore the conventional clothing of Gujarat, a white turban, a long coat, and under that a *dhoti*. I still value the signed
photograph of Lokamanya Tilak and Shri Khaparde, the president of the conference, which the former gave me as a memento.

DOMESTIC HAPPENINGS

My younger brother had gone to live with Gopal, my elder
brother. Gopal was, at this time, living a wild life. Dramas,
prostitutes, the gramophone, and treating his friends to tea parties were his principal amusements. My younger brother had also
begun to enjoy this dissipation, constantly surrounded by this life
as he was. During my occasional visits to Miraj he did not even
think it necessary to see me. He had begun to neglect school and
finally gave it up altogether. My younger brother was quite handsome and was becoming used to a life of luxury in Gopal's company. Naturally his mind was being distorted and he was also
developing a taste for concerts, dances, and dramas. Of course I
was opposed to all this. But any attempt on my part to advise
him had no effect. Not only that, he began to avoid meeting me.
When I spoke to my elder brother about this, he began to scold
the youngster and to beat him, even driving him out of the house
a few times. But as the elder himself was leading the same kind
of life, his remonstrance had no effect whatsoever. But Damu,
my younger brother, got tired of these constant bickerings.

I must note, however, that Damu, even though he was living
with Gopal, never did anything to interfere in the civil suit pend-
ing in the court. I finally gave him up as a hopeless case and
agreed with him to say nothing about the kind of life he was
leading. One of his friends had come into some money on attain-
ing his majority, and Damu then left my elder brother's house
and went to live with him. Of course this friend was not a very
virtuous sort of person. In fact, he and Damu kept a woman.

Damu somehow met some truck-drivers and even learned a few things about motor driving. Later on he became a driver and gradually acquired considerable skill in that profession, but he lost all regard for cleanliness. He used to smoke *bidis* the whole day long. Smoking is a habit which can never be got rid of once you acquire it. I have seen many people who smoke without letting others find out about it. They are even trying to deceive themselves. If somebody to whom they have been boasting about giving up the habit sees them smoking, they declare, "Everybody smokes from Jawaharlal [Nehru] to the humblest worker. Well, I am one of them. I am no Gandhi after all!" If they are not caught, they go on declaring that they have given up smoking. I knew all this about my brother and presented him once with a bundle of *bidis* with the remark, "I know you smoke. Only, please do not try to do it on the sly. You won't deceive anybody." Since then he has smoked in my presence. I felt that handing over Damu to Gopal's care when I went to Belgaum was an unfortunate thing.

My widowed sister was also in a sad plight. Gopal did not send money to her regularly, but she had to spend for her maintenance. She decided to file a suit against her late husband's brother and called me from Belgaum for consultation. Of course there was not even sufficient money for the expenses of the suit, and Gopal refused to advance any money unless she gave him a receipt for all the money she had received from him for her maintenance since her widowhood.

My attitude about the whole affair was that a girl should live with her husband's people even after her husband's death and be helpful to the other members of the family. I strongly disapproved of her going to a court of law to get money for her maintenance. If by private negotiations she could obtain some regular allowance, she should take it and live separately.

I therefore went straight from Miraj to Haveri to see my sister's brother-in-law. I suggested that one more person in a big family would not be a burden to them and that they should have my sister come to live with them. But I also added that they should fix a monthly allowance for her and allow her to live independently in case she found it impossible to pull on with the other members of the family. The gentleman agreed to all this and fixed Rs. 15 per month as her maintenance allowance, telling me that he would like her to live in his family and promising to treat her as an elder relative (she was the wife of his elder brother). I then came back to Miraj, persuaded her to accept the arrangement that I had made and took her to Haveri. At that time her mother-in-law was alive, and both she and the brother-in-law were very orthodox people. They would not allow a widow who had not shaved her head according to the ancient Hindu custom to live in their house. I tried my best to persuade her to shave her head, but she was adamant. Then, hoping that she, her brother-in-law, and her mother-in-law would come to some kind of agreement, I left her there at Haveri and went back to Belgaum. But only two or three days later she left Haveri by a night train without informing anybody and returned to Miraj.

Then somebody told her that a destitute person could make a declaration and file a pauper suit, but it was first necessary to get a court decision that she was penniless. Now although after the death of our mother we were orphans, I did not want the court to declare us paupers, but she would not listen to me. Once I suggested that she should accompany me to Belgaum and live in Gangadharrao Deshpande's house. But she would not hear of it.

After getting a decision from the court that she had no money to pay for the court fee stamp, she did file a pauper suit. The attorney agreed to plead on her behalf on condition that his fee would be paid later out of the maintenance allowance the court might grant her. Moreover, he regularly advanced some money to her for her living expenses.

In due course, the pauper suit was decided in her favour and she was granted a monthly maintenance allowance of Rs. 30. She was to receive that amount retroactively from the date of her husband's death; and for future payments her brother-in-law was to transfer to her name a farm on the Miraj state border which would give her an annual income of an equivalent amount. The attorney, who had become *diwan* in the meantime, took the money he had advanced her and his legal charges out of the allowance and undertook the management of her farm, letting her have about Rs. 20 a month. Even when her brother-in-law appealed in the high court against the decision of the lower court, he gave her every help, and fortunately the high court upheld the verdict of the lower court.

THE SUIT SETTLED AT LAST

In Belgaum I had got acquainted with a joint family of three brothers and their wives and children. There was a very pleasant atmosphere in the house, and one never heard harsh remarks or criticism made by members against each other. This naturally brought to mind the relations between us three brothers. It is such a wonderful thing for brothers to live together in such a loving atmosphere. Why could we not do the same? And I came to the conclusion that money was at the root of it all. Could I not give up my share altogether and persuade Damu to do the same and let Gopal have all the ancestral property?

With Gangadharrao's support and consent, I went to Miraj and told my plan to some of my own friends and to some friends of Father's. Most of them said, "You are mad to think of any such thing." Others said, "You will only be helping your elder brother to carry on his wasteful life." Then I saw my attorney and although he must have been displeased with the way things were turning out, he said, "Well, if the quarrels among you brothers are settled, why should I be the one to oppose a settlement?"

Then I marched Damu to the bank of the Krishna River and had a long talk with him. When I told him that I was going to give up my claim to the ancestral property he protested that he

alone would not be able to fight the law suit, that he had no idea
of civil court procedure and that he would probably be cheated
out of his proper share. Then I explained that I wanted him to
do the same. Frightened, he exclaimed, "That means that I agree
to become a beggar straightaway! How am I going to live? I
have learned nothing that will help me in earning my livelihood!"

Then I explained that even if the property that remained
after paying Gopal's debts (those that would be admitted by the
court as reasonable) were divided equally, the share of each
would be only a couple of thousand rupees and a third of the
house. He could not possibly expect to live on this for long. In
any case he would have to do something to earn his bread. Fortunately neither he nor I had others dependent on us.

Finally he consented to accept my suggestion. Next day we
went to the judge privately and told him what we proposed to
do. He also tried to dissuade us from our resolve, and my younger
brother began to get a little shaky. I explained to the judge that I
expected to establish friendly relations between us three by our
act of renunciation and that I attached far more importance to
that than to money. The judge was still unconvinced and told us
to see our attorney and take his advice. If the matter came up
formally before him, he would have to give a decision according
to the law.

When the matter did come up formally, the judge and the
attorneys came to an agreement that we should appoint arbitra-
tors, make a division of the property, and abide by that decision.
This was done and Damu and I each got nine hundred rupees in
cash, a one-third share in the house, and a one-third share in the
lands. All the movable property was given to our elder brother.
The pots and pans that had been taken from the house were returned to us. Later we agreed to buy the eldest brother's share in
the house, and a hundred rupees were deducted from Damu's and
my share for this purpose.

Out of the money received, I returned a hundred rupees borrowed from a neighbour, who very generously took no interest. Damu purchased an old motor car and ran it as a taxi, thus making a modest living. Until his death he never regretted the kind of settlement we had reached.

Damu, my sister, and I stayed in the house for some days and then dispersed. I went back to Belgaum, our sister went to Sangli, and Damu usually slept somewhere else. Sometime later I bought Damu's share in the house also and became its sole owner. As I lived away from Miraj most of the time, the house was uncared for, and in one rainy season practically the whole structure collapsed. Then people took away the doors, beams, windows, pillars, and anything else they could find; and when some years later I returned to Miraj, I saw that people were even using the place as a public latrine! To spare the land at least that dreadful fate, I later constructed a few rooms on it and rented them out.

STUMBLING BLOCK REMOVED

I could not forget my ambition of becoming an attorney, and very soon a fortuitous set of circumstances led to the removal of the stumbling block in my way—the absence of a proper dismissal certificate from my school.

In the plague epidemic that year in Miraj, the Chief and his family had hired a house outside Belgaum near Gangadharrao Deshpande's family's quarters. One day while I was out for a walk, I saw the prince riding a horse and greeted him. He invited me to his house to talk about old times. There I told him the whole story—how Shri Gogate had refused to sign a dismissal certificate; how he had charged that I exerted a bad influence on the prince while we were all living in Laxmeshwar; and all the rest of it. This so surprised and excited the prince that he asked me to accompany him to Miraj at once. We reached there the same night. The next day, as previously arranged, he went to see Shri Gogate at the school leaving me outside the office. There the prince charged Shri Gogate with his own allegations. At first he tried to deny them, but when I asked the prince to get the testimony of the other teacher who had been present during the whole scene, he confessed to having made the charge in a fit of temper. Finally, when the prince threatened to take the whole matter to his father, Shri Gogate had someone fill out the dismissal certificate, entered "best conduct" in the relevant column and signed it. Then he handed over the certificate to me and said he hoped that I would study hard in the future. I told him that I had no grudge against him and, in spite of the fact that two years of my life had been wasted, forgave him.

When I returned to Belgaum with this news, Gangadharrao Deshpande remarked only that the certificate would prove of no benefit to me. The major question of how to obtain money for my further education in Poona was still unsolved, and I could see no way to solve it.

STRUGGLE FOR FURTHER EDUCATION AND DISAPPOINTMENT

Finally, without further consultation with Gangadharrao, I left for Poona. I contacted the students from Miraj who were studying there, and on my suggestion we formed a kind of coöperative organisation to live and study cheaply in Poona. Over twenty of us hired a spacious room on the second floor of a musician's house and began a kind of common residence hall. Very soon, however, we discovered that the walls positively resounded with music. Our landlord practised on his instrument for about two hours a day and gave lessons for another two or three hours and we just could not concentrate on study at all.

So we decided to give up the room. In order to save the rent for a month's notice, during which we would have had to suffer the loud music, we decided to quit the room on the sly. Tying all our belongings into bundles, we lowered them through the window onto the street at dead of night and removed them to another room we had rented elsewhere. But to our utter disgust, this room was situated above a stable where a large number of buffaloes were kept, and the stink of the dung which was left heaped in a corner of the stalls was unbearable. Between the stench and the music, we preferred the latter. Using the same trick on our new landlord, we lowered our baggage with ropes onto the street, returned to our old place, pulled it up again, and pretended we had not left the place at all.

Soon, however, I began to have attacks of fever, probably malaria, and in spite of all the doctor's efforts I could not get rid of it. After about three weeks I decided to go to Belgaum until I felt better and then return to Poona. But even in Belgaum, I continued to have fever for about fourth months and all my dreams of completing high school were dashed to the ground. Even after my convalescence, I never again stirred up the enthusiasm to finish school.

Conditions in Champaran

At about this time, Mahatma Gandhi was working in the Champaran district of Bihar province. There were about sixty white planters in this district, who persecuted and ill-treated the people and subjected them to illegal taxes and levies. The following summary will give an idea of the conditions there:[33]

1. The planters compelled the farmers to pay an illegal tax called *"abvav."*

2. Each farmer was forced to grow indigo on a third of his land without any compensation from the planter, harvest the indigo, and deliver it at the planter's godown.

3. Whenever a new stove was constructed in the planter's house the farmers had to pay a stove levy.

4. There was another illegal tax called *"sarabeshi."*

5. Every year when the planter returned to the plains from his hot weather sojourn in the hills, the farmers had to go and pay homage to him—naturally some material offering.

[33] This summary is by the author, not the translator.

6. No person could use shoes or go in a vehicle on the road in front of the planter's bungalow. If anybody broke this rule, he was fined, absolutely without any kind of authority.

The population of Champaran, exasperated by this tyranny, requested Mahatma Gandhi to come to their aid. Gandhiji agreed to do this and with the coöperation of leaders like Babu Rajendra Prasad [34] went about the villages collecting authentic accounts of how the planters were treating the people. Lord Chelmsford was Viceroy at that time. The planters carried on a systematic agitation against Gandhiji and finally succeeded in getting the Provincial Government to serve a notice on him to quit Bihar, but Gandhiji decided to disobey the notice and suffer the consequences. He also made plans to establish three *ashrams* near the headquarters of three of the worst planters in Champaran district. One of these was at a village called Bhitiharva near the bungalow of a planter called Mr. Amon.

As soon as the notice of expulsion from Bihar was served on Mahatma Gandhi, he despatched to the Viceroy copies of the affidavits of seven hundred farmers which he had collected and prepared to go to jail for disobeying the order. Instead of trying him, the Government of India appointed a committee which included Gandhiji and some representatives of the planters. As soon as the report of this committee was received by Government, a special Act was passed making it illegal for planters to levy any unauthorised taxes and declaring as illegal many of their traditional ways. But to see that this act was properly administered and that the farmers and villagers were actually freed from tyranny was the work that Gandhiji's followers had to do.

In order to get workers to live in the *ashrams,* Gandhiji wrote to Gangadharrao Deshpande, who first selected Shri Babasaheb Soman.[35] I wanted to go too, but my ignorance of Hindi was a great barrier, so Ganhiji sent a worker from Bihar to Bel-

---

[34] India's first president after 1947. *Babu* is another title of respect roughly translatable as "Mr."

[35] Both Soman and Pundalik are mentioned in Gandhi's *Autobiography* as having been sent to Champaran by Deshpande.

gaum to teach Hindi to me and to anybody else that cared to learn.

As soon as I had a working knowledge of Hindi, I wrote a letter to Gandhiji in Hindi, and he called me to the Sabarmati Ashram. But apparently I had not got rid of my malaria, and at Sabarmati I began to have periodic attacks of fever. Gandhiji advised me to fast, but I was not very hopeful of the efficacy of fasting, particularly against malaria. Gandhiji then offered to get a doctor to treat me, but I told him that I would like to return to Belgaum. He permitted me to do so, and I returned to Belgaum.

DEPARTURE FOR CHAMPARAN

About two months later, when I was rid of my malaria and was back in normal health, I wrote to Gandhiji expressing my willingness to proceed to Champaran. A letter by return mail ordered me to proceed direct and not to stop at the Sabarmati Ashram. By this time, Shri Soman had come back from Champaran with a firsthand account of conditions there.

Shri Soman, Dr. Dev of the Servants of India Society, and Gandhiji's wife Kasturba had been living in grass huts in Bhitiharva and conducting a school. Someone had set fire to these huts, and the inhabitants had just managed to escape, although all their belongings were burned to ashes. The very next day Mr. Amon visited them and declared in a saddened tone, "I am sorry your huts have burned. I shall help you in building new ones." But they all decided to accept no help from him and instead to build brick structures. There was good ground to believe that Mr. Amon had made every effort to see that they did not get bricks in the neighbourhood, but when he realised that in desperation they would even order bricks from Bombay, he arranged for a local contractor to supply the bricks. Shri Soman had taken a prominent part in the actual construction of the huts. At the news of this, I felt a keen desire to embark upon a struggle with Mr. Amon.

According to Gandhiji's instructions, I picked up a companion named Kshire and proceeded to Motihari in Bihar, where we stayed in the house of a respected old leader in that region. When the question of who should go and live in the *ashram* near Mr. Amon's house arose, I insisted that I should be assigned to this work. In fact I even declared that if I was not given this job, I would prefer returning altogether. So ultimately I got what I wanted. My companion from Maharashtra also accompanied me partly to see the *ashram* and partly on account of his curiosity to see Mr. Amon.

The *ashram* at Bhitiharva had been constructed in a place central to about thirty-five villages near a temple. The nearest post office was situated in an out-building attached to Mr. Amon's bungalow, and the postmaster was also simultaneously Mr. Amon's clerk. The bungalow was about three miles from our *ashram*. The day after we reached Bhitiharva, we went to the post office and left a note there to the effect that any letters addressed to 1) Narayan Tamaji Katagade, and 2) Eknath Vasudev Kshire, and 3) Pundalik Katagade should be delivered at the *ashram*.

A few days later a police subinspector came to the *ashram* with about fifteen or twenty constables armed with long sticks and surrounded the place while the school I was conducting there was in session. The officer demanded, "How many persons came in your group from Maharashtra?"

"Initially Shri Kshire and I were the two persons who came. Shri Kshire has now gone to another *ashram,* and I am alone here," I replied.

"Don't try to deceive me. The police have very keen eyes, and their arms are also very long. Tell the truth."

"But if only two of us have come, how can I give you more names?"

He showed me the note we had left at the post office and asked, "Are there not three names on this note? Where is the third?" I explained to him that I was known by two names and that the note actually referred to only two persons. But the officer was not satisfied and proceeded to carry out a thorough search of the *ashram*. Of course he could not find anything or anybody, but for about two weeks after that the police kept a strict watch over the *ashram,* thinking that we had brought a third individual with us who was to attack Mr. Amon and then flee. Finally, however, getting no evidence to support this fantastic theory, they went away.

GANDHIJI'S BASIC METHOD

Gandhiji's idea about the work to be done in Champaran was actually quite simple. The people there had been so intimidated by the oppression and violence of the planters that they had become extremely cowardly and had no self-respect. They were suffering all kinds of indignities without the least protest. Even the fact that a self-respecting and independent person was living among them would itself be a kind of training for them. Gandhiji had also asked me to conduct a school for their children. Though we had no slates or pencils or books, the teacher was to tell stories to the children, play games with them, and occasionally use the board in the schoolroom to teach them the alphabet. The teacher was also expected to visit each of the neighbouring villages and try to teach the elements of hygiene to the people. He was himself expected to participate in sweeping the paths and cleaning the wells.[36] If any incident involving oppression or violence on the part of the planter took place, a report about it was to be sent to Gandhiji; but there were strict instructions not to send reports to the newspapers. One should, if possible, actually be present when incidents involving arbitrary or unjust action on the part of the planter took place.

---

[36] Considered an unclean and ritually defiling activity by higher castes.

After conducting the school at Bhitiharva for about a week, I informed Gandhiji that I did not see the point in remaining there as the children did not understand my language and I did not understand theirs. But Gandhiji sent a reply asking me to continue for a month and then to write him again about my experiences. Further he told me that Bihari (the local language) and Hindi were two branches of one and the same tree and that I already knew enough Hindi. Within one month, the children in the school taught me quite a lot of Bihari and I could speak it to some extent. The children in turn began to understand a little Hindi. After about a month, I wrote to Gandhiji, "What you said was right. Language cannot be a serious obstacle. I have now begun to understand Bihari to some extent." Often the pupils taught me more than I did them.

One day Mr. Amon came to visit the school, in reality to see me. The children were just coming in when Mr. Amon's servant came to announce to me that his master was about to visit the school and that we should all be orderly and neat. As it happened, I was clad in a loincloth and was in the midst of my daily exercises. The servant furthermore informed me that I was expected to go out and hold the reins of the *saheb*'s horse. I considered it and decided that I should not hold the reins of Mr. Amon's horse, but at the same time I told the children that they should stand up when the *saheb* entered. I explained to them that this did not involve any affront to one's self-respect. It was merely a matter of common courtesy. On hearing these instructions, the children began to whisper to each other that I was telling them to do something the previous teacher had never done. This gave me a slight shock. A moment later I saw the planter approaching the school on horseback. So I declared in the presence of the servant, "What right has this *saheb* to inspect this school? I will give you all a holiday. You may go out and play." Naturally they rushed out like young deer and began to play. When Mr. Amon entered the school, he saw only me, taking my exercises clad in nothing but my loincloth, and he had to go away with his entrance quite spoiled. The children were highly amused by this incident.

Once when Gandhiji was visiting the school, he asked the children, "Formerly the school building was a grass hut. Now it is constructed of bricks. Why was this necessary?"

"The grass huts were burned down," replied the children, "and in order to prevent its happening again, this brick building was built."

"Who do you think burned down the huts?"

"Mr. Amon, the planter, must have been behind it," all the children announced as one voice.

At this Gandhiji warned them never to indulge in such accusations, as there was no evidence for it. He also advised them to avoid the habit of blaming every misfortune on our adversaries. It is only then that we can succeed and make progress.

I lived there for about eleven months. My daily routine consisted of cooking my food and cleaning the vessels, visiting the nearby villages, and conducting the school.

My Pupils

The pupils who attended the school were from six to thirteen years old. In about a month's time their number reached about forty-five. Not much importance was attached in the *ashram* to the three R's. As soon as the students came to school, they had to clean their teeth with charcoal powder and ashes, the remnants from my hearth. If they were too young to brush their own teeth, I did it for them. Then they stood in a row and exhibited their clean teeth by making faces like a group of monkeys. Once a small boy of about six or seven asked me, "Teacher, let us see if *your* teeth are white also!"

Once one of the boys became ill while attending school and was not in a condition to walk back to his village home, so I put him to bed on my cot and went to sleep near him on the ground. At about eight in the evening the boy's parents came to the school in search of him. When they found him asleep on the cot while I slept on the ground, tears of gratitude came to their eyes. After that day he often stayed with me. Another boy, Mukut, had also grown very fond of me. He was very intelligent, and today both these boys are considered leaders in their respective villages and a source of strength to the Congress. In one year Mukut progressed up to the English second grade. He was then sent to Patna for further study, and Rajendra Babu took full responsibility for his expenses.

VILLAGE SANITATION AND CLEANING WORK

One of the items in the programme drawn up by Gandhiji for the volunteers in the *ashrams* was the cleaning of village roads and village wells. The children in the villages used to call me "Teacher" but the other villagers called me "Gandhiji's Vakilsaheb." [37] As soon as I began to sweep, a number of villagers also started to sweep the roads with brooms and clean up the space near the well. I did not have to continue the work for even a few minutes. The news that Gandhiji's Vakilsaheb had started sweeping the village spread very quickly to all the villages. In fact when it became known that I visited a particular village on a particular day, the village roads and well would be swept clean even before I reached it.

Although in Bihar, particularly in the villages, the women wore veils and were secluded from men, I was exempt from these restrictions. Being young in age, I was allowed to go into their part of the house. I was a daily visitor at Mukut's house. His mother reserved the milk of one buffalo just for my consumption. When she learned that I had no mother, she was particularly affectionate to me. Once when she learned that I was ill, she broke all the conventions about women's behaviour, came to the

---

[37] A *vakil* in modern India is a lawyer, but the term traditionally designated a representative of a great or wealthy man. It is in this traditional sense that Pundalik is addressed as Gandhiji's *vakilsaheb*.

ashram, and nursed me. When I went to Bihar again in 1934 I
made a special trip to visit her. She is very old now and is totally
blind. She recognised me, felt my hands and face and was over-
joyed at my visit. Mukut's house is a kind of centre in the village
of Bhitiharva. Fearing that I might go there and start sweeping
the roads, Mukut's mother would see that the villagers did the
sweeping, and if on my usual day I failed to turn up there she
managed to send word to me about it.

A BIZARRE INCIDENT

Within a week of my arrival at the Bhitiharva *ashram,* I
was to witness a strange occurrence. I was told that every young
girl had to be sent to Mr. Amon after her first flux. If that was
not done, the family's hut was burned down or she and her relatives were molested. She would spend one night at Mr. Amon's
bungalow and would then be sent home with some jewelry as a
present. Many such stories were told about Mr. Amon. Within a
week of my arrival Mr. Amon got news that the daughter of a
certain villager had had her first flux.[38] When an invitation from
Mr. Amon arrived for her, her father, terrified, came to me to
ask whether I could protect her honour. After hearing him out,
I realised the gravity of the situation. I did not know what I
could say to him. I was but an humble worker. What could I do
against this powerful Britisher? Still, I told the father to bring
the whole family to stay with me in the *ashram,* hoping that the
white man would not dare to attack the *ashram* itself. The father
agreed to this proposal, saying, "We will come here tonight. But
it may be rather late before we take our evening meal and reach
the *ashram.*" He was very thankful and bid me goodbye in deep
gratitude.

I remained awake waiting for the family nearly the whole
night. But in their village strange things were happening. Ap-

[38] In some orthodox families this occurrence is an occasion of celebration
known to everyone in the village.

parently the plan of going to the *ashram* had already reached Mr. Amon's ears.

Already by six o'clock in the evening, Mr. Amon's secret agents were loitering near the girl's house. The father was evidently molested and beaten, for as I was anxiously watching the road from their village, at about four in the morning I saw the girl, her father, and some servants of Mr. Amon's proceeding to his bungalow. But what could I, alone, do to intercept them? I learned later that the poor father was roundly abused by all the villagers for giving in to the planter and that they stopped all communication with him. He never came to see me again. It later came to my ears that a report had been sent to Government that I was trying to persuade his fellow villagers to excommunicate him. A couple of days later, the superintendent of police personally came to the village and interviewed some of the villagers, but no case was filed against me. Instead I got some publicity in a number of neighbouring villages and received invitations to visit there. Many new pupils from the surrounding villages began to attend my school.

Extreme Cowardice of the Villagers

Since most huts in the Champaran region were built of straw or hay which could easily be burned down if the planters had any cause for anger, all the inhabitants lived in a state of terror. Their ignorance was another cause of their fear. There was perhaps one person in ten or twelve villages who could read and write. When they came to the market, they used to bring with them letters they had received during the past several weeks in order to have them read out. This was an invitation to Mr. Amon's servants to take advantage of such ignorance. They used to show the villagers any typed sheet, or a piece cut from an English newspaper, or even a page from a railway timetable, pretending that this was a list of persons who were about to be prosecuted in a court of law. The "names" would be "crossed off" the "list" for pay-

ment of a small bribe. With all this extra income to be had for
the taking, Mr. Amon could get any number of people to serve
him on two or three rupees a month, as they could easily earn
about twenty-five rupees a month this way.

One day some police constables in one of the villages were
trying to extort some money from the owner of a goat which had
strangled itself by threatening to charge him with murder. The
man managed to escape by the back door while the police were
sitting at his front door and came running to the school. In
great haste he explained what was happening, saying, "Vakilsaheb, I confess that I have done wrong, but please help me to
get out of this. I can pay about twenty-five rupees, but they are
asking for two or three hundred, and where am I to get so much
money?" Surprised at this strange story, I accompanied him back
to his hut. As soon as the police saw me, they got up quietly and
left. Apparently nothing more was heard about the matter.

Some days later when Mr. Amon was passing another villager's hut on an elephant, he had occasion to stop the elephant
and call the man. The man, who was taking his meal, shouted,
"I am coming, Sir," but took some time to wash his hands and
come out. The *saheb*, thinking that the man was deliberately de-
laying in order to show insolence, got down from the elephant
and gave him a sound beating. Although many villagers were
standing around watching the scene, not one of them dared intervene or rescue the victim. One of the spectators, a pupil in my
school, came running to report the incident to me. Picking up my
long stick, I went rushing to the scene, but by the time I arrived,
Mr. Amon was already seated again on the back of the elephant.
I shouted from a distance asking him to stop, but he ignored me
and drove the elephant away at a fast pace. The people were still
gathered around the door of the man who had been beaten.
When I asked them about the whole incident, the reply was the
most curious I could imagine. They said, "Now look here, Vakilsaheb, it is very bad that the planter beat him. He should not
have been so hard. But after all, from another point of view, how

can you blame the *saheb*? When the *saheb* called him, he should immediately have gone out and stood before him. Instead, he merely called out, 'Coming!' After all, it is not as if we did not know the *saheb*'s temper! So naturally the *saheb* beat him! Well, let it be. After all, you can't undo the beating!"

DAILY ROUTINE IN THE ASHRAM

Gandhiji established certain unwritten rules for all workers who lived in any of the *ashrams* which may also make clear his way of thinking.

Every worker was expected to get up at five o'clock in the morning and after the morning wash to visit one village. There he was to explain the importance of cleanliness to the villagers and if necessary himself do the work of cleaning and sweeping the village so as to demonstrate to them how it should be done. He was to visit their houses to become acquainted with them and also to instruct them about public affairs as far as possible. By about nine or half past nine he was to return to the *ashram*. By that time the children would have assembled at the school. The school curriculum consisted mainly of telling stories and hearing the students' stories. While I was conducting school I used to put my rice pot on the fire to prepare my meal. Many of the children's mothers told them stories which they were specially asked to narrate to me. When I noticed this I had all the pupils ask their parents to tell them stories. In this way, I heard many very interesting tales. This solved my difficulty when my own stock of stories was exhausted. The children also told at home the stories I had narrated to them.

While all this storytelling was going on, I taught some of the older boys to write with the help of the board or the ground. I even taught a little English to those that had learned to read and write Hindi. Many of them later finished high school and are now responsible Congress workers.

After meals, I spent a little time either in reading or in writing letters. Soon the children returned to school after their mid-day meal. Some of them became quite bold and put their hands on my table, making it impossible to read or write, and pressing me to tell them stories. So I went on with storytelling, and then we played some games. I also taught them some drill.

In Bihar, many people kept elephants, just as in other parts people keep horses or bicycles in cities. In Champaran I could always get one to ride if the planter had called an assembly of the villagers. Often I took a few of the older pupils with me, as about six people could easily ride an elephant in addition to the driver. Afterward these boys usually discussed with the rest of my students the incidents in the assembly. No stories were told on such days, and occasionally proceedings became very animated.

In the evening I usually finished my supper and the cleaning of the pots by about six o'clock. I had a fisherman friend who would come to chat with me in the early part of the night. In a sweet voice he used to sing devotional songs, accompanying himself on a one-stringed instrument and becoming so absorbed with religious fervour that many times fifteen or twenty people assembled to listen to his songs as he nodded his head from side to side. That was my day at the *ashram*.

My First "Satyagraha" [39]

In Champaran, men and women, old and young, boys and girls all smoke the *hookah*. I soon became aware that all the pupils in my school were smoking the *hookah*. As I have mentioned, I had become very friendly with Mukut's family. This was one of the leading families in the village, with an annual income of at least twenty thousand rupees. The family also kept an elephant. The whole family had taken me to its bosom. Whenever there was a sweet dish prepared in the house, they invariably

---

[39] Literally, "insistence on truth." A program of planned nonviolent struggle. This is a term coined by Gandhi and his associates in South Africa for his campaigns.

invited me to partake of it. All the other villagers treated me with respect and affection because I had such friendly relations with a leading family. I used to go to the village very often. In order to save me the bother of boiling my milk, Mukut's mother boiled milk for me and even added to it some cream from other milk. In my campaign to eradicate the habit of smoking the *hookah,* I chose Bhitiharva village.

One day, I went to Mukut's house. Seeing a few villagers assembled there, I broached the subject of smoking. I explained to them the ill effects of tobacco on small children. And then I blurted out, "I will take my next meal only when you all give up this bad habit of smoking the *hookah.*" They did not take me seriously at first. I just got up and went back to the *ashram.* That was a Saturday. I pondered over the matter and went to bed. Next morning I began my daily routine. I did not eat anything for my noon meal, nursing a fond belief that some of the villagers would come to me, swear to give up tobacco, and then I would be able to eat my evening meal. But throughout the whole of Sunday nobody came except some of my pupils. Even the fisherman failed to turn up for the evening session of singing. None of the usual members of the audience turned up. As I was fasting, I did not go for my usual round of the village.

On Monday morning I was feeling very weak. I wrote letters to Gorakh Babu[40] at Motihari and to Gandhiji at Sabarmati explaining the awkward position I had got into. On Tuesday, when the children came to school in the morning, I did not get up but told them stories lying in my bed. Thinking that their teacher was ill, most of them went home earlier than usual, but Mukut and his cousin remained behind to ask what was the matter with me. When I explained the whole matter to them, they became quite frightened, as they also were smoking the *hookah,* and took an oath then and there never to smoke again. I told them my fast was not for the two of them. The whole Bhitiharva village must

---

[40] Gorakh Babu was the Congress leader in the district town and Pundalik's chief advisor and "straw boss."

take an oath not to smoke the *hookah* any more; then only
would I break my fast. These two went into the village and
described to the villagers their conversation with me. Expecting
that after the boys had explained the situation to the villagers,
at least a few individuals would come to see me, I went every
now and then to the window in order to see if anybody was coming to see me. When, three or four hours after the boys' departure, no visitor had appeared, I began to feel that my *satyagraha*
would be a failure. Actually, however, the villagers were deep in
discussion of the problem at that very moment.

About eight o'clock in the evening, some half a dozen respected members of the village community came to see me. By
that time I had become almost desperate. But as soon as they
arrived, I saw a ray of hope and was very happy. I explained to
them my thoughts and the resolve I had made. Mukut and his
cousin were standing in the shadow behind the group of elders.
Mukut's elder brother and two others were jointly trying to persuade me to give up my fast. They said, "Well, Mr. Teacher,
what you say is quite right. Smoking tobacco is very harmful to
men. Boys and girls particularly must never even touch a *hookah*.
It is urgently necessary to eradicate this evil. All school children
must be kept away from this habit, and you are perfectly right
when you say that this can never be achieved unless the elders in
the family set them a good example. But you must realise that
we have all been smoking *hookahs* for generations. We would be
unable to give up the habit just by your ordering us to do so. You
are Gandhiji's worker. We cannot tell lies to you. We would not
like to deceive you. Let us first stop the boys and girls from
smoking the *hookah*. But no fast is necessary for that. If you like,
let us write to Gandhiji and place before him our view and yours
and let us abide by what he says. At least give up this fast until
Gorakh Babu comes from Motihari. Please take food today and
you can start your fast again after a letter comes from Gandhiji
or Gorakh Babu. If you like, a half dozen of us will give up the

hookah right now but we do not think it is possible for the whole village to give up the habit."

I replied, "Well, I have made this resolve and I have also written letters to both Gandhiji and Gorakh Babu. But before I get replies from them, I cannot give up my fast. I don't care what happens to me. Please give me some hot water. That is all."

After sitting with me for some time, all these good people returned to Bhitiharva. I stretched out on my cot immersed in thought. Mukut and his cousin gave me some hot water. After about an hour, when it was a little dark, two or three bullock carts came from the village to my *ashram*. They contained the women of some of the leading families. Mukut whispered this information in my ear. All the ladies came into the room and sat down. Mukut's old mother came to me, passed her hand over my face and said, "I am an old woman, but I am ready to give up smoking. But at least for my sake, you must take food. Please do not bother about the villagers. Let them smoke or do whatever they like. We are really like a dog's curved tail. We may declare today that we have given up the *hookah* and start smoking it again tomorrow. I have been smoking a *hookah* from my child-hood. Let us, however, prevent the children, not only in our family but in the whole village, from smoking. It is good that you went on a fast for that. That is what I honestly feel. And, because you did not take any food today, all of us have also observed a fast." With these words, the old lady again passed her hand lovingly over my face. She added, "We have given up our customary *purdah* for your sake." Of course I realised the truth of what the men had said before and also of what the ladies told me. But I just could not think of something to say.

Mukut's mother went back to the group of ladies and held a consultation with them for a short while. Then she came back to me and said, "My dear boy, we have another suggestion. Will you accept it?"

I looked at her inquiringly and she proceeded, "We have

come here in a bullock cart. You and the boys should come with
us in that cart to the village and let us consider the whole matter
there." I at once gave my consent to this proposal, locked the
ashram, and went with them. A cot had been placed in the open
courtyard of Mukut's house and I stretched myself out there.
Very soon between two hundred and two hundred fifty villagers
assembled there. The pupils in my school took oaths to give up
smoking, as did some girls, including Mukut's sisters. Some of
the older people declared, "This habit of ours is of long standing,
but we will make a sincere effort to get rid of it." After this,
young Mukut came forward and asked, "Teacher, we have done
all that was possible. Will you take some food now?" Seeing that
I gave no reply, he said to his mother, "Mother, the teacher refuses to eat anything. Please bring the knife, and I will cut my
throat here and now."

It was quite a job for me to take the knife away from him
and in the course of it I impulsively announced that I would
break my fast. Everybody was delighted with this. They collected
milk from all the houses and made *khir* with wheat flour. Then
all assembled there took a meal consisting of one course only.
From that time Mukut was known in the village as "Bring-the-
knife." So ended my *satyagraha.*

As soon as Gorakh Babu received my letter in Motihari he
came to my *ashram.* Then two days later Mahatma Gandhi's
secretary, Mahadev Desai, sent a telegram asking for full details.
When I sent a detailed letter in reply to the telegram he wrote
back pointing out what I had done wrong under the caption "Under the instructions of respected Bapuji." [41] I remember the
points quite well even now:

a) This *satyagraha* dealt with a problem much beyond the
scope of the field of my service. It should have been confined to
the boys and girls in the school;

b) Notice of the *satyagraha* was not given to the villagers in
a proper manner, and so two or three days were wasted;

---

[41] An affectionate term for Gandhi, meaning Father.

c) That I went repeatedly to the window to see if anybody from the village was coming for a compromise proposal showed that I had not the true spirit of *satyagraha;*

d) The final compromise was arrived at in too great a hurry.

Of course I did not realise the importance of these false steps on my part at that time, but I am now in a position to appreciate the whole thing. Whenever I think of this experiment of my youth, I cannot help but laugh at myself.

IN THE MARRIAGE PARTY

Mukut's marriage was arranged while I was in Bhitiharva, and his mother insisted on my becoming a member of the groom's party. In Bihar in those days the bride's family not infrequently became bankrupt from the expenditure of her wedding. In an agreement drawn up between the two parties, a detailed statement was made about how many men, women, elephants, horses, palanquins, palanquin carriers, and others would form the groom's party.

During the days of the wedding, the elephants were supposed to be fed on rice and some sugar-cane fields were to be reserved for them. If both parties were very rich such matters caused no trouble. For Mukut's marriage, the groom's party consisted of twelve elephants, three horses, six palanquins, and about two hundred or two hundred and fifty persons. After the marriage ceremony, the older relatives of the groom sat down to a meal while the women sat behind a partition and sang ribald songs which they composed on the spot so as to include the name of each of the older relatives. Boys and girls were appointed to ask each man's name and convey it behind the screen. Anybody whose name was not thus included in a song considered it a slight. When one of the boys came to ask my name, I refused to tell it, but of course everybody had heard me being called Teacher (*Guruji*). The women concluded that this was my name and began a song describing the grief of Guruji when his wife

was kidnapped by the barber. I, a bachelor, was rather amused
at this.

It was also customary at such weddings for two learned *shas-
tris,* one from each side, to conduct a debate in Sanskrit. As I
had accompanied the groom, I was to act as the groom's *shastri.*
I knew that my opposite number had no very profound knowledge of Sanskrit, so I started reciting a Sanskrit verse, to which
the other *shastri* recited a verse he knew as a kind of reply. Then
I recited two verses, but as if I was speaking prose, upon which
my adversary immediately picked up a coconut and handed it
over to me as a token of my victory over him. Actually, it was a
convention that the groom's *shastri* should come out the victor,
so the bride's *shastri* did not feel any kind of humiliation about
it. When the groom's party was ready to return, as many people
from the bride's side as possible usually accompanied them for
a short way as a token of respect.

DISPUTE WITH THE SADHUBABA[42] AND A GIFT-DEED
OF THE ASHRAM LAND

The *sadhu* on whose land the *ashram* building had been constructed was a man of bad habits and character. It was through
the offices of the people in the *ashram* that a twice-weekly market
came to be held there as a convenience for the people of the surrounding villages. Naturally many people who came to the
market spent some time resting and talking in the *ashram.* They
ate their food there, told accounts of their life in the villages and
also made inquiries about Gandhiji's movement. Now this *sadhu*
began to levy a tax of one pice from each shopkeeper and merchant as ground rent. I called him to the *ashram* and suggested
that he charge a set amount for each market and that instead of
going round to the villages begging, which was his usual means
of livelihood, he should beg at the market and be content with

---

[42] *Sadhu*—ascetic; *-baba*—term of respect for an older man.

what people would give willingly. But even the begging should not be coercive. I even offered to guarantee that he would obtain every week double what would normally be required for his maintenance. He agreed to all this in our conversation but started to collect two pice instead of one from each merchant. The *sadhu* protested to me, "If my servant Japal collects the money, what can I do about it?" But when I made enquiries of Japal, he told me that he had strict instructions from the *sadhu* to collect two pice as rent. He continued, "After all, I am his servant. How can I go against his orders?"

So I called Japal and the *sadhu* into the *ashram*. There Japal repeated his story. I lost my temper completely and, catching hold of the *sadhu*'s beard, gave him several blows and slaps. All this happened in the door of the *ashram* with many spectators.

As a result, the *sadhu* began to nurture schemes for repossessing the *ashram*. When I learned of this, I again called him in and explained Gandhiji's movement to him, the work of the *ashram*, and how it was benefitting the people of Champaran. That particular day he had not smoked marijuana and was quite sober and appreciated the importance of all that I told him. He asked for forgiveness and said, "Teacher, today my reasoning faculties are working well. I don't know when that will change. So please take me to Motihari at once and get a gift-deed signed for whatever part of my land is required for the *ashram*. Let this be done in order to make the transaction final."

I at once had the land needed for the *ashram* measured out, and, armed with these notes, the *sadhu* and I caught the first available train to Motihari and went to Gorakh Babu. The *sadhu* and I remained there for about five days until the deed for the gift was signed and registered. Then the *sadhu* left.

Thereafter the *sadhu* behaved very well with me and with the village people. Until I departed from Bhitiharva he consulted me about everything and the villagers also grew to respect him. I bought good varieties of mango and jackfruit plants and planted them in the *ashram* compound. Some of them have now grown into beautiful trees, and the whole compound is even more lovely than before.

FURTHER IRRITATIONS FOR THE PLANTER

Whenever Mr. Amon called the people together in order to collect illegal and unjust taxes from them, I would try to go there on elephant-back to persuade the people to refuse to pay. As Mr. Amon was the contractor who had been entrusted by Government with collecting the land revenue of thirty-five villages, the farmers not only now refused to pay anything over and above due taxes, but began to demand formal receipts for their payments. Mr. Amon was convinced that these very people, who had formerly been mortally afraid of him but who now openly declared that he was extorting money from them illegally, had been influenced by our movement. I had given instruction to the father of each child attending my school to send the money for the land revenue with their sons and not to take it to Mr. Amon personally. Instead I accompanied the children, who were not afraid to insist on a proper receipt or to say that they would part with the money only when the receipt was given. Once when about twenty of my pupils and I were thus standing in front of Mr. Amon, he dissolved the meeting before any of the other villagers arrived so that what the children did would not influence them.

Gradually, preventing Mr. Amon from getting any money over and above what he, as a contractor for the land revenue, was entitled to became a kind of obsession with me, so I went to Motihari and consulted Gorakh Babu. Fortunately he did not dissuade me. In fact he suggested that I should get a written statement from such families as were willing to appoint me their legal manager and then go to Mr. Amon in that capacity with the money for the land revenue, also providing me with a draft statement for the purpose. He appreciated my idea of picking out the bolder of the children and sending the money with them and suggested that some people might also send the land revenue by postal money order. Finally, he told me that it would be worthwhile for some to send the money directly to the Government treasury, stating as their reason that they were afraid of ill-treatment at the hands of Mr. Amon and were therefore adopting that particular method of payment.

Following this, I had myself appointed manager for fifteen or twenty well-to-do families and informed Mr. Amon accordingly. Of course he was very angry about it all.

One day the *saheb*'s elephant drivers stopped in a village called Madhavpur to cut twigs from a *nim* tree to clean their teeth. The villagers of Madhavpur worshipped this *nim* tree and warned the drivers that they would not allow them to cut twigs from it. The drivers, on the other hand, threatened to have their elephant uproot the whole tree. The villagers replied that both the elephant and the drivers would be treated to a shower of stones and bricks. After this the drivers took the elephant to Mr. Amon's bungalow and reported the whole incident.

Now Mr. Amon was a particularly obstinate person. He at once drove to the village in his motor car, a distance of about a mile and a half, followed by the elephant and the drivers. The people would not yield, and while a discussion between Mr. Amon and some of the villagers was going on, others lifted up one side of the car and stood it on its side. I happened to be visiting that village that day on my usual round, and naturally Mr. Amon added another black mark against my name, sure that I was responsible for this outrage. He returned to his bungalow on the back of the elephant, and the driver, after setting the car on its four wheels again, drove it back.

Some of the older students in my school and I were also trying our best to prevent the *saheb* from realising other illegal and tyrannical levies he used to collect. The roads in these parts were divided into two sections. There was a slightly higher level used by the *saheb* either on elephant-back or in his car and the other, a little lower, was used by the villagers, their cattle and carts. In the evening when the cattle returned from grazing in the fields, if even one animal strayed onto the *saheb*'s section of the road, the whole flock was captured and put in a pound which was constructed especially for the purpose. The owner then had to pay a fine of eight annas for each cow or buffalo and two annas for each goat or pig to retrieve them.

Now my students and I decided to put a stop to this practice. I began to stand on the road in the evening. There one night I saw the Police Patel, the Government official in the village, himself driving the herds of cattle into the pound when one cow or goat strayed onto "Mr. Amon's part" of the road. Requesting the students to wait, I inquired of the Police Patel why he was driving the whole herd into the pound. He replied that it was the convention, and that it was under orders of Mr. Amon. The boys who were herding the cattle had begun to cry.

I suggested, "Let us count the number of animals and let the boys take away their cattle. I will myself accompany you to the *saheb,* and if he does not excuse the fine then it can always be paid." The Police Patel agreed to this proposal, and the boys, laughing and jumping for joy, took away their animals. I walked with the Police Patel for about half a mile and during the course of our conversation remarked, "What actual right has Mr. Amon to have a cattle pound? After all, he is not the government of the land. Then why should I have to come to his bungalow? I refuse to come. You can tell him what happened and when I meet him next, I will also tell him about it." With these words, I returned to the *ashram.* The Police Patel was not strong enough to drag me to Mr. Amon's bungalow and therefore could do nothing about it.

The news of the cattle rescue spread quickly to all the villages. From that day Mr. Amon's cattle pound was abolished, either because he himself realised that it might lead to serious trouble or because he received a gentle hint from Government to behave himself. Both parts of the road then came into use by the people, although some of them still used only the lower level, possibly as a result of fear or long habit.

Sometimes, when I was on my rounds, people said to me: "If you had gone to Mr. Amon's bungalow on that day, what would have happened? If Mr. Amon comes to you and questions you about it, what will you tell him? Oh! If we had done anything like this, he would have been wild with us. Anyway, please be very watchful. He is a very vindictive fellow, so you must be careful." Some others assured me that if anything happened to me, they would all be ready to come to my aid. Mukut's mother even sent two of her servants to sleep in the *ashram* for a couple of weeks for my protection.

But a new affair developed out of this. During my stay in the Bhitiharva *ashram* I sent detailed reports to Gandhiji about my dealings with the villagers, with government officials, and with Mr. Amon, including the various conversations which took place. I received replies regularly from Gandhiji which I kept carefully with me. Immediately after I went to Bhitiharva the police had made detailed inquiries about where I came from, who I was, and who had sent me; one copy of the statements I had made to the police was also sent to Gandhiji. On the other hand, Gandhiji had sent a letter to the Collector of Motihari, with a copy to me, stating that I was his representative. After I had informed him about my exploit in freeing the cattle, I was eagerly awaiting his reaction. I was sure I would be praised, because in one of his previous letters he had told me to serve the villagers in all possible ways without, however, coming into conflict with government officials.

Now Gandhiji had apparently communicated the whole episode to the Collector of Motihari, and I was astounded to read, in a copy sent me "for my information," that Gandhiji had suggested that I should be prosecuted for obstructing a government official in the execution of his duties! I was somewhat fearful of what would happen to me. I could not understand at all why Gandhiji had acted in this fashion. Further, in the copy he sent me, Gandhiji instructed me to go and see the Collector, admit all that I had done, suffer whatever punishment he awarded, and then return to the *ashram* to resume my work. In passing, I may mention that I wrote to Gangadharrao and others protesting against this attitude of Gandhiji's. He probably saw one of these letters.

Nevertheless I locked the *ashram,* took my belongings, and without telling anybody went to Motihari to see Gorakh Babu. He thought that a copy of the letter I received might also have been sent to the Collector. But I thought this was probably not the case, because the letter to me was in Hindi and was not typed; in any case he advised me to go and see the Collector according to Gandhiji's instructions. At about three in the afternoon I went to visit the Collector in Gorakh Babu's horse carriage. Before that, however, I rehearsed with Gorakh Babu an imaginary conversation in English with the Collector, as I was not very confident about my ability to converse fluently in English. The Collector asked me to sit down on a chair; and after about five minutes, during which he signed some papers, he said, "I have got a letter from Gandhiji yesterday in which a summary of the letter you wrote to him was enclosed. The cattle pound will not be kept any longer. If you have any complaints to make or have any difficulty, you should write directly to me. But you must not take the law into your own hands. If you do that, I will have to file a case against you. If you ever come to Motihari again, you may come and see me."

"Gandhiji has also issued instructions to me," I replied. "I will obey them. In case of need I will write to you. Also when I come to Motihari, if I have any business with you, I will gladly come and see you. Otherwise I would not like to take your time," and so saying I took my leave.

Later on I learned that Mr. Amon had instructed the Police Patel to make a complaint to higher police authority about my conduct.

I returned to Gorakh Babu's house, told him what had happened, and sent a detailed letter to Gandhiji. In reply Mahadev wrote, "So far so good, but be more careful in the future."

Another associate of Gandhiji's wrote me a letter explaining that Gandhiji's object in writing to the Collector and to me was to force me to confess to everything I had done and to suffer the consequences willingly. "In fact, it would have been better if you had been punished," he wrote, requesting me to explain to everybody connected with the *ashram* and to the pupils in the school the underlying principles in Gandhiji's letters.

The news of my interview with the Collector had spread to the villagers. Wherever I went, the villagers collected around me and inquired how the whole matter developed. They were all very glad that Mr. Amon's cattle pound was abolished at last. I can't say whether the cattle were glad, but I was sure the cattleherds were.

Mr. Amon also disliked to see anyone pass him on the road or pass by his house wearing shoes or riding any kind of vehicle. So I began to make propaganda that this was not a matter of what Mr. Amon liked or disliked but of people's convenience. Thus nobody should hesitate to walk on the road with shoes or to ride in a vehicle. Then people began to spread stories that so-and-so had gone to the post office in Mr. Amon's compound wearing shoes or that another walked past Mr. Amon wearing shoes on the station platform with impunity. Soon Mr. Amon began to feel a difference in the villagers' attitude. Seeing that his prestige and control of the people was suffering an eclipse, he became very agitated. In the end nobody except those who were his immediate dependents and employees kept up the convention of going barefoot in his presence. This, too, naturally enraged him.

MR. AMON'S TRICKS

Now Mr. Amon began to plan his revenge. I have already mentioned that I used to teach my pupils some drill by way of

physical exercise. This activity of mine soon became the focus of
rumours among the villagers. The First World War was then
about to end, but Mr. Amon gathered people from a large number of villages and distributed sweets to them, declaring, "I was
not on good terms with the teacher in Gandhiji's *ashram* for a
long time, but now things have changed. Now the teacher has
become a partisan of ours. He has agreed to train all the children
in his school and to send them as recruits to the army. That is
why he is teaching them drill. So everybody should see that his
children are sent to that school."

As a result of this propaganda, the simple villagers, without
any thought, stopped sending their children to the school. This
movement had not been started in Bhitiharva but only in the
outlying villages. The very people who had formerly welcomed
me into their houses and pressed me to drink milk now closed
their doors whenever I went to their village. At first I could not
understand this strange behaviour, but I soon discovered Mr.
Amon's craftiness. I tried to explain to some of the parents of
my pupils the ridiculousness of the whole affair by drawing their
attention to the war situation, to the impossibility of a worker
in Gandhiji's *ashram* doing anything of the sort, to the nature of
the drill I was teaching, and finally to the absurdity of children
of seven to fifteen years of age having anything to do with the
army. After about a month and a half the pupils again began to
attend the school. To convince the people, I substituted the
Indian game of *kabaddi* for the drill.

I have already mentioned that in the beginning I was full
of fear of Mr. Amon and was very alert to possible danger. But
one incident eliminated that fear. As I was returning from a
neighbouring village to the *ashram* one evening, Mr. Amon
passed by on horseback through the jungle. Seeing him in that
lonely spot I became very nervous, sure that he would do me
harm. The *saheb* pulled up his horse, took the reins in his left
hand, and pretended to feel in his pocket for his pistol with his
right hand. I took all this to mean that I would die if I did not

attack first—not through boldness, but mainly out of fear. So I raised my stick and took resolute steps in his direction. Seeing me thus advancing towards him, he turned his horse in the opposite direction and rapidly galloped away. I then realised that in fact he was not a very courageous man and that he was afraid of me.

After that I did not mind going alone even at night to the post office to get my letters. If he saw me, he would close his door, and this made me bolder still. Until that time I had intentionally avoided visiting Amolva, the village near Mr. Amon's bungalow; but now I began to visit it every other day. This seems to have increased his irritation, for it appeared that he had drawn up a plan to give me a sound beating. Whenever I went to Amolva village, one of his servants quite openly followed me about. The villagers, sensing that something was going to happen, did not speak to me as usual when they saw this man following me. But one or two of them called me into the inner parts of their houses, offered me milk, and implored me to stay with them for the night. Realising that they were all sick of Mr. Amon's tyranny, I continued to go every evening to the post office and to visit Amolva village almost every morning.

But my impression that Mr. Amon was rather afraid of me or perhaps that Gandhiji's letter to the Collector had produced a warning to him was soon proved wrong. Hardly had I settled myself on the bed one night when I heard whispering outside the door. Putting on my loincloth I went cautiously to the door, where I heard the words "You call him." I was genuinely frightened but stood there noiseless, my whole body wet with perspiration while I tried frantically to think of some way to save my life. The thought that it was the work of ghosts even passed through my mind.

But I did not remain in suspense for long. A voice from outside said, "Teacher, will you please open the door for a short while?"

"Who are you? How many of you are there? What do you

want with me? Why have you come at this late hour?" I reeled
off my questions. "Open the door," came the answer. "We have
some business with you." The words were so threatening and
malicious that I was afraid to open the door. There was no other
way of escape. Without waiting longer, I raised the wick of the
oil lamp, caught hold of my stick, put on my shirt, placed my
shoes near the door so that I could flee quickly after opening it
if that became necessary, and prepared to open the door.

"Oh, we are only two, Teacher."

I then opened the door and saw that there were seven outside and that three of them had light axes which many farmers
often carried about with them. I tried to argue with myself that
this might be nothing unusual, but without much success. I then
invited them all in and asked them to sit down. I also sat down
on my cot. For a few moments nobody spoke. Although I was
shaking with fear, while all of us sat crowded into the small
room, of course I tried to put on a bold appearance and I must
have succeeded to some extent.

Then I began the conversation by asking why they had
come and what they had to tell me. I also mentioned that people
did not usually pay courtesy visits at that time of night.

"Teacher, you can take it that your life span is now at an
end. Nobody who has opposed Mr. Amon has been able to sur-
vive in these parts," said my visitors.

"Well, let Mr. Amon come here and do what he wants to
me. After all, we all belong together. What harm have I done
to you? I am only teaching the children of your brother-villagers.
I brush their teeth, I wash their faces. Am I not trying to free
you all from Mr. Amon's tyranny even at the risk of my life?
Gandhiji and all my family have sent me here to serve you in con-
fidence that you will stand by me and protect me. Of course
I will not beg Mr. Amon for my life, but I will certainly do that
of you. After all, if you people protect me, I have no fear of
Mr. Amon."

In this strain I spoke in the Bihari dialect to them for some

fifteen or twenty minutes. It had its effect first on an old man
among them, for tears began to stream down his cheeks. So I
bowed my head in front of him and said, "Kill me, old Father.
If I have to die at your hands, well, that also would be a good
thing." At these words he put aside his axe, took my face in both
hands and began to sob violently. This brought tears to the eyes
of the others too. Feeling somewhat relieved, I made a grand
gesture and threw my stick out of the room. Then I invited all
of them to go out into the veranda and sit more comfortably.

Then they said, "Teacher, please go away from here. Your
life is in danger."

But I replied, "No. I can't do that. All of you must protect
me. If I have been the cause of ill to the villagers, you should
punish me. But why should anybody be ready to kill me at the
instigation of Mr. Amon?"

When finally they bid goodbye to me to return to their
village, I asked them to wait for awhile and then told each one
to take a different route, thinking that it was not impossible for
them to hatch some new plot if they returned together. The last
to leave was the old man. He embraced me and declared, "My
boy, you are like a son to me. Don't be afraid."

After they had all gone, I locked the *ashram* and went to
Bhitiharva, thinking it safer to be in the village. When I reached
Mukut's house, everybody awoke and I related the whole episode
to them. The next two hours were spent in telling stories of
Mr. Amon's atrocities. Finally about one o'clock in the morning
we all went to sleep. After that about ten or twelve people from
the village slept at the *ashram* to protect me.

I informed Gandhiji first by telegram and then in detail by
letter about this incident. I also wrote to Rajendra Babu and to
Gorakh Babu. Gandhiji telegraphed in reply, "Act and speak
without flinching from truth. God with you." In replying to my
letter, he asked me to stay on boldly at the *ashram*. If I lost my
life I would acquire great merit by my service to Champaran. He
also instructed me to obey any notice or order that I might receive

from Government. Both Rajendra Babu and Gorakh Babu came
to Bhitiharva to assure themselves of my well-being.

My next encounter with Mr. Amon was in the village of
Mitni, where three or four days later, while everybody was out
working in the fields, all the huts caught fire and burned down.
I arrived in the village about two hours after the fire but five or
ten minutes after Mr. Amon. The students riding with me on the
elephant begged me not to get down, fearing that Mr. Amon
might urge his elephant to trample me in an "accident." The fire
had brought all the villagers from the fields, and they were all
crying out loudly at the total loss of all their earthly goods. Mr.
Amon's followers said it was God's wrath. I, however, declared
in Hindi in a loud voice that even a child could understand that
the huts had been set on fire, so that Mr. Amon could hear me.
Suddenly one of his servants came to me and said, "Sir, please
direct your elephant over there, the *saheb* is calling you."

"Tell your *saheb* that if he wants to meet me, he should
come to the *ashram*."

I invited the Mitni villagers to build their huts in the
ashram compound and turned to go. As we passed Mr. Amon's
elephant he said, "Mr. Teacher, what do you think of all this?"

"I think you are responsible for this fire. That is the honest
opinion of myself and my people. But of course we have no evidence." With these words, my elephant sped on to the *ashram*.

Although Mr. Amon's activities gradually became a little
more bearable from the point of view of the villagers, both he
and the Government officers were plotting to drive me away from
the Bhitiharva *ashram*. The police kept a watch on the *ashram*,
and there was always a shadow behind me whenever I went into
the villages. The people whose houses I visited were called to the
police station and statements taken. I reported all these develop-
ments regularly to Gandhiji; in fact Mahadev instructed me to
send in a report regularly every Monday and also wrote to
Gorakh Babu to visit the *ashram* once every fortnight.

About this time, I ran completely out of money. Although

Gorakh Babu was coming regularly to the *ashram,* I felt some hesitation in asking him for money. But I found that in that region milk and milk products like butter and *ghi* were available at very cheap rates. So I purchased six large tins of *ghi* on credit and sent them to Banaras with Shri Kshire to be sold on my account. This transaction brought a profit of twenty-four rupees.

I had written to Dr. Dev of the Servants of India Society, Rajendra Babu, Gandhiji, Babasaheb Soman, and Gangadharrao Deshpande about my financial predicament. And surprisingly enough, every one of them sent me money. In this way I collected nearly a hundred and twenty-five rupees! Then I wrote to Gandhiji that I now had plenty of money and asked whether I could close the school for a fortnight to attend the Delhi session of the Congress.

He replied with permission and added, "It would indeed be a wonder if, with so much money in your pocket, you were not to think of attending the Congress session! But you should go only if the Reception Committee accepts you as a volunteer. Otherwise, you should attend to your work and not consider going to Delhi."

MY STAY IN BIHAR ABRUPTLY ENDED

When I returned to Bhitiharva from Delhi, the whole situation appeared to have altered. My friends were all nervous. Everyone told me that Mr. Amon was very angry and there was no telling what he would do next. One had, therefore, to be very cautious.

The *ashram* was under constant watch by the police, and every evening I heaved a sigh of relief that nothing untoward had happened—but was apprehensive about the next day.

On the second or third day, a lean, fair young man in a long *khadi* shirt, a cap, and a beard came to me carrying nothing except a brass water pot. He put his head on my feet and said, "I wish to serve the country in some way and so to make my life meaningful. I shall be greatly obliged to you if you will consent to keep me with you. I shall gladly do everything that you ask me to do. I value greatly any experience that I may get in your company. I am also prepared to go anywhere that you ask me to go. Actually, after being trained under your guidance, I wish to serve my fellow-countrymen in Champaran. If, with your help, I could have the good fortune of living for some time with Mahatma Gandhi, I will consider myself very lucky. But first I would request you to let me stay here with you and only if you find that I am worthy of your trust, then you could recommend me. Otherwise you can keep me here. But I have one earnest request. You must let me do some personal service for you."

At this, my head was turned. I did not even stop to think whether I was a fit person to have a disciple. The more he praised me, the more pleased I became. For two or three days, he cooked in the *ashram* for both of us. At night, when I went to bed, he insisted on massaging my feet and legs. Casually he asked, "How are we going to rid ourselves of Mr. Amon's tyranny?" to which I answered, "He deserves to be whipped. His tyranny will only disappear when he disappears. The villagers must be made to feel this way. Otherwise, some one like us must take it upon himself to do that work and be ready to suffer the consequences. Naturally, he must be prepared for every kind of hardship. Then alone he should think of doing this act of liberation." Not that such thoughts of doing away with Mr. Amon had not been present in my mind! It was not that I gave expression to these thoughts merely because I wanted to say something radical.

Once my disciple asked, "Who do you think burned down the huts in Mitni village?"

"Oh! That must have been Mr. Amon's work," I replied. "He could not extort money from the villagers. They began to show some spirit. So the *saheb* got irritated and arranged to set fire to the village. He will only come to his senses when the villagers retaliate by setting fire to his bungalow. You know, once his elephant's stable was burned down. That fire really originated in the people's hearts."

My new-found disciple also persuaded me to show him some of Gandhiji's letters, made inquiries about who paid for my stay in Champaran, how and why I happened to come there, and who selected me. On the fourth morning he went out to relieve himself and never came back. The whole affair remained a mystery for me until I next went to Motihari when I was informed that the C.I.D. had made a report about me. Then I realised that the "disciple" who had stayed with me was a C.I.D. officer. I did not mind that the C.I.D. had made a report against me or that on the basis of that report a case might be filed against me. But I was humiliated that a clever man had made a fool of me just by uttering a few words of praise. The more people learned about it, the more I hung my head in shame.

About a fortnight after this incident, as I was on my way from Bhitiharva to Motihari, a notice was served on me to quit Bihar Province in thirty-six hours. I returned immediately to Bhitiharva. Thirty armed policemen were sent to Amolva by the same train. Fifteen of these went to Mr. Amon's bungalow for his protection, and fifteen followed me to the *ashram*.

During the evening, I went to one or two neighbouring villages and met a few friends. I sent word to the other villages that I was going to leave the *ashram* the next afternoon and a trusted messenger to Motihari with a letter arranging my departure from Motihari by the evening train. Many villagers came to the station to see me off. Mukut's elder brother accompanied me part of the way. Before the train started, Mukut's mother put a red mark on my forehead and offered me fifty rupees. If I had accepted this gift, many others might have given me money also. On the train, the police accompanying me debated whether I should be taken away via Motihari or via Kanpur. They finally decided on Kanpur, probably fearing that a crowd might gather to see me at Motihari. On the way, I inquired of the police whether I was in their custody, as my second class ticket had been purchased by Government. The police officer replied that although I was not under arrest, I would be under watch until I left Bihar Province. I would not, therefore, be allowed to go anywhere I liked, though, with his permission, I could see anyone I wanted. We all got down at Kanpur. There, with the consent of the police, I visited the office of the *Pratap,* a well known Hindi newspaper. Then I was set free on the Banaras railway station platform in the United Provinces.

To my surprise, Shri Kshire, my co-worker in Champaran, was standing on the station platform. He said that as soon as people in Motihari learned that I had been taken by way of Kanpur they had arranged for him to come straight to Banaras from Motihari. As we left the station in a horse carriage, a police agent took the seat by the driver and ordered him to drive to the police station. At first I thought he was a friend of the driver who wished to get down at the police station and that was why the carriage was going there. Kshire and I were busy talking. When the carriage halted before the police station and the man told the driver to wait there until he returned, we realised what had happened. So we said to the driver, "We have hired your carriage for the two of us and do not wish to take along anyone else. If you do not drive on this very moment, we won't pay you any fare."

The agent on the other hand warned the driver of dire consequences if he moved from his place and then walked away in the fashion of a high officer. He did not return for nearly forty-five minutes, and the driver hadn't the courage to drive off. There was no possibility of getting another carriage there, so there we sat. Then I was called into the office, and the police superintendent asked me where I proposed to stay. As I did not know what arrangements Shri Kshire had made for me, I told the superintendent to send somebody with us to see for himself where I was staying. Then the same man who had accompanied us from the railway station again accompanied us to the house of a *pandya.*

Just as I was getting up from an after lunch nap that afternoon, a gentleman came to make inquiries about my programme,
asking whether I was scheduled to participate in some agitation
or whether I proposed to go back to Motihari. I said I had no
definite programme but that I would bathe in the sacred river
Ganges, visit the temple, and then decide. Then the gentleman
declared that he was a C.I.D. agent and warned me to tell the
truth. He pointed to a heap of handbills in a corner of the room
and declared that they must be announcements of a lecture I was
going to give. The C.I.D. agent, a little crestfallen to discover
that they were only handbills advertising the *pandya*'s business of
performing religious ceremonies for pilgrims, then took his leave.
But needless to add, a detective was stationed there to keep a
watch on me.

When I returned to Bombay after my forcible eviction from
Champaran, I went straight to see Mahatma Gandhi. I found him
sitting on a simple wooden cot with a white sheet spread on it.
He greeted me with, "Oh! Here comes the young man who has
been externed from Champaran."

He told me that I should give him only a brief account of the
happenings in Champaran as he had only twenty minutes to
spare, but later, when he had more time, he would hear a detailed story. So I gave him a very short account; even while I was
telling that he showed some impatience and pushed me on with
such remarks as "Yes yes, I know that" or "What then?"

Training in the Sabarmati Ashram[43]

When I described the events in Champaran to Gandhiji
I told him that I had been prepared to disobey the order of
expulsion from Bihar and would gladly have gone to jail for
three years. But before I could conclude my account, Gandhiji

---

[43] The Sabarmati Ashram was Gandhi's headquarters during this stage of
his political career. Pundalik went there to be trained in the Mahatma's constructive work program.

said, "You will get all the experience of jail routine at Sabarmati."

After five days in Bombay, Gandhiji sent me to Sabarmati Ashram. When Gandhiji arrived there the day after I did, he immediately set to work.

The routine of the *ashram* went on like clockwork. The general manager of the *ashram*, Shri Maganlal,[44] was the soul of the establishment. He continuously visited all the various departments and personally supervised everything. He probably did not get more than four hours of sleep a night. It was his pride that he could himself do all the different chores that the inmates in the *ashram* were asked to carry out. As soon as he saw that a knowledge of carpentry was necessary for carrying out his duties, he learned that craft. He was already adept at spinning and weaving. When he thought a knowledge of music was necessary for conducting the prayer meetings, he took music lessons even at an advanced age and made considerable progress. He never showed partiality to any of the *ashramites,* but he was very strict about having everybody's work done in the correct manner down to the most minute detail. If he was not satisfied, he used such harsh language in reprimanding the culprit that the latter often became furious with suppressed rage. He liked people who feared him and was angered by those who tried to evade work or cheat him.

He had an assistant called Chhotalal. This man was also an indefatigable worker. He was always clad only in a *pancha*. It was said that when Chhotalal was arrested, the police did not let him sleep for a full three months. Every half hour, a warden would come and wake him by prodding him with a stick. He was in solitary confinement all this time. All this had affected Chhotalal to such an extent that he never again laughed. One or two inmates did say that they had observed a faint smile on his face once or twice, but that was all. As he was Maganlal's

[44] Maganlal Desai, later president of the Gujarat National University, the Gujarat Vidyapitha.

deputy, he had occasion to assign duties to the persons living in the *ashram*. But if he saw that the work was not being done, he would himself start it, and it was his peculiarity that once he began something he always insisted on going on with it till it was finished.

Even Bapuji, if he had occasion to send for Chhotalal, always told the messenger, "Tell Chhotalal to come over, only if he is not presently engaged in doing something and is free." Chhotalal was never found spending his time chatting with people or describing his past life. He also never criticised the opinions or actions of other people. He was in charge of the *ashram* library and also of training the inmates in weaving. But of course he also did any other duty Shri Maganlal assigned him. He was very particular to see that he never, by speech or action, offended or troubled anybody else, and even respected Bapuji always pointed to him as an example in this respect. Many years later, when he was ill in the Wardha Ashram[45] he worried so about having to accept service from others that he jumped into a well and committed suicide.

In the *ashram* everybody got up and started their duties at four in the morning. But I was doing no work yet. I took my meals, loitered about, and slept, so I went to Gandhiji one morning and asked him to assign some regular work to me. Maganlal was passing by just at this moment and Gandhiji pointed to him and said, "Go to Maganlal. He will give you work."

Accordingly, I went to Maganlal and said that Gandhiji wanted him to assign me some work also. He continued his walk and while I was accompanying him inquired about my name, where I came from, and what work I had done in Champaran. (He had lived in that part of Bihar to help organise the workers in the indigo plantations owned by the British planters and had

---

[45] The Wardha Ashram was Gandhi's headquarters during the latter part of his political career.

become very popular among the people there as a courageous and honest worker.) Then he asked me whether I had taken my bath and had my breakfast.

Soon we arrived at a row of eight or ten latrines. Maganlal opened them all and said, "Now you take up the work of cleaning these latrines." Looking at me, he continued, "You probably do not know how to clean a latrine. So please note carefully what I say." I was listening all the while, not looking at his face. "These latrines have been constructed on a new pattern," he told me. "Inside, in a bucket or box is kept some dry soil. Under the seat are two buckets, so placed that the urine collects in one and the solid matter in the other. The former is covered with a hollow lid with a hole in the centre so that the urine does not splash about. This arrangement prevents the formation of a mixture of the solid matter with the urine and the water used for cleansing the body in our country; this mixture has a very offensive odor and is also difficult to clean. Everyone who uses the latrine has to cover the solid matter with dry earth to prevent the bad odor. But no earth is to be put in the urine bucket. The water used afterward also goes into this bucket and thus serves to dilute it and keep down the odor. You have to wash the area where the two buckets are kept in each latrine. The latrine itself should also be scrubbed after you pour in a bucket of water. Both buckets in each latrine must be scoured and cleaned. See that there is enough dry earth in each latrine. The ground near the latrines needs to be swept every other day only. The urine and solid matter from the latrines are to be dumped into a pit that you should dig over there. One big pit will be adequate for these latrines for about four days. Of course it will depend on its size. So that a new pit is not dug on the site of an old pit, you should put some mark on it after it is filled in." After firing all these instructions at me, Maganlal started off at a rapid pace.

I ran after him and caught up with him to ask, "Have I to start this work today or tomorrow?"

"The cleaning has already been done today, so you can begin from tomorrow. Find out who is doing this work now and get further directions from him."

"Then have I no work for today?"

"Well, I am making my rounds just now; if you like, you can accompany me."

We then toured the whole *ashram;* the room where the weaving machines were kept, the yarn store, the workshop which turned out spinning wheels, the library, the office, the kitchen. We have a saying, "The mare died of carrying the burden while the foal died of following its mother around." So I got tired merely from walking about with Maganlal. He stopped a couple of minutes at each place to give instructions. Even Chhotalal, although he was in charge of the weaving section, had his own stool and received some instructions. In the yarn store, Maganlal helped in the proper storage of the yarn, and, shamefacedly, I also had to lend a hand. In the workshop he started some carpentry because he was experimenting with a new type of spinning wheel. At that time, they were using machine-made yarn for weaving and Maganlal wanted to replace it by handspun yarn. Then we went into the library, and he asked Chhotalal to dust all the books. He added, "Pundalik will help you in this work, for he is free today." And then he went into the kitchen, washed his hands and feet, and sat down to prepare *chapatis.*

I went to my room and sad thoughts came to my mind. "Oh! that patriotism should have brought this scavenger's work to me! If I have to do all this work of cleaning the latrines every day according to the instructions I have received, it will take at least four hours. What kind of training for patriotic work am I going to get out of this? It is fortunate that at least there is nobody from my home town to watch me here. But in any case, I must not return to Belgaum a dishonoured failure. How can they assign such menial work to a person who was sent to Gandhiji's *ashram* by a noted and respected patriot like Ganga-

dharrao Deshpande? Of course Gandhiji is extremely busy, and
he cannot possibly have time to look to these little things."

Next day, I started to clean the latrines. It began at about
eight in the morning and continued for over two hours. Putting
fresh dry earth in the boxes in the latrines and digging pits for
the night soil and urine had to be done in the afternoon. That
took from thirty to forty-five minutes. On the first day, after
I had finished the work, I swam across the Sabarmati river and
sat weeping on the other bank—but not for long. For one must
not be late for the evening meal. However often I washed my
hands and whatever quantities of soap I used, I had the feeling
that a telltale odor would persist, so I began using a spoon to eat
my meal of rice and split peas. After a couple of days this feeling of disgust lessened somewhat.

On the third day, just as I was finishing my work, Maganlal
came by on a tour of inspection. He took up the buckets and
smelled them and then went into each latrine to see that it had
been properly cleaned. Still standing in a latrine holding the
bucket for the night soil, he said, "Well, you have done the work
well, but you must pay more attention to some points. You must
try to see that the buckets don't smell. Take a tuft of grass in
one hand and hold the bucket firmly with the other. Then use
some sand and give it a thorough scrub. When it is clean, spread
a little dry earth at the bottom and put it back in the latrine. The
corners inside the latrine are often full of dirt, so sweep out
carefully. Also, you must sweep out any earth that has dropped
on the floor from filling the boxes. If anybody forgets to spread
earth over the solid matter, you should mention this matter after
the evening prayers, because then all the inmates come together,
and, even if you do not know the particular individual, a general
request can be made. Moreover, you should take an inspection
tour in the afternoon, so that if somebody has not put down earth
you can do it yourself. Otherwise, you have done your work
well."

Four or five days later, while I was accompanying Gandhiji on his evening walk, he asked me, "Well, what work are you doing nowadays?" I looked down and answered, "Latrine cleaning." He replied, "That is your great good fortune!" I did not even utter a single syllable to indicate my agreement with him, but he continued, "What valuable service our brothers the scavengers are rendering to society! And society treats them as untouchables. If the work is dirty or involves unsanitary conditions, we must introduce improvements in it."

"Oh! That must be done," I blurted out, "and how long must I continue to do it?"

"Not for very long, just one lifetime," he replied.

The words gave me a shock. I felt as if I had been reborn the son of a scavenger. So I would have to continue doing this dirty work at least until the end of my stay in the *ashram!* But what could I do, and to whom could I turn?

After another four or five days, Gandhiji asked me of his own accord, "Well, how are you getting along with your work?"

"It is quite all right now. I don't mind the bad smell so much now and also do not have such a feeling of disgust."

When the evening walk was over that night and we were about to part, Gandhiji said, "Change your work tomorrow. You must get experience for some other kind of work."

Although I was relieved to some extent by this order, I spent the night worrying about what the new chore would be. The next day, after the early morning prayer, Maganlal announced, "Pundalik will take over the work of filling water pots in the *ashram* from today." I thought that this was in addition to my usual work of latrine cleaning and merely remarked, "I am entrusted with cleaning the latrines," and waited for some answer.

"Somebody else will do that work," Maganlal told me.

I did the work of latrine-cleaning for fourteen days. I consider this experience a valuable episode in my life.

STORING WATER IN THE ASHRAM

Maganlal took me around to show me where water was
stored. The vessels used for water storage had to be cleaned
inside and out. Then I also had to fill the vessels in the house of
Imamsaheb, a former associate of Gandhiji in South Africa. In
the kitchen of the *ashram* there was a big copper vessel of
seventy-five to eighty gallons capacity which also had to be
scoured daily inside and out. In all about forty or forty-five
buckets of water were required during the day. These had to be
drawn from the well by means of a hand wheel and rope. I did
all this work very diligently, and Maganlal once even gave me
high praise for it.

But one day I thought, "What is the point in scouring a big
vessel like this every day? After all if it is polished on the outside and not on the inside, nobody is likely to know if the inside
has been scoured or not." But that very day Maganlal came to
inspect the vessel a little before meal time. He said, "The vessel
is beautifully polished on the outside. I hope you cleaned it
equally well on the inside also!"

"Well, it was not quite empty and I thought the water need
not be wasted. So I poured in fresh water and filled it up," I said
after a moment's silent debate about whether to tell a lie or to
state the actual state of affairs and finally blurting out the truth.

"Then pour out all that water, clean the inside carefully
and fill it up again," Maganlal ordered.

Infuriated, I went straight to Gandhiji, told him all that had
happened and remarked, "Shri Maganlal appears to take pleasure
in persecuting people. Why should he mistreat people like that?"

"Isn't that water used in the kitchen? Fetch a couple of
buckets of fresh water for immediate use there and then empty
the big vessel and clean the inside later at your convenience.
By then the vessel will be half empty in any case. And tomorrow fill it only half full. See that there is just enough water

to last till the following morning. Ask everybody to use water from it for cleaning the pots and pans so that most of the water will be used up."

Still very angry, I emptied the vessel, cleaned the inside, and filled it up with fresh water. By that time, however, I had cooled off a bit and so did not quite fill it up.

I had now become quite used to this work, and pulling up fifty or sixty buckets one after the other was just in the day's work for me. But this was hard physical labour which made me very hungry. I was not very fond of rice and preferred to eat the thin wheat bread in the Gujarati style, as did my friend Manindra. Naturally preparing the bread took more time and work than rice and Maganlal hinted to us to eat more rice and less bread. We did not say anything and also did not follow his suggestion. Finally Maganlal took the matter to Gandhiji. One day after prayer, Gandhiji asked me about it in front of all the assembled inmates.

I explained to him about the strenuous work I was doing and about the usual diet of people from my part of Maharashtra. Then I said, "I do not like rice in such large quantities. And I am not sure eating so much bread without enough *ghi* is a good thing." [46] (Maganlal's idea was that if one chewed the bread well, one would eat less of it, and the labour of the cooks would be lessened.) But Gandhiji's decision was, "Well, if they want more bread, let them have it and more *ghi* too."

I did the work of supplying water for about a month and then I was transferred to the flour-milling department. One day, after the bell had announced the beginning of work, Maganlal told me to begin grinding flour. He said to get instruction from the people who were working the mills and then departed. These grinding stones were quite different from those to which I was accustomed; they were mounted on a wooden base about fifteen inches high with a device for regulating the friction of the

[46] There is generally current in India the notion that if wheat bread is eaten without adequate quantities of *ghi,* it will not be properly digested.

stones. The mills were operated by pairs of workers. We had to
do this work for two or three hours both morning and afternoon.
So many thoughts crowded into my head while I was turning the
mill that often my speed increased tremendously. I would think,
"How am I going to liberate my country by turning a flour mill?
Haven't women in every house done this work for centuries?
How can I, a worker in the cause of the liberation of my
Motherland, do such work? However can a hatred for the
British be generated in the minds of the people by my working
a stone flour mill? Can it be said that the day of independence
comes nearer in proportion to the time we spend in grinding
corn?"

This train of thought came again and again to my mind and
I used to dispute with an imaginary adversary who maintained
that cleaning latrines, drawing water from the well, and grinding corn in a stone mill were necessary preparations for independence. But, like the stone mills, my thoughts also went round
and round.

There were four or five grinding mills in the room. If one
could not get a companion, he had to work the mill alone,
though usually one did get a helper. These four or five pairs
would hold discussions on various topics while they worked.
Naturally I got the benefit of all this, and incidentally my
knowledge of Gujarati also improved. I used to participate in
the discussions in Hindi, and then the others would also speak
Hindi. Gandhiji visited us three or four times a week to ask,
"Well, how is the work going on?" After spending a few moments with us he would go away.

Maganlal of course came every day and took up a pinch of
flour to see that it was not too coarse. Once he said to me,
"Pundalik, you are not used to this work. Every now and then
you should feel the flour to make sure that it is fine enough. And
you should regulate the amount of fresh grain you put in according to the texture of the flour. Or else adjust the centre disk

occasionally. If the flour is too coarse, you will have to grind it again and that is very bothersome." I listened to this sermon with my head bowed and then asked, "How fine must the flour be? Please look at the flour in my mill." What I wanted was to know once and for all what was required and not be rebuked again and again. Maganlal examined my flour and said, pointing at another mill, "Your flour ought be finer than this. Look at the flour in that mill. Come on! Get up!"

When I returned to my mill, I found that Maganlal had taken my place. After about ten minutes, he said, "Just look at the flour now. It should be as fine as this." Occasionally he sat down to turn the mill while chatting with somebody and easily did the work for half an hour or so. Whenever he came into the room, I felt a little nervous. "Why is he particularly bent on persecuting me?" I would think. But after about a week, my anger cooled down, and I became used to the new work.

After about a month of this, I was asked to begin sweeping the *ashram* and its surroundings. Said Maganlal, "You should finish the sweeping by evening. Each place has its own broom. You should return it to its proper place after use. You must also clean the broom before putting it away. If the straws or coconut sticks in the broom come out, do not let them fall into the refuse. Tie them securely to the broom. In fact, once a week the brooms should all be retied. If a broom gets wet, put it in the sun to dry. If a broom is worn away, get a new one from the storehouse. The sweepings must not be collected in a corner and left there; deposit them in the garbage. If you see a scrap of paper while going through the *ashram,* pick it up and put it in the waste basket. All waste baskets must be emptied into the garbage every day." With these detailed instructions he left me. Then Chhotalal took me around to show me what to clean. I swept for about fifteen days. Fortunately we had long handles to the brooms and did not have to bend down. Every now and then, while making his rounds, Maganlal would tell me that a room had not been swept properly. And he always returned once more to that room to see that I had cleaned it properly.

One day, while I was sweeping a path in the *ashram,* an untouchable woman was sweeping the nearby road leading to the Sabarmati Jail. She had put her baby in a hammock and hung it up on a tree. When she had moved quite far away, the baby started to cry. I tried to calm him by swinging the hammock to and fro, but that did not help. So I stopped sweeping and tried to talk to him. Then he smiled at me and was quite content. In a few moments the mother returned, and Maganlal also appeared. I expected to be given a sharp reprimand for not minding my business, but on the contrary, Maganlal praised me and even reported the incident to Gandhiji.

By the time the whole *ashram* was swept and clean, I would be very tired and my back would ache. I had to spend the whole day at it. I could get no time for reading and, even if I did find time, I was too tired to do any serious reading. But gradually I became used to this also. Then I began to think of ways of finishing the work more speedily. I began my work even before the work bell rang in the morning. I found that if one was careful to pick up scraps of paper and trash every time one went by the paths, there was no need to sweep them every day. If it rained, it was unnecessary to sweep the paths, but then the verandas had to be swept twice a day. Whenever anybody noticed any dirt or waste matter anywhere, they began to stare at me. Then I would feel insulted. I did not mind sweeping even a few more rooms, but that everyone should be free to throw litter about and look at me as if I were responsible for it was a thing I could not stand. But even this chore I did to the satisfaction of Maganlal.

Weaving at the Ashram

Before I was actually allowed to work on a loom, I had to learn the various preliminary processes of loosening the yarn, soaking it, weaving thick, narrow ribbons for chair seats or mattresses, folding cloth, and trimming the yarn ends sticking out of the woven cloth. Then I was given a loom to work. I had already mastered the general principles while weaving the thick ribbons. The loom I was assigned was near the side of the building where the *ashram* library was also situated. My whole attention was centered on this library. While dusting the books with Chhotalal, I had learned its contents. Of course until I was set to working a loom there was no possibility of devoting time to reading, as the previous jobs had taken up all my time and energy. But stationed before the loom, I could hold a book in my lap and learn parts of it by heart while working the loom. I had long cherished a desire to learn the Upanishads by heart and now it seemed possible for me to devote considerable time to this without attracting criticism. I read several of the Upanishads while sitting in front of the loom; some I even learned by heart. I also devoted some time to Hindi grammar.

None of this escaped Maganlal, of course. Chhotalal once spoke to me about it and told me it was improper not to give my full attention to weaving, but as was his nature, he did not refer to the subject again. Finally Maganlal called me to his room and said, "You have so far done all your assignments, even those requiring hard physical labour, with great diligence. Why then are you not attending to the weaving with all your enthusiasm? Don't you wish to enjoy the sight of a whole piece of cloth you have woven? If I see you reading a book again when you should be weaving cloth on the loom, I will have to take you to Bapuji."

"Supposing," I asked, "I just repeat God's name 'Rama' while I am weaving, will that be all right?"

"Yes," he replied, "that will not be objectionable."

"Then," said I, "if I look at a hymn in the Upanishads and repeat it, what harm is there in that?"

"But you just don't weave. That is what I am objecting to," he replied.

Finally I promised to do the weaving while learning the

Upanishads by heart. But because I did not pay much attention to the loom, the woof was rather irregular and the cloth was naturally nothing to admire. Unfortunately the queer piece of cloth on my loom with the weft making an acute angle with the warp came accidentally to Gandhiji's notice. He smiled and said, "I am afraid all that must be undone. But please see that you don't break the yarn. It does not matter if you take a lot of time over it." It took me three or four days to get the weft out of the piece, and I must say I was very much irritated.

About this time Gandhiji received a request from Madras for the services of a weaving instructor, and somebody told me that he had decided to send me there. What did I know about weaving? What would I do in Madras? It would only expose me. So ran my thoughts; and while accompanying Gandhiji on his evening walk I said, "Although I have been working at the loom for some months, I must admit that I have neither worked assiduously nor learned much. So it would be better if somebody else is sent to Madras."

"It does not matter even if you have to tell the people in Madras all this," he said. "But you must go there. Then, when you have explained your inability to them, you can return."

"Oh, well, if I must go, then please allow me a couple of weeks and I will learn everything here. And then I will be willing to go to Madras," I replied.

Accordingly I saw Maganlal, took measurements of the looms, learned how to repair them, prepared notes on all the steps of the weaving process, and even dismantled and fitted two or three looms by myself. Maganlal spent a lot of time with me. But by the time I was ready, somebody else had already been sent to Madras. Nevertheless, I had to weave a certain length of cloth every day as a matter of course.

About the same time I was drafted into the weaving section, a committee was established to clean the cooking vessels. The chairman of this committee was Vinoba Bhave,[47] and I was the

---

[47] Later famous as the originator of the Bhudan or Land-Gift movement.

secretary for some time. Normally, at meal times, food was served only once, but in case anyone wanted more one person remained to serve it. Gandhiji himself undertook to serve the inmates. Each one went up to the table with his plate and bowl and asked for the quantity he wanted. Gandhiji had learned how much each of us usually ate, and even before one said, "I want so many pieces of bread," Gandhiji would ask, "I suppose you want so many pieces of bread." If somebody asked for less than usual, Gandhiji would ask, "Why one piece (or two or three pieces) less today?"

Once Gandhiji's grandson asked for more *ghi* during the meal, but Gandhiji refused to give him any. He said, "The money we spend here is public money, and we must be careful how we spend it. If I give you more *ghi,* I will have to give it to everybody else, because all these others are as near and dear to me as you are." But the boy would not give up his demand and pushed back his plate saying, "I am going to fast till evening." Gandhiji then took his plate away. After a couple of hours the boy was very hungry and was ready to eat, but Gandhiji did not allow him to eat until evening. He tried to impress upon his grandson that once a vow is taken, it must be kept. If he had decided not to eat until evening, he must keep to his vow. Even the intercession of Gandhiji's wife on the boy's behalf was of no avail.

As we all took whatever we wanted right at the start, the big cooking pots were emptied even before we had finished our meal, and each one of us had to clean one of them. It was the business of the pot-scouring committee to see that the cleaning was done properly. Our chairman used to say that one should be able to see one's face in the mirror-bright surface of the pot. Every day, one or two members had to repeat the process because the chairman had not approved the pots. Very often I was one of those who had to clean his pot a second time. Once I told him in exasperation, "You have a dark complexion and that is why you can't see your face in the surface of the pot!" But he remained quite unperturbed and replied, "I think a dark complexion is advantageous from the point of view of seeing a reflection in the pot!"

At last I decided that instead of trying to find time for my reading by not attending to my work properly, I should refer the matter to Gandhiji and obtain permission to do my reading at some specified time. So I went to him and asked for some free time for reading. He asked, "How much time do you think you will want every day?"

"About three hours will be enough," I replied.

"I don't think that will be difficult. I think I can easily manage to give you that much time. Now, when you get up at four, how much time do you take to wash your face and so on?"

"I should think about fifteen minutes."

Gandhiji replied, "The prayers don't begin until four-thirty. You can get at least ten minutes here. Then when do you take breakfast after the prayers? How much time would you get between prayers and breakfast?"

"Perhaps fifteen minutes."

"There. Already you have twenty-five minutes!" he said triumphantly.

In this way, by adding up the time between different items in the daily routine he could bring the total to nearly three and a half hours.

"But," I protested, "how can I concentrate on what I am reading?"

"That is very important. If one does his work with devotion, one can concentrate on anything he takes up, even reading. Moreover, I do not attach so much importance to reading as an activity in life. Contemplation is more important, and action is most important. It is thinking about things that one has read and appreciated, and even more the practice of those things that is really of use in life. And moreover, after you have worked in all the sections of the *ashram* you can stay on here for, say, six months, just for reading. But you must never be indifferent to the job in hand."

After that I never gave Maganlal any occasion to complain about me to Gandhiji. And still I cannot say that my reading suffered to any very great extent.

I Become Prompt to Prayers

Maganlal was very particular that every inmate of the *ashram* should attend both morning and evening prayers regularly. During prayers, his attention was fixed not on the proceedings, but on who was absent and whether they had a valid excuse; and he appeared to be more concerned about this than about the prayers. He always caught the person concerned some time during the day and asked for an explanation of his absence. I never used to attend the early morning prayers. Sabarmati was very cold, and my supply of clothes was very meagre—and of course my laziness was not an unimportant reason too. Once or twice Maganlal advised me not to miss early morning prayers.

"I just do not wake up as I am dead tired by the day's work," I told him plainly. "If somebody would undertake to wake me up, I would be glad to come."

"Oh, that is easy," he replied, "you can sleep anywhere in the veranda, and anyone can wake you up. As a matter of fact, I myself will do it."

"But I have a keen desire to enjoy Kakasaheb's company," I said hastily, naming an inmate who was suffering from what we suspected to be the first stage of tuberculosis. Naturally nobody disturbed him in the morning; in fact, everybody saw to it that he was not awakened. I knew that if I slept in his house, nobody would disturb me either. Maganlal was well aware of this. Finally he took the matter to Gandhiji. To Gandhiji I repeated the same things. But he said, "You see, if you are really serious about attending prayers, you will wake up at the right time, wherever you may sleep."

"It is not as if I do not wish to attend morning prayers," I replied.

"Then I will tell you what to do. You take up the job of

ringing the rising bell at four o'clock. Whenever you cannot do it, I will myself ring the bell."

It was impossible for me to put such a great man to this trouble, and so somehow I began waking with a start, even at a quarter of three. Once, thinking that I had not arisen, Gandhiji started for the bell from one direction while I approached it from the other. Seeing him approaching, I ran to the bell and rang it before he could reach it. He laughed heartily at this, and I assured him that he need have no anxiety about the bell. I would ring it at the proper time without fail. Later this chore was entrusted to another inmate, but still I never missed the morning prayer session.

V. MADHAV TRIMBAK PATWARDHAN,
Poet

INTRODUCTION

Lilabai Patwardhan gives us a sketch of the mode of life of an early twentieth-century intellectual in India in this short selection from the story of her married life with Professor M. T. Patwardhan, a noted Marathi poet, author, and Persian scholar. Patwardhan was born in Baroda in 1894 of a poor Brahman family and, after receiving the M.A. degree, became a professor in Fergusson College in 1918. As he had been admitted to the Deccan Education Society, he would normally have continued with the College until his retirement. What seems today a trivial incident—an entirely innocent friendship with a girl student in the College—led instead to his resignation in 1924 and to times of considerable hardship for him. The entire incident and in fact much of the selection which follows illustrate the restricted numbers and importance of personal relationships which characterized the intellectual community in Poona. These same features may be found today in many regions of India which are struggling to establish a modern literary tradition in their regional languages.

Professor Patwardhan's literary accomplishments include a translation of Omar Khayyám's *Rubaiyat* into Marathi poetry, a Persian-Marathi dictionary, and a volume in Marathi on poetics. His original poetry was considered representative of a new school in the twenties and thirties which attempted to break away from old traditions by the use of new forms of structure and imagery —in his case, by the adaptation of Persian poetic forms into

Marathi. Professor Patwardhan's reputation is confined to readers
of Marathi, for although he was educated in English, he wrote
by choice in Marathi. The rejection of English—and therefore of
a national audience—in favor of the regional language as a mode
of literary expression has been an important concomitant of the
nationalist movement in India. Its political, linguistic, and intellectual consequences, both good and evil, have been of incalcu-
lable importance and are a prominent feature of the scene in the
various regions and at the national level in India today. The small
literary circles who gathered in private homes to read their latest
poems in their regional languages in Poona and hundreds of
other cities throughout India could not have foreseen that the
impetus they gave to the development of these languages would
contribute to one of the most vexing internal problems of India's
national unity today—the language problem.

Professor Patwardhan, in any case, overcame his early difficulties and was elected president of the annual Marathi Literary
Conference in 1937, thus signifying recognition of his intellectual
eminence and acceptance by polite literary society. He died at the
height of his intellectual powers in 1939.

His wife Lilabai's *Amchi Akara Varshe* [*Our Eleven Years*]
was published in 1945 (by Y. G. Joshi, Poona); the selection
which follows takes us into the middle-class life of modern India
and suggests some of the personal problems created for the sensitive and reflective Indian woman by the new social mores.

E. M.

OUR ELEVEN YEARS

Lilabai Patwardhan

I had seen Madhavrao, my husband, in 1927 about a year before our marriage. In that year, the Marathi literary conference was held in Poona, and the famous poet Tambe came especially to attend it. Tambe was a very dear friend of my father and was staying in our house. One day a poets' afternoon was arranged at our place, and many noted poets gathered to recite their latest poems. When somebody asked Madhavrao, whom I did not know, to recite some of his poems, I inquired his name of a friend who was sitting near me. I was informed that this was the well-known poet whose pen name was "Madhav Julian." Then a few days later Madhavrao again came to our house to see Mr. Tambe, and my father introduced him to me. During several subsequent visits to Mr. Tambe we formed a slight acquaintance. My first impression was that he was a little nervous, spoke very little, and was an introvert. He also gave the impression of being irritated by little things and appeared rather unsociable.

After the conference was over, my professor in the Women's College, Professor Joshi, suggested to my father that I should marry Madhavrao. A couple of days later Father told me about Madhavrao's life including the incident in the Fergusson College which had led to his resignation. After listening calmly to him, I told him plainly that I did not think it advisable to give further consideration to the proposal, and Father did not insist. But Professor Joshi apparently had a very good opinion of Madhavrao, and, when Father informed him of my refusal, he said I was a fool. He told Father that the exaggerated stories being circulated about Madhavrao's supposed exploits in the Fergusson College were not true and that he was a very straightforward man. He repeated that Madhavrao would make a very good husband for me and undertook to correspond with him, but this correspondence was kept a secret from me.

In 1928 I appeared for the final examination of the Women's College but unfortunately failed in English. This was due mainly to carelessness on my part, as I wrote the answers to the questions printed on one side of the question sheet but completely forgot to read the other side. I thus finished my paper early and left the examination hall. When I realised what I had done, I became so nervous that I could not write the next paper, which was also in English, and was declared Failed in that subject. Before that time I had managed to pass all my examinations and it was a severe blow to me. I planned to take the examination again the next year.

In the meantime Father was making inquiries about suitable bridegrooms for me, and, to tell the truth, I was not averse to the idea of marriage. I was confident that Father would do only what was in my best interest, but somehow nothing came of his efforts. Some young men turned me down because I was not considered particularly handsome, others apparently objected to the fact that my father had married a widow, my present stepmother, and I myself said no to a few because I did not like them or their families. After some time, Father again suggested Madhavrao's name to me. At that time he was serving as a teacher in a high school in Poona and living in a small room not far from our house. While he was serving as an examiner for the Bombay University with Professor Joshi, the latter took the opportunity to say, "Mr. Garud (my father) is willing to give his daughter to you. I would recommend that you give serious consideration to the proposal."

Some days later Madhavrao wrote to Father requesting a
meeting. In that meeting Madhavrao told Father that he had a
slight acquaintance with me and that if, even knowing his past
history, I was prepared to accept him, he would be willing. This
time I gave my consent and with Father's permission Madhavrao
used to visit me. It appeared that a few other offers had been made
to him, but he had turned down some, and in one or two cases
the girls had flatly refused to consider his case. In our meetings
Madhavrao told me the full story of his resignation from the
Fergusson College without any reservations.

It was during the seven years from 1918 to 1924 that he and
a few other poets in Poona established "The Circle of the Sun's
Rays," a group devoted to the new school of poetry then coming
into vogue. Madhavrao popularised the Persian (*gazzal*) verse
form in Marathi, as well as new varieties of love poems. He had
become very popular among the younger generation of readers
and equally unpopular among the older, traditionally inclined
people. The members of the Circle used to meet on Sunday after-
noons for tea and literary discussions. Very often the wives of the
members and a few rather bold girl students from the colleges
also attended. One of them, an accomplished tennis player and
a good conversationalist, became friendly with some of the members and their wives. One of the poets—not Madhavrao—even
wrote a poem about her.

All these things and Madhavrao's *gazzals* in Marathi were
frowned upon by his colleagues in the College, where there had
been for some years two parties among the life members. Nobody
had accused Madhavrao of immoral conduct, but the social atmosphere in the early twenties was quite different from what it
is now[1] and even minor incidents were magnified into indis-
cretions. So finally the disapproval of a majority of his colleagues
forced Madhavrao to resign from the Fergusson College. This
brought about a kind of social boycott and by 1924–1925
Madhavrao had become the subject of whispered remarks, when-

---

[1] 1945.

ever people who knew him met together. Even some of his erst-
while friends tried to avoid him, looking the other way if they
happened to pass him in the street. After his resignation
Madhavrao served for a year as a teacher in a high school in
the northern part of Maharashtra and then returned to Poona,
where he taught in a local high school.

Madhavrao not only told me the whole story but introduced
the girl whose name had been connected with his in the episode
and the two of us had a long and frank talk together. I may
mention here that she was later married and is very happy in
her family. Madhavrao plainly told me that I should think carefully before coming to a decision. "Marriage," he said, "is a
final step. The decision affects the whole of your life. Therefore,
you can say 'No' at any time before the actual ceremony." There
was almost nobody whom I could consult, as they were all preju-
diced against him. But his frankness impressed me, and I decided
to give my consent to the marriage proposal. When I informed
him of my decision he replied, "I have now made up my mind
to shoulder this responsibility, and I shall never fail in my duty."
I was satisfied with this frank declaration of his.

One day before our marriage when Madhavrao came to see
me, I had the impression that he was greatly agitated. He said,
"The Rajaram College at Kolhapur[2] is in need of a lecturer in
Persian, and some friends have suggested that I apply. But I am
not very keen on serving in an Indian state. What do you think?
I would give up my present teaching job if you say so, but
actually I have had enough of a professor's post."

I was a little uncertain at first. For a moment I thought that
I should advise him to apply, but when I saw his troubled face
I came down to reality and said, "If you do not feel happy about
the professor's job, please do not apply. I will be satisfied with
your present way of life." He seemed to be more composed and
after a short while said, "You are very good natured. I was greatly

---

[2] At this time Kolhapur, about two hundred miles south of Poona, was
a princely state not under direct British jurisdiction.

impressed by the high opinion that Professor Joshi had of you. One of my colleagues did not think very highly of your looks, but I told him I was marrying you more for your good nature than for your looks. I hope you will prove to me the correctness of my decision." I was both flattered and a little shocked, and I assured him that I would do my best.

Madhavrao wanted to have a civil marriage registered according to the new Act, but my father was traditionally minded in these matters. He would not agree to a civil marriage and insisted upon having the old religious rites. But, as he had married a widow, none of the really orthodox priests would come to our house to officiate at our wedding. A teacher in Professor Karve's school near Poona, who was also well versed in the old Sanskrit lore, finally agreed to serve as a priest, and the ceremony was performed on May 29, 1928. Very few members of Madhavrao's family attended, probably because some opposition had been caused by the fact that he and I belonged to two different Brahman castes. A professor from the Fergusson College, a former senior colleague of Madhavrao's, acted as the groom's father.[3]

I remember that very little publicity was given to the ceremony, and only the closest friends and relatives were invited. After the ceremony was over, we were about to go into the marquee to greet friends and visitors when Madhavrao looked at me and said, "The *kunku* on your forehead is a bit too large. Make it a little smaller and then come out." Immediately the thought came into my mind, "Until now I have obeyed the directions of my parents. Now I have to obey my husband. As the ancient sage said, 'A woman does not deserve freedom'!"

I can hardly describe the state of my mind at that time. Madhavrao was in every way better than my fondest expectations —in looks, in education, in his literary achievement. But I con-

---

[3] In the Hindu marriage rite the role of the parents is most important. The bride's father gives his daughter away, and the groom's father must be present to accept the new daughter-in-law.

fess that the rumours about his friendship with the other girl
disturbed my peace of mind and until some years after marriage
when I had come to know him better and learned to respect his
integrity and simplicity, there was always a small corner of my
mind that remained a little apprehensive.

In the afternoon of our wedding day Madhavrao, to my surprise, informed me that he had sent an application for the post
at the Rajaram College. He remarked, "I have acted foolishly
on several occasions in my life so far, and I am suffering on that
account. If, for a change, taking the advice of friends is going to
bring me better luck, let us give it a chance."

For a fortnight after our wedding, we visited friends in response to tea and dinner invitations almost daily, and finally I
protested to Madhavrao that I would fall ill if we accepted any
more such invitations. Then he said, "Oh, I realise that you
should have been consulted in the matter! I have lived as a
bachelor so long that it will require some time for me to get
used to consulting another person about such things." From
that time we stopped accepting invitations—with, however, one
exception. The old lady who conducted the boarding house
where Madhavrao used to take his meals pressed him to come to
dinner with the new bride. Remembering our talk, he accepted
the invitation on his own behalf and agreed to convey the message
to me. I was at first a little reluctant to accompany him, but I
did go, and, when the old lady saw us, tears of joy came to her
eyes. As it happened, all her regular boarders had finished their
meals, and we partook of the special dishes she had prepared
alone. After dinner I received the traditional coconut and blouse-
piece and a little garland of flowers for my hair.

I had been brought up by my mother's grandmother, as my
mother died when I was very young. The old lady had taught
me to undertake many fasts, but Madhavrao was a rationalist in
these matters. When I asked about it he told me, "I do not go
in for these fasts. I do not believe that one will go to Heaven
after death or that God is pleased by such observances. If we

can assume that there is a God, He may very well be pleased with good deeds, but certainly not by eating certain things and abstaining from certain others. I think you should give up these fasts."

About eight days after the wedding came a religious holiday, and I undertook a fast along with my stepmother. In my conversation with Madhavrao I casually referred to the fast.

At once he asked, "But why did you fast?"

At first I did not understand the significance of the question. I answered simply, "Because all married women fast on this day."

Then he gave me a long lecture. "Have you ever thought about the underlying principle? You women fast and pray that you get the same husband in future births. Have you ever considered whether we really want to be tied up with you? And how could you come to decide that you wanted me as your husband in future births so soon after our marriage? Supposing you were to discover later that I am after all not such a good husband, then you would not want to live with me even for a single day, let alone seven future births! You are merely deceiving yourself by undertaking this fast. I can only admire your traditional attitude as a Hindu wife eternally loyal to her husband!" This homily made me feel very peculiar, but after giving much thought to the matter I realised the rationality of his argument. From that time I did not fast on that day. But somehow I could not give up all the old traditions and continued to observe many other fasts.

Early in June, 1928, my husband received an order to join duty at Kolhapur, and I experienced the peculiar grief a young bride feels when she leaves her parents' house and goes to her husband's house for the first time. Only grown-up Hindu brides can know what it is: the final break with familiar surroundings and the beginning of life with one's husband, whom one has known for such a short time.

After staying for about a week with a friend at Kolhapur we took a second-floor apartment. Our baggage consisted of two steel trunks and a bedroll. I did not possess even a single pot in which to cook. The day we moved into our new rooms we purchased an iron stove, some charcoal, a cooking pot, some rice and split peas, and I produced my first meal of rice and split peas cooked with salt and spices at 2:30 p.m.

I was now on my own for the first time in my life. Madhavrao usually went to the college after the morning meal, which we ate together. Sometimes, if everything was not ready, he took his meals first and I ate afterwards. I had no idea what preferences and dislikes he had for food. But when I asked him, he merely said, "People who have eaten in boarding houses for a large part of their lives have hardly any choice about food. They have to eat what is placed before them. So you just go ahead and prepare anything you like." On the whole he was indifferent about food and would eat anything that I made. When he went to visit his nonvegetarian friends, he ate fish and meat also, but I was a strict vegetarian.

He wanted me to spend some time reading and writing and urged me not to be doing housework all the time "like uneducated women," but I hardly ever found it possible. Then he began to bring home books from the college library and set passages for me to read every day. I had to look up all the words which I did not understand in the dictionary and note down their meanings. This meant that I had to give up my afternoon nap, but I gradually got used to it. One day while he was reading Shakespeare's *Cymbeline* with me he became very angry because I had not looked up one word in the dictionary, forgetting himself so far that he seized my ear and twisted it. This was an entirely new experience for me, for, although Father had often taught me, he had never given me the slightest physical punishment. My eyes filled with tears of humiliation and anger. Madhavrao also realised that he had behaved improperly. After this one incident he always remained calm when he was teaching me. Sometimes I could see from his face that he was impatient and angry, but that was all.

Later, when the two children came, I could hardly get any time to read or write, but Madhavrao always insisted on my keeping up with it. He used to say, "Who knows what one will have to face in life? It may be that in some difficult situation you may have to take service!" How prophetic these words of his proved to be! He died on November 29, 1939, and I took service as a teacher in the following February.

There was a funny incident during the first couple of weeks after we went to Kolhapur. According to the usual custom my first name Gangu had been changed to Malati at the time of the wedding ceremony. I did not want people to use the shorter, more familiar form, Malu, but that is exactly what happened. One day, Mr. Shahane, with whom we had lived during our first week at Kolhapur, came to our house and addressed me as "Malutai," adding the usual suffix *-tai* meaning sister to the short form Malu. I did not like this form of my name at all, and we let it be known to friends that I did not. But ultimately Madhavrao thought it best to change my name to Lila, and since then I have come to be known by that name.

Our days between June and October, during the first semester at Kolhapur, proved to be a great strain on me and I began to get low fever. I thought it best to go to Poona to my father's house for a change, and Madhavrao at once gave his consent. I thus went to Poona before the end of the semester, leaving Madhavrao behind. Sometimes I felt that the old traditional marriages, when girls were married off young, were better in some ways. They enabled the young brides, who were more adaptable, to get used to their new homes and new relatives. On the other hand the marriages of grown-ups, particularly educated people, when both the man and the woman had already become fixed in their habits and attitudes, were more difficult and placed a greater strain upon them. Even when one made conscious efforts to adapt himself to his partner, there were more chances of sparks flying and the relations becoming strained in such a marriage, particularly if there was no one else in the family.

Madhavrao used to get fits of depression in the early days

of our marriage. One such occasion was a letter he received from the father of a young widow. The gentleman obviously did not know of our marriage and wrote to Madhavrao asking him whether he would marry his widowed daughter. Madhavrao's idea had been to have a "love marriage," or if that was not possible, then to marry a widow and thus be instrumental in bringing new hope into a woman's life. But he could realise neither of these desires and married me according to the new tradition[4] that was becoming common in Hindu middle-class society. His determination to forget all these things and live a satisfied life with me was apparently disturbed by the letter. He did not speak to me for a whole day, and when he finally got over his agitation, he asked me not to mind these fits, adding that he hoped to get over them in the course of time.

Occasionally he would go out for long solitary walks and I did not know what to do in the strange town. I used to cry and then consoled myself by saying that there was nothing that I could do about it. I used to wait for him with food ready cooked, standing by the window for hours on end looking out into the street until he returned. Often he replied to my query, "I am still not used to the fact that I am no longer alone. Please do not be angry," and then I could say nothing. It took him nearly two years to get full control over this "devil," as we used to call it; after 1930 he never had these fits. It was during this period that he wrote the Marathi translation of Omar Khayyám, publishing it on my birthday, August 15, 1929.

In Kolhapur we made history by going out for walks together, going to cinema shows in each other's company, and attending public meetings together. Also, when I began to wear a raincoat and slippers people stared at us in the streets, but I ignored them. In the cinema theaters (there were only silent films

---

[4] The new tradition to which she refers is a sort of modified arranged marriage. The girl's father, in consultation with her, selects a suitable young man, and the engaged couple are then allowed to see each other more or less regularly. They thus do not come to marriage total strangers, as was often the case in a traditional arranged marriage.

in those days), women used to sit apart from men behind some thin curtains. But I always went and sat by my husband in the men's part, to everyone's surprise. Usually a couple of seats near me were left vacant and people would stare at us before the film started and during the intermissions.

Madhavrao was very particular about money matters. He disliked having to buy groceries for me twice during the month. Also he was insistent on saving something every month and paying the installment on his insurance regularly. He never spent much on his own clothes, but allowed me a liberal amount for my clothes and the children's. He used to give me Rs. 100 for the monthly expenses of the household, insisting that I had to manage on that.

It was after the children came that I saw what a kind and considerate family man Madhavrao was. He looked after the children in all ways. I never had to get up at night to give them their milk. They would remain awake until he finished his studies and was able to put them to bed. Even in his last illness, almost until the end, he faithfully put the children to bed as they asked. When one or the other of them was ill he would sit near the bed and worry, and tears would come to his eyes when he saw the little one suffer. When he was deeply engrossed in writing some book and had a deadline to meet, he would send me and the two children to Poona to be free to devote all his time to his work.

During the last couple of years many of his relatives became frequent visitors at our house. The small house which we had built at Poona became the scene of many family gatherings during the vacations which we always spent there. In 1939 we celebrated our son Dinu's thread ceremony, and many friends and relatives gathered on that occasion. Madhavrao gave presents to everybody and tried to show his gratitude to all those who had helped him in any way.

Only about a month after this ceremony Madhavrao fell ill. It was the same year that he received the D. Litt. degree of the

Bombay University for his book on figures of speech in Marathi. Two years before that, in 1937, he had been elected president of the Annual Marathi Literary Conference and was thus accepted by all and acknowledged to be at the height of his productive period. At first no one thought the slight attack of jaundice was at all serious, but he became weaker and weaker. The doctors did everything that was humanly possible but they could not check the gradual advance of the liver ailment. He died on November 29, 1939.

GLOSSARY OF VERNACULAR TERMS

Appa—elder brother.

ashram—Hindu retreat; home of a holy man or a sort of monastic community.

ambadi—a hind of hibiscus; hog-plum.

–baba—suffix of respect.

Babu (also suffix)—term of respect; clerk.

bai—meaning "woman" attached to proper names in Maharashtra.

bajri—millet.

Bapu—father; title for Gandhi.

baya—term of endearment for a girl or woman.

bhakri—wheat or millet *chapatis* of rough, home-ground grain.

bidi—hand-rolled cigarette.

chapati—unleavened wheat bread baked in rounds like tortillas.

chivda—Maharashtrian snack dish or appetizer of puffed wheat, coconut, and spices.

Dada (also suffix)—elder brother; also term of respect.

darbar—convocation.

Dasara—the martial autumn festival symbolizing the victory of the god Rama over the forces of evil. A tradition continued from the days of the *peshwas*.

Desh-sevak—Servant of the Country (a newspaper).

dharmashala—public rest house.

dhoti—basic men's garment in India; a length of white cloth wound about the midsection and reaching to the knees or ankles.

dipmal—stone pillar with protuberances for oil lamps.

Diwali—the festival of light, symbolizing in Maharashtra the coming of the goddess of fortune, Sri. October or November.

diwan—chief administrative officer of a princely state.

doli—box-like structure in which individuals are transported on the shoulders of porters.

gazzal—a Persian verse form similar to a sonnet.

ghi—clarified butter.

hookah—hubble-bubble pipe.

jambul—a plum-like fruit.

-ji—suffix of respect; Mr. or Sir.

joda—red leather slipper with the toe turned up.

jowar—millet.

kabaddi—Indian team sport, something like hockey.

karma-yoga—the path of action; the philosophy of doing one's duty. One of three ways to salvation in Indian religious philosophy.

khadi—handspun; a symbol of the nationalist movement.

khir—milk pudding.

kirtan (hari-kirtan)—religious discourse, with songs.

Konkanastha—from the Konkan, a coastal strip south of Bombay.

kunku—red powder used in Maharashtra to mark the foreheads of unmarried girls and women whose husbands are living.

Lokamanya—title of respect; Approved by the People.

Maharashtra-mitra—Friend of Maharashtra (a newspaper).

Maharshi—title of respect; Great Sage.

Mahatma—title of respect; Great Soul.

mela—country fair, either religious or secular in nature.

Modi—obsolete cursive script in which Marathi was once written.

mot—large water bucket drawn from a well by bullocks.

namaskar—respectful salutation.

nim—the margosa tree.

pan—betel leaf with ground areca nut and spices.

pancha—short *dhoti* or loincloth.

Pandit—title of respect; learned (sir).

Pandita—title of respect; learned (lady).

pandya—priest who performs ceremonies for pilgrims at places of pilgrimage.

-pant—suffix of respect (men only).

pat—marriage of a widow of certain Maharashtrian castes, always clearly differentiated from a first marriage.

pattewala—uniformed servant or "wearer of the belt."
pedha—a milk confection distributed on ceremonial occasions.
purdah—literally, veil or screen; seclusion of women.
-rao—suffix of respect (men only).
Rashtroddhar—Rescue of the Nation (a play).
sadhu—monk, holy man.
Saheb (also suffix)—term of respect for whites and Indians alike.
sanyasi—ascetic.
sari—Indian women's garb.
sati—immolation of a widow upon her deceased husband's pyre.
satyagraha—planned, organized campaign of nonviolent resistance.
shastri—man learned in the Sanskrit classics.
shira—a confection of wheat flour, *ghi,* and sugar.
Shravan—Hindu lunar month, about August.
Shri—Mr.
soubhagyavati—a married woman whose husband did not predecease
    her.
supari—refreshing after-meal spice mixture.
swadeshi—homemade.
Tai (also suffix)—older sister.
tamasha—travelling musical play or show popular in rural areas.
tonga—horsedrawn taxi or hack.
Tukaram—medieval saint-poet of Maharashtra; name of a play.
Vaishakh—Hindu lunar month, about May.
vakil—lawyer, personal representative of an important person.
Venisamhar—a Sanskrit drama.
Zunzarrao—Marathi version of *Othello.*

TABLE OF MONETARY UNITS

(for the period before Independence)

3 pies	....	1 pice
4 pice	....	1 anna
16 annas	....	1 rupee
1 rupee	....	about $ .20
5 rupees	....	about $1.00

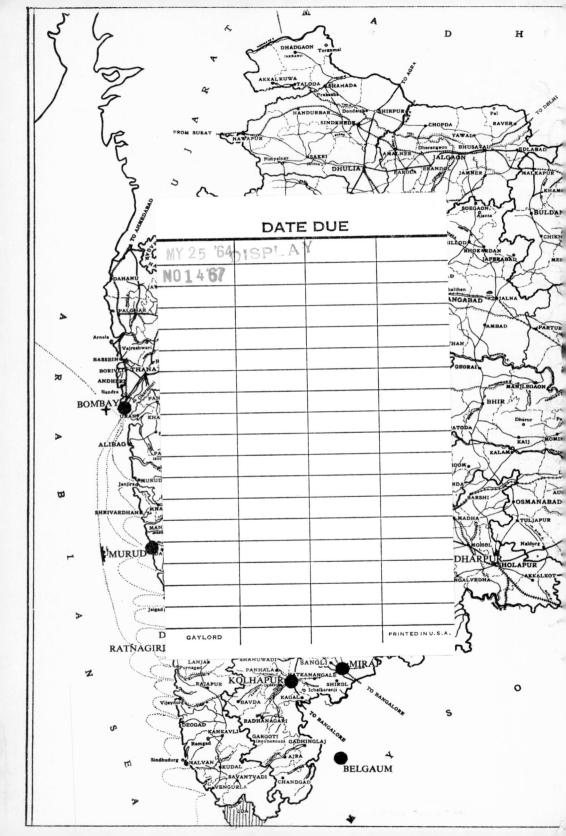